# RESEMBLANCE AND REPRESENTATION

# Resemblance and Representation

## An Essay in the Philosophy of Pictures

*Ben Blumson*

http://www.openbookpublishers.com

© 2014 Ben Blumson

The text of this book is licensed under a Creative Commons Attribution 4.0 International license (CC BY 4.0). This license allows you to share, copy, distribute and transmit the work; to adapt the work and to make commercial use of the work providing attribution is made to the author (but not in any way that suggests that he endorses you or your use of the work). Attribution should include the following information:

Blumson, Ben, *Resemblance and Representation: An Essay in the Philosophy of Pictures*. Cambridge, UK: Open Book Publishers, 2014. http://dx.doi.org/10.11647/OBP.0046

Please see the list of illustrations for attribution relating to individual images. Every effort has been made to identify and contact copyright holders and any omissions or errors will be corrected if notification is made to the publisher.

In order to access detailed and updated information on the license, please visit: http://www.openbookpublishers.com/isbn/9781783740727#copyright

Further details about CC BY licenses are available at: http://creativecommons.org/licenses/by/4.0

Digital material and resources associated with this volume are available at http://www.openbookpublishers.com/isbn/9781783740727#resources

ISBN Paperback: 978-1-78374-072-7
ISBN Hardback: 978-1-78374-073-4
ISBN Digital (PDF): 978-1-78374-074-1
ISBN Digital ebook (epub): 978-1-78374-075-8
ISBN Digital ebook (mobi): 978-1-78374-076-5
DOI: 10.11647/OBP.0046

Cover image: Kazimir Malevich, *Suprematist painting (with black trapezium and red square)* (1915). Stedelijk Museum, Amsterdam. Wikimedia Commons: http://commons.wikimedia.org/wiki/File:Kazimir_Malevich_-_Suprametism.jpg

All paper used by Open Book Publishers is SFI (Sustainable Forestry Initiative), and PEFC (Programme for the Endorsement of Forest Certification Schemes) Certified.

Printed in the United Kingdom and United States by Lightning Source for
Open Book Publishers (Cambridge, UK).

*For my father, Richard Blumson*

# Contents

| | |
|---|---|
| List of illustrations | ix |
| Acknowledgements | 1 |
| Note on the text | 5 |
| 1. Introduction | 9 |
|    1.1 An ostensive definition of depiction | 10 |
|    1.2 The analysis of resemblance as sharing properties | 13 |
|    1.3 An intuitive taxonomy of representation | 21 |
|    1.4 The methodology of analysis | 23 |
|    1.5 Conclusion | 28 |
| 2. Defining Depiction | 31 |
|    2.1 Grice's analysis of speaker meaning | 32 |
|    2.2 The intended effect in Grice's analysis | 35 |
|    2.3 The salient feature in Grice's analysis | 39 |
|    2.4 Abell's analysis of depiction | 44 |
|    2.5 Conclusion | 49 |
| 3. Depiction and Intention | 51 |
|    3.1 Objections to the necessity of intention | 52 |
|    3.2 Objections to the necessity of an audience | 57 |
|    3.3 Objections to the sufficiency of intention | 60 |
|    3.4 Objections to the necessity of reasons | 63 |
|    3.5 Conclusion | 66 |
| 4. Depiction and Convention | 67 |
|    4.1 Goodman's definition of symbol systems | 68 |
|    4.2 Formal definition of languages | 70 |
|    4.3 Lewis' analysis of convention | 73 |
|    4.4 Analysis of depictive symbol systems | 77 |
|    4.5 Conclusion | 81 |

## 5. Symbol Systems — 85
- 5.1 Analysis of conventional language — 86
- 5.2 Analysis of symbol systems in use — 88
- 5.3 Depiction outside of symbol systems — 92
- 5.4 Meaning outside conventional language — 94
- 5.5 Conclusion — 96

## 6. Depiction and Composition — 99
- 6.1 Theories of representation — 102
- 6.2 The finite axiomatization constraint — 105
- 6.3 The mirror constraint — 108
- 6.4 The structural constraint — 111
- 6.5 Conclusion — 114

## 7. Interpreting Images — 117
- 7.1 Compositionality and language understanding — 118
- 7.2 Compositionality and understanding pictures — 122
- 7.3 Understanding pictures without compositionality — 126
- 7.4 Understanding language without compositionality — 130
- 7.5 Conclusion — 136

## 8. Intentionality and Inexistence — 139
- 8.1 Analysing depiction in intentional terms — 141
- 8.2 Denying depiction is relational — 145
- 8.3 Denying relations are between existents — 148
- 8.4 Depiction of states of affairs — 151
- 8.5 Conclusion — 157

## 9. Perspective and Possibility — 159
- 9.1 The possible worlds analysis of content — 159
- 9.2 Centred properties and possible worlds — 161
- 9.3 The two-dimensional analysis of content — 168
- 9.4 Structured intensions and impossible worlds — 172
- 9.5 Conclusion — 177

## 10. Pictures and Properties — 179
- 10.1 Predicate nominalism — 182
- 10.2 Class nominalism — 185
- 10.3 Scientific realism — 188
- 10.4 Inegalitarian nominalism — 193
- 10.5 Conclusion — 196

References — 199

Index — 207

# List of illustrations

| | | |
|---|---|---|
| 1 | A white sphere in front of a black sphere. From Jeff Ross (1997), *Semantics of Media* (Dordrecht: Kluwer), p. 73. © Kluwer. With kind permission from Springer Science and Business Media. | 161 |
| 2 | A black sphere in front of a white sphere. From Jeff Ross (1997), *Semantics of Media* (Dordrecht: Kluwer), p. 73. © Kluwer. With kind permission from Springer Science and Business Media. | 161 |
| 3 | A black sphere to the left. | 163 |
| 4 | A black sphere to the right. | 163 |
| 5 | A black sphere to the left from above. | 164 |
| 6 | A black sphere to the right from above. | 164 |
| 7 | An impossible triangle. Image from Wikimedia: http://commons.wikimedia.org/wiki/File:Pentriangle.svg | 172 |

# Acknowledgements

This book has had a long gestation, and I have needed a lot of help, so there are a lot of people to thank. Much of the philosophy of language and mind I draw on in these pages I learnt as an undergraduate at the University of Queensland. I thank especially Deborah Brown, William Grey, Dominic Hyde and Gary Malinas for everything they taught me. I also met many of my closest friends at the University of Queensland – I would especially like to thank June Mahadevan.

The first version of the book was my PhD thesis at the Australian National University (ANU). I especially thank my supervisors Daniel Stoljar, David Chalmers and Martin Davies. Andy Egan, Frank Jackson and Robert McRoberts read entire drafts, while Catharine Abell, Jake Beck, Elizabeth Coleman, Daniel Friedrich, Brendan Jackson and Uriah Kriegel gave me comments on various chapters. The examiners also gave me helpful comments on the finished thesis.

I learnt as much at ANU from my fellow students as my teachers. In particular, Jens Christian Bjerring, David Bourget, Campbell Brown, Carl Brusse, Jacek Brzozowski, Brett Calcott, Yuri Cath, Philippe Chuard, Aisling Crean, Nic Damnjanovic, Ben Fraser, Akira Inoue, Ben Jeffares, Mitch Joe, Ole Koksvik, John Matthewson, Yujin Nagasawa, Karen Riley, Kelly Roe, Stewart Saunders, Martin Smith, Nic Southwood, Weng Hong Tang and David Wall all helped me more than they know.

In addition, I am very grateful to Magdalena Balcerak, John Bigelow, David Braddon-Mitchell, Tyler Dogget, Christoph Fehige, Alan Hajek, Bernard Nickel, Daniel Nolan, John O'Dea, Brad Richards, Denis Robinson and Declan Smithies for discussions at ANU. When Yuri Cath saw the thesis acknowledgements he accused me of thanking everyone indiscriminately. But this list is just a small fraction of the people I spoke to at ANU – I am very sorry to all those I have omitted.

I finished the first draft of the book, conceived as such, as a postdoctoral fellow at the University of Sydney. I'm grateful to Uriah Kriegel, Raamy Majeed and Luca Moretti for discussions during this time. I also thank Axel Gelfert, John Holbo, Wang-Yen Lee, Mike Pelczar, Neil Sinhababu and especially Tang Weng-Hong for taking part in a reading group on the book at the National University of Singapore, and Gabriel Greenberg, Raamy Majeed and David Wall for comments on the draft.

Finally, I am grateful for conversations at conferences and seminars with Catharine Abell, Rafael De Clerq, Mitchell Green, Robert Hopkins, John Kulvicki, Paisley Livingston, Dominic Lopes, Dan Marshall, Michael Newall, Josh Parsons, Michael Rescorla, John Williams, Alberto Voltolini and John Zeimbekis. And I'm grateful to very many – but unfortunately not to all – referees who read the book manuscript or drafts of the papers mentioned below.

Parts of chapters one, two and three appeared previously as "Defining Depiction" in the *British Journal of Aesthetics* (2009a). This paper was presented at the Australasian Postgraduate Philosophy Conference in Melbourne, the University of Queensland and the Singapore Management University in 2005, at the Australian National University and the British Society of Aesthetics in 2006, and at "Images and Intentionality", a workshop I organised at the University of Sydney in 2008.

Parts of chapters four and five appeared as "Depiction and Convention" in *dialectica* (2008). This paper was also presented at the Australasian Association of Philosophy Conference in Canberra and at the Australian National University in 2006. The final paragraphs of chapter four are from "Depictive Structure?" in *Philosophical Papers* (2011). This paper was presented at the American Philosophical Association Pacific Division in 2009 and at the University of Western Australia in 2010.

Parts of "Maps and Meaning" from the *Journal of Philosophical Research* (2010a) are reused in chapter six. I thank Daniel Friedrich and Uriah Kriegel for reading this paper. Chapter six in its current form, "Depiction and Composition", was presented at the Australasian Association of Philosophy Conference in Sydney in 2010, the University of Copenhagen and the London Aesthetics Forum in 2011 and the Victoria University of Wellington in 2013.

Chapter seven, "Interpreting Images", was presented to the American Society of Aesthetics Pacific Division in 2009, at a workshop, "Depiction and Description" in Singapore in 2010, and to the International Society of

Philosophy and Literature in Singapore and at the University of Western Australia in 2013. I thank Liz Blumson for reading this chapter. Chapter eight previously appeared as "Images, Intentionality and Inexistence" in *Philosophy and Phenomenological Research* (2009b) and was presented at the University of Sydney and the Australian National University in 2007.

Chapter nine was published as "Pictures Perspective and Possibility" in *Philosophical Studies* (2010b). This paper was also presented at the New Zealand division of the Australasian Association of Philosophy in 2007 and the University of Sydney in 2008. Chapter ten was presented at a workshop at Lingnan University in Hong Kong, "Art and Metaphysics", and at the University of Sydney in 2012.

It's difficult to acknowledge family without sounding like one is winning an academy award rather than writing an academic monograph. Nevertheless, Elizabeth, Erica and Emily Blumson are the best mother and sisters one could ask for. While a quick look at my thesis convinced my nephew that it was mind-numbingly repetitive (no doubt some other readers will be sympathetic), my father patiently read it all, and corrected several mistakes. This book is dedicated to him.

# Note on the text

I use single quotation marks to mention an expression. So whereas Boston is a North American city, 'Boston' is the name of a North American city. I use double quotation marks to quote what another person said. For example, Quine said that quotation "… has a certain anomalous feature …" (Quine, 1940, 26). I use corner quotation marks when I need to use a variable or subscript within a quoted expression. So ⌜the bank$_1$ is open⌝ and ⌜the bank$_2$ is open⌝ refer to disambiguations of 'the bank is open'.

I also use corner quotes for substitutional quantification. In particular '($\prod \phi$) ⌜$\phi$⌝ in English means that $\phi$' asserts that for every English sentence $\phi$, writing $\phi$ (not '$\phi$'!) in quotation marks, followed by 'in English means that', followed by $\phi$ without quotations marks results in a truth. In particular, it asserts that 'snow is white' in English means that snow is white, that 'grass is green' in English means that grass is green, … and so on.

The passage just quoted from Quine continues "A quotation is not a *description*, but a *hieroglyph;* it designates its object not by describing it in terms of other objects, but by picturing it" (Quine, 1940, 26). Though I mostly follow Quine's recommendations for the usage of quotation marks I cannot agree with this: in fact I take quotation as a paradigmatic example of descriptive, rather than depictive, representation. I think this presupposition is defensible, but also dispensable, so I won't defend it here.

*The fact is that on that night I laughed at the axiom Quae sunt aequalia uni tertio sunt aequalia inter se ("Things which are equal to a third thing are equal to each other"), for the portrait resembled M. M. and it also resembled the strumpet, and the latter did not resemble M. M. Murray admitted it, and we spent an hour philosophizing.*

Giacomo Casanova, *History of My Life*, volume 4, chapter 10

# 1. Introduction

It's a platitude – which only a philosopher should dream of denying – that whereas words are connected to what they represent merely by arbitrary conventions, pictures are connected to what they represent by resemblance. The most important difference between my portrait and my name, for example, is that whereas my portrait and I are connected by my portrait's resemblance to me, my name and I are connected merely by an arbitrary convention. The first aim of this book is to defend this platitude from the apparently compelling objections raised against it, by analysing depiction in a way which reveals that it really is mediated by resemblance.

It's natural to contrast the platitude that depiction is mediated by resemblance, which emphasises the differences between depictive and descriptive representation, with an extremely close analogy between depiction and description, which emphasises the similarities between depictive and descriptive representation. Whereas the platitude emphasises that the connection between my portrait and me is natural in a way the connection between my name and me is not, the analogy emphasises the contingency of the connection between my portrait and me. Nevertheless, the second aim of this book is to defend an extremely close analogy between depiction and description.

The main strategy of the book is to generalise ideas from the philosophy of language to encompass pictures. Depiction is representational in the same sense as description, except whereas the latter is mediated by convention, the former is by resemblance. It turns out, I will argue, that many ideas from the philosophy of language apply directly to depiction, with only superficial amendments or the incorporation of resemblance. And it turns out that the apparently compelling objections raised against the platitude that depiction is mediated by resemblance are merely manifestations of, and amenable to the same solutions as, familiar problems from the philosophy of language.

This chapter introduces the central themes of the book. The first section clarifies the subject with an ostensive definition of depiction. The second section introduces the analysis of resemblance as sharing properties and explains how it underlies the most compelling objections to the platitude that depiction is mediated by resemblance. The third section provides a brief taxonomy of kinds of representation, and discusses the place of depiction within this taxonomy. The fourth section elaborates and defends the method of analysis, which is the central method of the book. The fifth section outlines the remaining chapters of the book.

## 1.1 An ostensive definition of depiction

Depiction is a distinctive kind of representation. Figurative painting and drawing are the paradigm example, but figurative sculpture, photographs and maps are also central examples. Language is the paradigm of non-depictive representation, but symbolic notation – whether in mathematics or music – and indication – as when clouds represent rain or smoke represents fire – are also central examples. In contrast, material objects such as rocks, tables and planets are not examples of either kind of representation, but are at most degenerate cases of indication. The rest of this section clarifies and defends this ostensive definition.

Three clarifications. First, although figurative painting and drawing is the paradigm example of depiction, defining depiction as a kind of representation means that not all paintings and drawings are depictions. Although figurative and abstract painting, for example, have much in common, abstract paintings are not counterexamples to the thesis that depiction is mediated by resemblance, because figurative and abstract paintings intuitively don't belong to the same kind of representation (Lopes, 1996, 5-6). Figurative and abstract paintings are similar because they are flat surfaces marked with paint, not because they represent in the same way.

Second, defining depiction as a kind of representation means depictions may belong to any media (Hopkins, 1994, 1; Kulvicki, 2006, 106-114).

Although sculptures, for example, are not flat surfaces marked with lines or colour, this does not disqualify sculptures from being depictions, since it is plausible that figurative sculptures and pictures represent in the same way. Similarly although most music, for example, is neither depictive nor representational, program music is an important exception. Most dance is not representational, but mime is depiction in the medium of movement. And movies are plausibly depictions in the medium of film (Currie, 1995, 2).

This point is methodologically important. John Hyman, for example, begins a very different inquiry when he writes "Is an apple red because of the visual sensation it produces in us when we see it, or does it produce this sensation in us because it is red? All pictures – whatever kind of substance they are made of – consist of colour distributed on a plane. So this is the right way for a study of depiction to begin" (Hyman, 2006, 7). If the subject of inquiry is a kind of representation, rather than a representational medium, the right way to begin is not to inquire into the nature of perception and colour, but into the nature of representation in general.

Third, while depictive and descriptive representation are distinct kinds, I allow that they may overlap. Take, for example, a picture of a signboard which reads 'danger'. The picture both represents a signboard and represents danger. But whereas the signboard is represented depictively, danger is represented merely descriptively, since it is represented by the appearance of the word 'danger' within the picture. Similarly the Soviet flag represents a hammer and sickle as well as representing the Soviet Union: the hammer and sickle are represented depictively, but the representation of the Soviet Union is arguably merely conventional (Peacocke, 1986, 383).

Allegorical representation is the reverse of this pattern. The words of the fiction are paradigmatically descriptive, but the events described also represent a real situation. While the representation of the fiction is descriptive, the representation of the real situation is depictive, and plausibly mediated by resemblance. *Animal Farm*, for example, describes in language the takeover of a farm by pigs (Orwell, 1945). The events described in turn depict the Russian Revolution, perhaps in virtue of the resemblance between the events of the story and the events of the revolution. So allegorical stories are plausibly a kind of depictive representation.

If it's insisted that depiction must be a kind of visual representation, then this could be accommodated by substituting resemblance below for resemblance in visible respects. Although *Animal Farm* and the Mona Lisa, for example, have in common that they both represent what they do by resemblance, they differ because whereas the Mona Lisa resembles Lisa in respects which are visible, the story of *Animal Farm* resembles the revolution in respects which are invisible. So although the analysis below does not distinguish between depictions in different media, it can be easily modified if it's desirable to do so (Abell's (2009) analysis, for example, adopts this suggestion).

One objection. Beginning with an ostensive definition of depiction which – whether by accident or design – classifies all and only representations which are mediated by resemblance as depictions might be thought to beg the question in favour of the platitude that depiction is mediated by resemblance. If the main objections against the resemblance theory were about which representations it classifies as depictions, then this objection would be right: choosing figurative painting and drawing as paradigm examples of depiction would stack the deck in favour of the platitude that depiction is mediated by resemblance.

But the most compelling objections against the platitude that depiction is mediated by resemblance aren't merely about its classification of different kinds of representation, but purport to show that it's impossible for any kind of representation to be mediated by resemblance. If successful, these objections would show that depiction is not mediated by resemblance, no matter which representations are classified as depictions and no matter how depiction is ostensively defined. So in the context of rebutting these objections, beginning with an ostensive definition of depiction doesn't beg the question in favour of the platitude that depiction is mediated by resemblance.

Beginning with an ostensive definition of depiction which – whether by accident or design – classifies all and only representations which are mediated by resemblance as depictions may also be thought to beg the question against other theories of depiction, according to which what is distinctive of depiction is a distinctive kind of perceptual experience (Wollheim, 1980; 1987), a special kind of syntactic and semantic structure (Goodman, 1968; Kulvicki, 2006), or a peculiar kind of perceptual processing (Schier, 1986; Currie, 1995; Lopes, 1996; Newall, 2011). Since these theories disagree in their classifications, my choice of examples may also stack the deck against them.

But if a different choice of ostensive definition leads to a different final classification, and thence to a different theory, this only shows that the different definition ostended a different class of things, for which a different theory is appropriate. If, for example, one begins with an ostensive definition of depiction which includes abstract painting and excludes figurative sculpture, then one will end with a different classification and a different theory of depiction. But that theory of depiction would not disagree with the theory I argue for here, because it has a different subject matter. Beginning with an ostensive definition doesn't beg the question, but merely describes the subject.

Because different theories of depiction – whether or not they agree about which things they classify as depictions – are not obviously inconsistent with each other, I will not adopt a last man standing approach, which seeks to establish the resemblance theory by first refuting every other plausible theory, and mention alternative approaches only when they're relevant to the exposition of my own. If there's an analysis of depiction in terms of resemblance which captures the classification outlined here, discovering that analysis suffices for success. If there are other analyses or theories in other terms which capture other classifications, discovering them is an even greater success.

## 1.2 The analysis of resemblance as sharing properties

The naïvest analysis of depiction in terms of resemblance simply assimilates depiction to resemblance (Goodman, 1968, 3). According to it:

(1) Something depicts another if and only if the former resembles the latter.

The Mona Lisa, for example, is supposed to depict Lisa simply because the Mona Lisa resembles Lisa. Counterexamples to the necessity and sufficiency of this analysis illustrate some of the most compelling objections to the platitude that depiction is mediated by resemblance.

In turn, the naïvest analysis of resemblance simply assimilates resemblance to having properties in common. According to it:

(2) Something resembles another if and only if the former has a property in common with the latter.

Peas in a pod resemble each other, for example, because they have the properties of greenness, roundness and yuckiness in common. So according to the naïvest analyses of depiction and resemblance, the nature of depiction ultimately depends on the nature of properties.

But there are rifts in our conceptions of properties. A first is the rift between sparse and abundant conceptions of properties (Lewis, 1983a; 1986, 59-69). According to an abundant conception of properties there's a property corresponding to each (possible) predicate, and so the number of properties is the number of (possible) predicates. Just as there's a property of being white which corresponds to the predicate 'is white', for example, there is also, according to abundant conceptions of properties, a property of being a raven or a writing desk, corresponding to the predicate 'is a raven or a writing desk'. So properties, according to the abundant conception, are ubiquitous.

(A predicate is just a sentence with a name removed. The predicate 'is white', for example, results from removing 'snow' from 'snow is white'. Likewise, the predicate 'is a raven or a writing desk' results from removing 'Edgar' from the sentence 'Edgar is a raven or a writing desk'. The semantic value of a predicate is often thought of as a property: the semantic value of 'is white', for example, is the property of being white, whereas the semantic value of 'is a raven or a writing desk' is the property of being a raven or a writing desk. So abundant conceptions of properties are motivated in part by the need to find a semantic value for every (possible) predicate.)

Sparse theories of properties deny there is a property corresponding to every possible predicate, and so deny the number of properties is the number of possible predicates. Which predicates correspond to properties, according to sparse theories, is revealed *a posteriori* by total science (Armstrong, 1978b, 7-9). Whether the predicate 'is white' corresponds to a property of being white, for example, is an *a posteriori* question; the existence of the property of being white cannot be deduced from the existence of the predicate 'is white', and no property of being a raven or a writing desk corresponds to the predicate 'is a raven or a writing desk'.

Whereas an abundant conception of properties is considered most appropriate for the analysis of predication, it's the sparse conception which is considered appropriate for the analysis of resemblance. As David Lewis, for example, writes "Because properties are so abundant, they are undiscriminating. ... Thus properties do nothing to capture facts about resemblance. That is work more suited to the sparse universals" (Lewis, 1983a, 13). But it's almost as difficult to square the analysis of resemblance as having properties in common with a sparse as with an abundant conception of properties. So, until chapter ten, I'll attempt to stay neutral on this issue.

A second is the rift between the subjective and objective conception of properties. According to subjective conceptions of properties, whether a particular instantiates a property is dependent on us, whereas according to objective conceptions of properties, whether a particular instantiates a property is a fact independent of us. According to a subjective conception of colours, for example, whether a particular is red depends on whether it is disposed to appear red to us under certain conditions, whereas according to an objective conception of colours, whether a particular is red depends on whether it is disposed to reflect light of a certain wavelength.

The platitude that depiction is mediated by resemblance is often associated with an objective conception of properties. In his criticism of the resemblance theory, Michael Newall, for example, says "I will call all theories that hold that a viewer-independent resemblance between a picture and its referent is necessary for depiction resemblance theories. ... Viewer-independent resemblances involve identity in some respects – a sharing of viewer-independent properties ... Viewer-independent resemblance is close to the everyday meaning of the term 'resemblance', and it is this that resemblance theorists employ" (Newall, 2011, 67).

Likewise, in his defence of the resemblance theory, Hyman writes "I shall argue that there is a strict and invariable relationship between the shapes and colours on a picture's surface and the object which it depicts, which can be defined without referring to the psychological effect the picture produces in a spectator's mind ..." (Hyman, 2006, 73). But although it's natural to combine the platitude that depiction is mediated by resemblance with an objective conception of properties and resemblance, the platitude that depiction is mediated by resemblance is equally compatible with the subjective conception, and so I will also attempt to stay neutral on this issue.

In light of the analysis of resemblance as having properties in common, the necessity of the first analysis is not obvious, because it's not obvious which properties pictures have in common with what they represent. As Robert Hopkins, for example, writes: "Resemblance must be resemblance in certain respects. If two things resemble, they must do so in respect of some property or other, perhaps in respect of many. Unfortunately, when we ask in what respect picture and object resemble, it is easier to find difference than likeness" (Hopkins, 1998, 11). Whereas most pictures are flat and rectangular, most of the things they represent are neither flat nor rectangular.

But although explicitly specifying the respects of resemblance between many pictures and what they represent is difficult (see Hyman (2006, 73-112) and Newall (2011, 66-94) for detailed discussion of particular examples), whether there is an in principle problem for the necessity of resemblance for depiction depends on one's conception of properties. If it's combined with a sparse theory of properties – according to which whether there is a property corresponding to each (possible) predicate is revealed by *a posteriori* scientific investigation – the problem is severe. I will return to the problem posed by sparse conceptions of properties in chapter ten.

But if it's combined with an abundant theory of properties – according to which there is a property corresponding to each (possible) predicate – the analysis of resemblance as sharing properties entails that everything resembles everything in some respect, so the necessity of resemblance for depiction is guaranteed. If properties are abundant, then a raven resembles a writing desk, for example, because the raven and the writing desk both fall under the predicate 'is a raven or a writing desk'. Likewise, the Mona Lisa resembles Lisa because the Mona Lisa and Lisa both fall under the predicate 'is the Mona Lisa or Lisa'. In this case, the problem of necessity evaporates.

The insufficiency of the first analysis *is* obvious, because resemblance is ubiquitous. Members of the same family resemble each other, but do not depict each other; twins resemble each other almost exactly, but still do not depict each other. Automobiles from the same assembly line resemble each other very closely, but rarely represent each other. Most paintings bear a closer resemblance to other paintings than they do to what they represent (Goodman, 1968, 4-5). And all white things resemble each other in virtue of sharing the property of being white, but not all white things depict each other. Sharing a property is sufficient for resemblance, but not depiction.

If it's combined with an abundant theory of properties – according to which there is a property corresponding to each (possible) predicate – then the analysis of resemblance as sharing properties entails everything resembles everything in some respect, which exacerbates the insufficiency of resemblance for depiction. Although if properties are abundant the Mona Lisa is guaranteed to resemble Lisa, for example, since the Mona Lisa and Lisa both fall under the predicate 'is the Mona Lisa or Lisa', a raven is also guaranteed to resemble a writing desk because both fall under the predicate 'is a raven or a writing desk'. But ravens do not depict writing desks.

Since resemblance is not obviously necessary and obviously insufficient for depiction, it might be thought that an analysis of depiction should specify some relevant respects in which all depictions resemble what they represent. Hopkins, for example, writes "One reaction would be to abandon hope that there is any one respect in which all pictures are experienced as resembling their objects. Sometimes colour is the key, sometimes tone, sometimes shape. However, it is clearly desirable to resist this retreat if possible. Supposing that we still hope for a single respect relevant to all depiction, where should we look for it?" (Hopkins, 1998, 51-52).

But the quixotic search for a specification of a relevant respect in which all depictions resemble what they represent is superfluous to defending the platitude that depiction is mediated by resemblance. If depiction is mediated by resemblance, every depiction resembles what it represents in some relevant respect. But it doesn't follow that there is some relevant respect in which all depictions resemble what they represent, because the respects relevant to each different depiction may be different. And even if there is a relevant respect in which all depictions resemble what they represent, a specification of the respect cannot establish the sufficiency of resemblance for depiction.

Two counterexamples, which rely on the reflexivity and symmetry of resemblance, illustrate this point. First, Aristotle resembles himself, but Aristotle does not depict himself. Moreover, since all things share all of their properties with themselves, it follows from the definition of resemblance as sharing properties that resemblance is a reflexive relation: everything resembles itself. In contrast, depiction is not a reflexive relation: not everything depicts itself. So the insufficiency of resemblance for depiction follows simply from the fact that resemblance is reflexive whereas depiction is not (Goodman, 1968, 4).

Just as resemblance is reflexive, so is resemblance in specific respects. Resemblance in respect of colour, for example, is reflexive, because everything is the same colour as itself. In general, everything shares its own properties with itself, so everything resembles itself in respect of every kind of property. So just as resemblance simpliciter is not sufficient for depictive representation, no specific respects of resemblance are sufficient for depictive representation either: even if there were a relevant respect in which all depictions resembled what they represent, resemblance in that respect would not provide a sufficient condition for depiction.

Second, just as the Duke of Wellington's portrait resembles the Duke, the Duke resembles his portrait. But while the portrait depicts the Duke, the Duke does not depict his portrait. Since whenever one thing shares a property with a second, the second shares that same property with the first, resemblance is symmetric: whenever one thing resembles a second, the second resembles the first. In contrast, depiction is not a symmetric relation: not all things depict the things which depict them. So the insufficiency of resemblance for depiction follows merely from the fact that resemblance is symmetric whereas depiction is not (Goodman, 1968, 4).

Just as resemblance is symmetric, so is resemblance in specific respects. Resemblance in respect of being green, for example, is symmetric, since if one pea shares the property of being green with another pea, then the second pea must also share the property of being green with the first. In general, if something shares a property with another, then the latter shares that property with the former, so if something resembles another in some respect, then the latter resembles the former in that same respect. So specifying particular respects in which depictions resemble what they represent can't exclude examples of insufficiency arising from the symmetry of resemblance.

So analysing depiction in terms of respects of resemblance is inadequate not because there's no relevant respect in which all depictions resemble what they represent, but because no respect of any kind could be sufficient for representation. A similar point is made by Nelson Goodman in *Languages of Art*, where he writes that: "The plain fact is that a picture, to represent an object, must be a symbol for it, stand for it, refer to it; and that no degree of resemblance is sufficient to establish the requisite relationship of reference" (Goodman, 1968, 5). An adequate analysis of depiction in terms of resemblance must combine resemblance with representation.

But effecting a combination of resemblance with representation is not straightforward. The simplest way to effect the combination is simply to conjoin resemblance with representation, leading to the following analysis (Schier, 1986, 3):

(3)     Something depicts another if and only if the former resembles and represents the latter.

This analysis accommodates the point that depiction is a kind of representation straightforwardly since, according to it, the Mona Lisa, for example, depicts Lisa not merely because the Mona Lisa resembles Lisa, but also because the Mona Lisa is a representation of Lisa.

This analysis also escapes the obvious counterexamples to the sufficiency of the first. Members of the same family and cars off an assembly line do not depict each other, since although they resemble each other, they don't represent each other. Paintings resemble each other more than what they represent, but they still do not depict each other unless they represent each other. Aristotle does not depict himself, since he does not represent himself. And although the Duke of Wellington resembles his portrait as much as it resembles him, the Duke does not depict his portrait, since only the portrait represents the Duke, and not vice versa.

But there are less obvious counterexamples to the sufficiency of the second analysis, which show that it doesn't escape the problems of the first. The sign-language sign for a rabbit, for example, resembles a rabbit, but it does not depict a rabbit because the resemblance of the sign to the rabbit is noticeable only if one already knows what it represents (Lopes, 1996, 16). Similarly, all onomatopoeic words resemble what they represent, but not all depict what they represent, because the resemblances responsible for their origin have ceased to be relevant: the resemblance of 'woof' to a dog's bark, for example, is no longer relevant to its representation of a dog's bark.

Likewise, if properties are abundant, the analysis of resemblance as sharing properties entails every representation resembles what it represents in some respect. But even if properties are abundant, not every representation is a depiction. If properties are abundant, then the name 'rosemary' resembles rosemary, for example, since both the name 'rosemary' and rosemary fall under the predicate 'is 'rosemary' or rosemary', and so have the corresponding property of being 'rosemary' or rosemary. But even if properties are abundant, the name 'rosemary' does not depict rosemary. Resemblance and representation, like resemblance simpliciter, is insufficient for depiction.

Moreover, there are counterexamples to the combination of representation with any specific respect of resemblance. The phrase 'this phrase', for example, both represents and resembles itself, so the analysis predicts that it depicts itself. Furthermore, since resemblance is reflexive, the phrase 'this phrase' resembles itself in every respect. Nevertheless, 'this phrase' is obviously not a depiction of itself, since the fact that it resembles itself is merely incidental to the fact that it represents itself. So simply conjoining resemblance and representation cannot escape the basic problem posed by the insufficiency of resemblance (Goodman, 1970, 437).

A simple way to attain sufficiency would be to stipulate that the resemblance of a symbol to what it represents is not incidental to how it represents. Take, for example, the following analysis (Sachs-Hombach, 2003, 171):

(4)  Something depicts another if and only if the former represents the latter in virtue of the former resembling the latter.

Since 'this phrase' does not represent itself in virtue of resembling itself, this version of the analysis escapes the insufficiency of the second analysis by guaranteeing a non-incidental connection between resemblance and representation.

Likewise, although onomatopoeic words resemble what they represent, but do not all depict what they represent, this is because they have ceased representing what they do in virtue of resembling it, and now represent what they do merely conventionally: the resemblance of 'woof' to a dog's bark, for example, is not any longer relevant to its representation of a dog's bark, and so 'woof' does not represent a dog's bark in virtue of resembling it. And even if the name 'rosemary' resembles rosemary in respect of the property of being 'rosemary' or rosemary, it's obviously not in virtue of this resemblance that 'rosemary' represents rosemary.

But although this analysis escapes insufficiency, it's not an informative response to the objection. The objection, supported by examples such as 'this phrase', claims that resemblance is in general incidental to the way that symbols represent what they do. By defining depiction as that kind of representation in which resemblance plays a non-incidental role, this version of the analysis states there is a non-incidental role for resemblance in depictive representation, but it doesn't elaborate on what that role is. An informative analysis, in contrast, would specify what the non-incidental role of resemblance in depictive representation is as well as stating that it has one.

## 1.3 An intuitive taxonomy of representation

Representation is not a fundamental feature of the world, which suggests it should be analysable in terms of more fundamental features. In order to effect this reduction, it's helpful to divide representation into various kinds. The broadest division into kinds of representation is between natural and non-natural representation. Intuitively, natural representation divides into depiction and indication, and non-natural representation divides into conventional and intentional representation. Conventional representation is analysed in terms of intentional representation, whereas intentional representation is analysed in terms of natural representation.

It's common to combine the platitude that depiction is mediated by resemblance with the thesis that depiction is a kind of natural representation. The following passage, for example, neatly exemplifies the intuitive connection that many feel between the two theses: "As opposed to conventional symbols there are the so-called *natural* symbols, in which there is some non-conventional or natural relation (usually either of resemblance or causal connection) between the symbol and the thing symbolized" (Hospers, 1946, 30). Depiction, this suggests, is a kind of natural representation, and the role of resemblance is analogous to the role of causation in indication.

The paradigmatic example of natural representation is indication. Whereas depiction is mediated by resemblance and language by convention, indication is mediated by causation. Smoke is a natural representation of fire, for example, because smoke is caused by fire. Similarly, clouds naturally represent rain because rain is caused by clouds. And the number of rings in a tree's trunk is an indication of the age of the tree because of the causal connection between the number of rings and the age of the tree. If indication is simply causation, then indication is ubiquitous, since nearly everything physical is causally connected to something.

So the obvious way to analyse depiction as a kind of natural representation is to argue that just as indication is simply causation, depiction is simply resemblance. But this naïve suggestion – as the last section argued – cannot offer sufficient conditions for depiction, and so cannot support the platitude that whereas description is mediated by convention, depiction is mediated by resemblance. This suggests that unless one's willing to accept the consequence that just as resemblance is ubiquitous, depiction is ubiquitous, depiction should not be analysed as a kind of natural representation, like indication, but as a kind of non-natural representation, like description.

Even if it's denied that depiction is a kind of natural representation, photography – an important kind of depiction – plausibly is. Since there's a causal connection between photographs and what they represent, photographs are indications. This suggests that depiction must be analysed at least partially in terms of indication or causation: just as painting and drawing might be analysed by combining resemblance with non-natural representation, photography can be analysed by combining resemblance with natural representation. I'll argue in section 3.3 that this suggestion cannot be carried through: photographs are depictive only insofar as they are non-natural.

Just as natural representation is traditionally – but incorrectly – divided into depiction and indication, non-natural representation is traditionally – and correctly – divided into conventional and intentional representation. Language is the paradigm example of conventional representation, but there are numerous other examples, such as Morse code and semaphore, musical and mathematical notation, and various traffic signals or gestures. The hallmark of conventional representation is arbitrariness: my name, for example, is conventional, because my name was chosen arbitrarily; if my parents had chosen another name, it may have suited me just as well.

It's natural to combine a close analogy between depiction and description with the thesis that depiction is a kind of conventional representation, so I have to emphasise this is not my position: whereas my name and I, for example, are connected merely by an arbitrary convention, the connection between my portrait and me is non-arbitrary – my portrait represents me because it resembles me. Although some depictive symbol systems are partly mediated by convention – it's a convention, for example, that the top of a map represents the north – I will argue in section 5.2 that not every depictive symbol system is mediated (even in part) by convention.

Although depiction is not a kind of conventional representation, chapters four and five argue that there's a close analogy between depictive symbol systems and conventional language: if the component of the analysis of conventional language which ensures its arbitrariness is substituted for resemblance, then it applies instead to depictive symbol systems. And if the component of the analysis of conventional language ensuring its arbitrariness is removed altogether, it applies not just to depictive symbol systems but to symbol systems in general, including those – such as innately known languages or symbol systems – which are mediated by neither convention nor resemblance.

The fact that linguistic expressions may be used non-literally, with meanings which differ from those attached to them by convention, attests conventional representation is not the only kind of non-natural representation (Grice, 1957, 215). If, for example, I said, pointing into the sky, 'that aeroplane is a kilometre long', then I would typically only mean that it was much longer than the usual aeroplane, though the conventional meaning of the sentence is that the aeroplane is a whole kilometre in length. This type of representation is not mediated by convention, but by the intentions and purposes of the representation's perpetrator.

Although the paradigm example of intentional representation is non-literal language, there are numerous other examples. Whereas it's a convention for an audience to clap (or to knock on the table) to express appreciation, it's not a convention for speakers to clear their throats in order to signal they're about to begin, since because a clear throat is a prerequisite of speaking, an audience can recognise a speaker's intention to speak by hearing them clear their throat. I will argue in chapters two and three that depiction is a kind of intentional representation, and the role of the resemblance of depictions to what they represent is to facilitate the expression of intention.

## 1.4 The methodology of analysis

The central method of this book is philosophical analysis, which calls for clarification in order to avoid some common misunderstandings and misgivings. An analysis is a statement of equivalence between an analysandum and analysans. The following, for example, is an analysis of bachelors: bachelors are unmarried men. The analysis says what bachelors are by stating that bachelors, the analysandum, are equivalent to unmarried men, the analysans. Similarly, an analysis of depiction should state an equivalence between depiction, the analysandum, and a combination of resemblance and intentions, the analysans.

An analysis of depiction should not only state an equivalence between depiction and something else, but should state the conditions under which something depicts another. The Mona Lisa, for example, should not merely be classified as a depiction, but as a depiction of Lisa. That suggests that the analysis should be in the form of a biconditional stating that something depicts another if and only if ..., where the ellipsis on the right hand side is replaced by the analysans. The first analysis above, for example, replaced the ellipsis on the right with 'resembles' to form the statement that something depicts another if and only if the former resembles the latter.

Biconditional analyses should be interpreted as strict biconditionals, which state necessary equivalences between the analysandum and the analysans, rather than material biconditionals, which merely state a contingent coincidence between the analysandum and analysans. The biconditional 'snow is white if and only if grass is green', for example, is not an adequate analysis of snow's being white in terms of grass' being green, since although 'snow is white' and 'grass is green' are the same in truth-value, it isn't necessary that this is so. Illuminating analysis requires a necessary and not merely contingent coincidence between the analysandum and the analysans.

Even a strict biconditional does not always suffice for an illuminating philosophical analysis: it is a simple matter to find strict biconditionals which fail to provide an analysans which illuminates the nature of the analysandum. Take, for example, the analysis: something depicts another if and only if the former depicts the latter. This analysis obviously states a necessary equivalence between the analysandum and the analysans, since its left and right side cannot differ in truth-value. But because the analysandum and the analysans are stated in exactly the same terms, the analysis is uninformative: it contributes nothing to a philosophical understanding of depiction.

The fourth analysis above – which states that something depicts another if and only if the former represents the latter in virtue of resembling the latter – displays a similar defect, despite being a strict biconditional. In this case the terms of the analysans are distinct from terms of the analysandum. But the analysis is insufficiently illuminating since what is sought from a philosophical analysis of depiction – an explanation of how something may represent another in virtue of resembling it – is not provided in the analysans, but simply assumed to be available. An adequate analysis of depiction, in contrast, can be expected to provide an explanation of how depictions represent.

Some analyses are illuminating but uninteresting. No doubt it's possible, for example, to analyse bottles in terms of the purely physical. But the analysis would not be worth the difficulty of obtaining it: although an analysis of bottles in terms of the physical would show bottles are physical, the physical nature of bottles is not something we're inclined to doubt. An illuminating analysis of depiction in terms of resemblance, in contrast, would be interesting, because – as the objections raised against it show – the platitude that whereas description is mediated by convention, depiction is mediated by resemblance is something we're inclined to doubt.

The illumination of analysandum by analysans may be of two kinds: an analysis may be either reductive or reciprocal, depending on its goals. Reductive analyses require the terms of the analysans to be metaphysically, epistemologically or conceptually prior to the terms of the analysandum, whereas reciprocal analyses are just required to illuminate how the analysandum and analysans are interrelated (Avramides, 1989, 19-24). Defending the platitude that depiction is mediated by resemblance and a strong analogy between depiction and description requires merely a reciprocal analysis of depiction in terms of resemblance and intention.

Nevertheless, the analysis of non-natural meaning in terms of intentions and beliefs is generally considered as the first stage of a larger reduction of all representation – mental, descriptive and depictive – in terms of the physical (Schiffer, 1972, xi-xxix). If the second stage of this reduction – the analysis of intentions and beliefs in terms of the physical – is successful, then the analysis of depiction in terms of intentions and beliefs could likewise be considered as a step towards reductive physicalism, which would establish the epistemic, metaphysical or conceptual priority of mental over depictive representation. This is desirable, but not a requirement of success.

In particular, it's often objected that analyses of depiction in terms of resemblance and intention cannot be epistemologically reductive, since the terms of the analysans are not epistemologically prior to the terms of the analysandum: the resemblance of a depiction to what it represents and the intentions of its perpetrator, according to the objection, are only discoverable because the depiction represents what it does, rather than the reverse (Lopes, 1996, 16-20). The analysis below isn't committed to the epistemic priority of intention over representation, but merely, I will argue in section 2.2, to the epistemic priority of resemblance over depiction.

Four objections. First, analysis is often misleadingly called "conceptual analysis", as if the analysandum were a concept and the analysans were the conditions for the application of that concept. This leads to the idea that the subject of investigation is not depiction itself, or whatever is being analysed, but merely the concept of depiction, or the concept of the analysandum. Given that one might easily have had a different concept of depiction and that it's possible that not everyone expresses the same concept using the word 'depiction', this suggests analysis is merely an exercise in autobiography, rather than a method of philosophical inquiry.

But analyses, on the face of it, state equivalences between analysanda and analysans, rather than conditions for the application of concepts. So there's no reason to suppose that concepts, rather than analysanda themselves, are the subject of investigation. It might be true, and explain the use of the title "conceptual analysis", that knowledge that an analysis is true is based on grasping the concepts expressed in the analysis. But even if this epistemology of analysis is correct, it needn't follow that concepts are the subject of analyses. So it needn't follow that analysis is merely an exercise in autobiography, rather than a method of philosophical inquiry.

Second, analysis is often criticised on the grounds that it leads to dialectical deadlock, where it becomes impossible to assess rival positions. Robert Hopkins, for example, writes that "Provided that rival views avoid obscurity and obvious failure to cover more than a fraction of picturing [depiction], there is little to help us choose between them. At most they may differ about quite where the boundaries of depiction lie. The debate between them will then reduce to trading intuitions about which peripheral cases do or don't count as depiction. Experiences of such discussions elsewhere in philosophy suggest that they are rarely productive" (Hopkins, 1998, 23-24).

It is true that rival analyses disagree on the classification of which examples count as depictions. But this is no different from the disagreement of rival scientific theories over how to interpret the results of particular experiments: one theory may discard as noise what another regards as extremely significant. Just as it's still possible to assess rival scientific theories which disagree over the results of particular experiments by conducting further experiments and appealing to theoretical virtues such as simplicity, rival analyses may still be assessed by appeal both to further examples and, when only peripheral examples remain, to general theoretical virtues.

Third, continued disagreement between proponents of rival analyses even after all examples and theoretical considerations are taken into account sometimes indicates verbal disagreement about what the terms of the analysandum refer to, rather than substantive disagreement about its nature. If this is the case, it's better to resolve the dispute by accepting both analyses as successful accounts of distinct analysanda (as I suggested in section 1.1). But philosophical progress may continue by assessing the consequences of each analysis for the further questions they were intended to resolve, so that the method of analysis is able to resolve substantive questions even in the presence of verbal disagreement (Chalmers, 2011a).

So even if the dispute about whether depiction is mediated by resemblance turns out to be a merely verbal dispute about which kind of representation 'depiction' refers to, it does not follow that there are no substantive questions which an analysis of depiction – or of one disambiguation of what 'depiction' refers to – in terms of resemblance can resolve. In particular, there is substantive disagreement about the question of whether any kind of representation at all is mediated by resemblance, so disagreement over whether depiction is mediated by resemblance could continue even if it were discovered the original disagreement is partly verbal.

Fourth, it might be objected that most philosophical analyses are unsuccessful. There are nearly always counterexamples which show that the truth of the sentences on each side of the biconditional used to give an analysis may differ, so that the two sides are not equivalent. Furthermore, this usually proves to be the case independently of the complexity of the analysis or the number of revisions it has undergone. Given this history, it is very unlikely that an analysis of depiction which is both informative and truly necessary and sufficient will ever be given. If this is the case, then it seems that analysis is a poor choice of method for examining the nature of depiction.

But failure comes in degrees. Some counterexamples damage the succinctness of an analysis, but don't interfere with its ability to clarify the issues it's proposed in order to resolve. It's sometimes pointed out, for example, that colours cannot be analysed in terms of reflectance properties, because stained glass windows have their colour due to filtering rather than reflecting light (Hyman, 2006, 15). But this counterexample does not affect the spirit of the analysis, since it's not an obstacle in principle to the project of analysing colours in terms of their effect on light or, more generally, in terms of whatever physical properties are normally correlated with colours.

But some counterexamples show, not just that the analysis of a given thing is likely to be cumbersome, but that it is in principle impossible to give an analysis of that thing in the relevant terms. The existence of a possible world, for example, which is a physical duplicate of our own but lacks conscious experience, is a counterexample to any analysis of consciousness in physical terms, regardless of the complexity of such an analysis (Chalmers, 1996). The example, if successful, shows that the analysis of consciousness in terms of the physical is not merely cumbersome, but impossible in principle.

An adequate analysis of depiction should not be vulnerable to this second kind of counterexample. There may be counterexamples which show the correct analysis must be cumbersome and unwieldy, but there should be no counterexamples which show it's impossible in principle to analyse depiction in terms of resemblance and intentions in parallel with the analysis of non-natural meaning. So although the analysis of depiction below is unlikely to be more than approximately true, it may still be sufficiently close to the truth to support a strong analogy between depiction and description and to defend the platitude that depiction is mediated by resemblance.

## 1.5 Conclusion

The following chapters pursue an analysis of depiction which combines the platitude that depiction is mediated by resemblance with a close analogy between depiction and description. The second chapter argues for defining depiction as a kind of intentional representation, by adapting a Gricean analysis of meaning and communication (this part of the book shadows Abell 2005a; 2009, as well as Blumson 2009). Chapter three defends this analysis from familiar objections to intentionalism in philosophy of art. I argue that these objections are really objections to intentionalism in general, and have already been answered by proponents of the Gricean program.

The Gricean program in the philosophy of language employs a strategy of divide and conquer by distinguishing speaker meaning, which is analysed in terms of intention, from sentence meaning, which is analysed in terms of convention. Whereas chapters two and three extend the Gricean analysis of speaker meaning in terms of intention to encompass depiction, chapters four and five modify the Gricean analysis of sentence meaning in terms of convention by jettisoning arbitrariness in favour of resemblance to form an analysis of depictive symbol systems. By jettisoning resemblance as well, chapter five extends this analysis to symbol systems in general.

Languages are striking for their compositionality: the meaning of sentences depends upon the meanings and arrangement of their parts. Chapters six and seven pursue the analogy between depiction and description to its extreme by arguing that depictive symbol systems, like languages, are compositional. Chapter six argues that both depiction and description have compositional structure and chapter seven argues that compositional structure has the same role in the interpretation of both depiction and description. The platitude that depiction is mediated by resemblance is neglected in these chapters, but the pursuit of a strong analogy between depiction and description continues.

The platitude that depiction is mediated by resemblance is often doubted because it's not obviously consonant with the possibility of depicting inexistents, the possibility of depicting something without depicting something in particular, and the possibility of depictive misrepresentation. In chapter eight, I argue that these problems are merely manifestations of the problem of intentionality in general and, in chapter nine, I argue that the analysis of content in terms of possible worlds resolves this problem in a way which is consonant with the platitude. Chapter nine also addresses problems raised by pictures in perspective, and the possibility of depicting impossibilities.

Just as it's a platitude that depiction is mediated by resemblance, it's a platitude that a picture is realistic to the degree to which it resembles what it represents (in relevant respects). But if properties are abundant and degrees of resemblance are proportions of properties in common, then the degree of resemblance between different particulars is constant (or undefined), which is inconsonant with the platitude. Chapter ten argues this problem should be resolved by revising the analysis of degrees of resemblance in terms of proportion of properties in common, and not by accepting a sparse theory of properties or denying the platitude.

# 2. Defining Depiction

"The aim of philosophy …", according to Wilfrid Sellars, "… is to understand how things in the broadest possible sense of the term hang together in the broadest possible sense of the term" (Sellars, 1962, 369). One way of pursuing this aim is to pursue the reductive analysis of everything in terms of the more or most fundamental things. The aim may, for example, be a reductive analysis of everything in terms of the physical, or the phenomenological, or a combination of the physical and the phenomenological. As I conceive of it, the purpose of the philosophy of pictures is to complete one small step in this ambitious reductive program.

The reductive program may take various paths. In philosophy of mind and language, it's common to distinguish the Sellarsian program, which pursues a reductive analysis of mind in terms of language, from the Gricean program, which pursues an analysis of language in terms of mind (see McKinsey (1983, 1-2) and Bennett (1976, 24-27)). Whereas the Sellarsian program analyses the belief that it's raining, for example, in terms of the assertion that it's raining, the Gricean program analyses the assertion that it's raining in terms of the belief that it's raining. The next four chapters pursue an analysis of depiction as part of this Gricean program.

The Gricean program in the philosophy of language employs a strategy of divide and conquer by distinguishing speaker meaning, to be analysed in terms of intention, from sentence meaning, to be analysed in terms of convention. Whereas this chapter and the following extend the Gricean analysis of speaker meaning in terms of intention to encompass depiction, chapters four and five modify the Gricean analysis of sentence meaning in terms of convention by jettisoning arbitrariness in favour of resemblance to form an analysis of depictive symbol systems. The analysis of pictures, I will argue in these chapters, slides seamlessly into the Gricean program as a whole.

http://dx.doi.org/10.11647/OBP.0046.02

So this chapter argues for defining depiction as a kind of intentional representation. In particular, it argues for defining depiction by combining resemblance with an analysis of speaker meaning in terms of intentions (following Abell, 2005a; 2009; as well as Blumson, 2009). The Mona Lisa depicts Lisa, for example, because Leo intended his audience to infer from the Mona Lisa's resemblance to Lisa his intention to induce an effect in them, by means of recognition of his intentions. This analysis, I will argue, supports both a close analogy between depiction and description and the platitude that whereas description is mediated by convention, depiction is mediated by resemblance.

The first section introduces the analysis of speaker meaning in terms of intention and argues for its application to depiction. The second section takes up and argues against the natural suggestion of defining depiction by substituting experienced resemblance for the intended effect in the analysis of speaker meaning. The third section argues for defining depiction by substituting resemblance for the intended feature of utterances in the analysis of speaker meaning from which the speaker's intentions are intended to be inferred. The fourth section compares the analysis with Catharine Abell's (2009), which also defines depiction by combining resemblance with speaker meaning.

## 2.1 Grice's analysis of speaker meaning

There's an important distinction between the meaning of sentences, called "sentence meaning", and what speakers use those sentences to mean, called "speaker meaning" (Grice, 1957, 217). Suppose, for example, I say, after Smith's just insulted me, 'Smith is a fine friend'. The sentence means that Smith is a fine friend, but this is not what I mean by the sentence: rather, my utterance of the sentence on this occasion means that Smith is a foul friend, for having insulted me. It's plausible that speaker meaning should be analysed directly in terms of intentions, whereas sentence meaning should be analysed jointly in terms of convention and speaker meaning.

This order of analysis is justified by the dependence of meaning on use: the purpose of linguistic utterances is to achieve various effects in audiences. Indicative sentences, for example, are usually uttered to produce beliefs. Imperative sentences, in contrast, are usually uttered to produce actions rather than beliefs. If, for example, I mean you to stop by uttering 'stop!', then my purpose is to induce you to stop. This suggests that a person means something by an utterance if and only if the person intends to induce an effect in an audience (Grice, 1957, 217). I might mean that it's raining by uttering 'it's raining', for example, because I intend you to believe it's raining.

But the following is a counterexample. Suppose that I want to frame you for a murder I've committed. In order to do so I leave your handkerchief at the scene of the crime, stained in the blood of the victim. I intend to induce the police to believe, on finding the bloodstained handkerchief, that you are the murderer, so the conditions of the analysis are met. Nevertheless, it is not the case that by leaving your handkerchief at the scene I mean that you are the murderer. I intend my action to produce an effect in my audience, but I nevertheless do not mean anything by my action, so intending to induce an effect in an audience is insufficient for speaker meaning (Grice, 1957, 217).

The problem the example raises is that it is not sufficient for an utterance to have meaning that it be used for a certain purpose, even if that purpose is characteristically linguistic, because it's always possible to achieve that purpose in some other way, without communicating one's intentions. The example shows an adequate analysis of speaker meaning has to characterise not only the effects, such as inducing beliefs and actions, that meaningful utterances are intended to accomplish, but also the distinctive way in which meaningful utterances bring about those effects. Merely causing beliefs and actions is not the same as communicating them.

In meaning something by an utterance, one's intentions are explicit in a way one's intentions in other actions aren't: telling someone something, for example, is explicit in a way that tricking someone is not (Grice, 1957, 218). This suggests:

(5) A person means something by an utterance if and only if the person intends the utterance to produce an effect in an audience by means of recognition of this intention (Grice, 1957, 220).

So I mean that it's raining by uttering 'it's raining', for example, because I intend to induce you to believe that it's raining by means of recognition of my intention.

Requiring the intended effect of an utterance to produce an effect in an audience by means of recognition of intention captures the distinctive way in which meaningful utterances produce their effects, because it captures the fact that one's intentions in meaning something by an utterance are explicit in a way one's intentions in other actions aren't. In leaving your bloodstained handkerchief at the scene of the crime, for example, I don't mean that you're the murderer, because although I intend the police to believe that you are the murderer, I don't intend this effect to be produced by means of recognition of my intention.

Depictions, like sentences, are aimed at the production of various effects. Maps, for example, are depictions aimed at producing beliefs in audiences about terrain. Lego instructions are depictions which are intended to induce audiences to arrange Lego in a certain way, rather than to induce them to believe that Lego is arranged in that way. Caricatures, like jokes, are aimed at producing amusement. This suggests analysing depiction, like speaker meaning, in terms of the effects pictures are intended to induce in their audiences, by means of recognition of these intentions: depiction, in other words, should be analysed as a special case of speaker meaning.

It would be a problematic disanalogy with meaning if there were any depiction which did not have the purpose of producing an effect in its audience. The fact that the purposes of some depictions are exclusively aesthetic, rather than directed towards a practical end such as belief or action, might be thought to show this. But, firstly, this is not a disanalogy since there are examples of descriptions, such as in poetry or song, which are also exclusively aesthetic and, secondly, even a depiction with an exclusively aesthetic purpose is at least intended to produce some aesthetic effect, such as pleasure or amusement, concerning what it represents in its audience.

An example analogous to the example of the handkerchief shows that depictive, like descriptive, representation requires the effect in the audience to be induced explicitly and openly. Suppose that I have a secret tunnel in my office. One panel of the wall is actually the door to the secret tunnel, which I have disguised to look exactly like an ordinary part of my bookshelf. Hence, the tunnel door is intended to look and be like an ordinary part of my bookshelf and to induce visitors to believe it is an ordinary part of my bookshelf. But the tunnel door doesn't depict an ordinary part of my bookshelf, since I don't intend it to induce this effect by means of recognition of my intention.

A deeper reason that the analysis of speaker meaning ought to be applied to depiction is its general nature. There is no distinctively linguistic or verbal element in the analysis of speaker meaning except for the word 'utterance', which is used in an extended sense to cover any kind of action, including dropping handkerchiefs and drawing pictures as well as writing and talking (Grice, 1969, 92). This means that the analysis should be expected to apply not just to language but to all communication, including pictorial representation. Different kinds of representation – like depiction and description – can then be defined as different kinds of speaker meaning.

So the analysis of speaker meaning should be applied to specifying how depiction is representational. As Catharine Abell writes: "... in the case of depiction 'the maker $A$, means picture $Y$ to depict an object, $Z$' is roughly equivalent to '$A$ produced $Y$ with the intention of inducing a belief about [or other effect concerning] $Z$ in the observers of $Y$ in virtue of those observers recognizing this intention'" (Abell, 2005a, 59; see also Novitz, 1977, for a similar account). So the Mona Lisa, for example, depicts Lisa because Leo intended to induce an effect – such as the belief that Lisa smiled – in his audience, by means of recognition of his intention.

But exactly how to apply the analysis of speaker meaning to the analysis of depiction is not obvious: simply conjoining resemblance with speaker meaning is no better than merely conjoining it with representation. The sentence 'this sentence is thirty-five letters long', for example, resembles itself and may be written with the intention of inducing in audiences the effect of believing that it is thirty-five letters long, by means of recognition of this intention. But, like the phrase 'this phrase', the sentence does not depict itself, because its resemblance to itself is incidental to its representation of itself. The problem of insufficiency is still unresolved.

## 2.2 The intended effect in Grice's analysis

A common way to analyse a particular kind of meaning or representation is by specifying the intended effect in the analysis of speaker meaning. Assertions, for example, are those utterances which are intended to induce beliefs by means of recognition of intention, whereas commands are those utterances which are intended to induce actions by means of recognition of intention. Similarly, jokes are utterances intended, by means of recognition of intention, to induce amusement. This suggests depiction might also be analysed by an appropriate specification of the intended effect in the analysis of speaker meaning.

To take a more exotic example, fiction can be analysed by substituting imagination as the intended effect in the analysis of speaker meaning (Currie, 1990, 18-51). So, for example, it is fictional in *The Adventures of*

*Sherlock Holmes* that Sherlock Holmes is a detective because the reader is intended, on the basis of recognition of that intention, to imagine that Sherlock Holmes is a detective. If there is some effect on the audience that is distinctive of depiction, as imagination is an effect distinctive of fiction, then that could be combined with the analysis of speaker meaning to provide an analysis of depiction.

Robert Hopkins (1998, 50-51) suggests that audiences of depictions experience them as resembling what they represent. This suggests substituting experienced resemblance for the intended effect in the analysis of speaker meaning as follows:

(6) Something depicts another if and only if the former is intended to induce the former to be experienced as resembling the latter by means of recognition of this intention.

So the Mona Lisa, for example, is supposed to depict Lisa because Leo intended it to be experienced as resembling Lisa, by means of recognition of his intention.

One clarification. An experience of resemblance does not require both the thing that resembles and the thing that is resembled to be present. If somebody is familiar with a company logo, for example, then whenever they see that logo their experience is likely to represent it as having the property of resembling the instances of the logo that they have seen in the past (Peacocke, 1987, 385). So experiencing a resemblance is not just experiencing similar things simultaneously. Rather, it's having an experience which represents something as having the property of resembling another, which may or may not be present.

By specifying experienced resemblance as the intended effect in the analysis of speaker meaning, this analysis seems to provide for a non-incidental connection between resemblance and representation. Although the sentence 'this sentence is thirty-five letters long', for example, resembles itself and is intended to induce an effect in its audience by means of recognition of intention, the intended effect is not for it to be experienced as resembling itself. This suggests that substituting experienced resemblance for the effect in the analysis of speaker meaning escapes the counterexamples to straightforwardly conjoining resemblance with representation.

But the following counterexample shows that it doesn't. Suppose I sincerely write: 'I intend this sentence to induce itself to be experienced as resembling itself by means of recognition of my intention'. Since I do intend the sentence to induce itself to be experienced as resembling itself by means of recognition of my intention, the analysis predicts that I have not only written that sentence, but also depicted it. But although the sentence is sincerely intended to be experienced as resembling itself by means of recognition of my intention, it is not a depiction of itself. On the contrary, it's a paradigm example of a non-depictive, descriptive, representation.

In this case, the fact that the sentence is intended to be experienced as resembling itself is incidental to the way that the sentence represents itself in the same way that the fact that 'this sentence is thirty-five letters long' resembles itself is incidental to the way that it represents itself. The problem with the analysis is that it specifies the distinctive feature of depiction by specifying what depiction is used to do. But depiction is distinctive, not because it is used to do something special, but because it achieves what it is used to do in a special way. So depiction cannot be analysed by specifying the intended effect in the analysis of speaker meaning.

Four objections. First, perhaps the counterexample can be avoided by denying that things can be experienced as resembling themselves, and thus denying that I can sincerely intend my sentence to be experienced as resembling itself by means of recognition of my intention. But since there are pictures that represent themselves (Walton, 1990, 117-121), denying that things can be experienced as resembling themselves is not an available response. One might just deny that this particular sentence can be experienced as resembling itself. But there is no principled reason to do so, nor to think that this would solve the underlying problem.

Second, perhaps the argument tacitly relies on the false premise that nothing can be both a depictive and a descriptive representation. Pattern poems, for example, often represent their subjects both through the conventional meaning of their words and the arrangement of those words into patterns that resemble what they represent: John Hollander's (1981, 31) pattern-poem *Pattern Poem*, for example, makes its point by both describing itself as making a point and depicting itself as making a point, in virtue of resembling itself in respect of being point shaped. I don't want to deny that such pattern poems are both descriptions and depictions of their subjects.

But the argument doesn't rely on the premise that nothing can be both a depiction and a description. I don't deny that the sentence 'I intend this sentence to be experienced as resembling itself by means of recognition of my intention' is a depiction merely because it is a linguistic description, but because both the resemblance of the sentence to itself and the fact that the sentence is intended to be experienced as resembling itself are incidental to its representation of itself: the sentence refers to itself only because of its use of the demonstrative expression 'this sentence' to refer to itself.

So the fact that the sentence is a paradigmatically linguistic representation doesn't exclude the sentence from being a depiction, and the claim that linguistic representations cannot also be depictive representations is not a premise of the argument. The fact that the example is an explicit and paradigmatically linguistic representation plays only a heuristic role: it makes it more obvious than another example would that the sentence's being intended to be experienced as resembling itself and its resemblance to itself are incidental to the way it represents itself.

Third, it might be objected that the argument proves too much, because it undermines the analysis of fiction as well. Suppose I say 'I intend you to imagine that it was a dark and stormy night, by means of recognition of this intention'. It might be argued that, despite meeting the conditions of the analysis of fiction, what the sentence says is not fictional, because a person sincerely uttering it would be telling the truth: the sentence would be a factually correct account of that person's intention. So explicitly stating that the conditions of the analysis of fiction are met appears to produce an analogous counterexample to its sufficiency.

But the sufficiency of the analysis of fiction may be defended by arguing that my utterance of 'I intend you to imagine that it is a dark and stormy night by means of recognition of my intention', as well as accurately reporting my intentions, really does make it fictional that it is a dark and stormy night. The example is not one in which an utterance of non-fiction meets the conditions of the analysis of fiction, but is an example in which someone meets the conditions of the analysis of fiction by simultaneously speaking the truth and explicitly creating a fiction.

The following example illustrates the plausibility of this response. The first sentence of *If on a Winter's Night a Traveller,* by Italo Calvino, is 'You are about to begin reading Italo Calvino's new novel, *If on a Winter's Night a Traveller'* (Calvino, 1982, 1). Like a sentence that explicitly states the conditions of the analysis of fiction are met, this opening is at once a statement of fact, since normally the reader is about to begin reading the book, and an explicit announcement that the author is engaging in fiction, since it states that you are reading a novel.

Fourth, it might be objected that the argument proves too much because it undermines the analysis of speaker meaning in general. Suppose I sincerely say 'I intend you to believe that it's raining by means of recognition of my intention'. It follows from the analysis of speaker meaning that the person has said that it's raining. But intuitively, runs the objection, by uttering that sentence I would not mean that that it's raining. Rather, I would mean that I intend you to believe that it's raining by means of recognition of my intention.

But the sufficiency of the analysis of speaker meaning may be defended by arguing that by uttering 'I intend you to believe that it's raining by means of recognition of my intention' as well as explicitly stating my intentions, I also mean that it's raining. As for the analysis of fiction, the response becomes plausible if one considers explicit performatives. 'I hereby declare that there is a cat on the mat', for example, is at once a declaration that there is a cat on the mat and a report that the speaker declares that there is a cat on the mat (Schiffer, 1972, 64-68).

Note that the argument applies not only to experienced resemblance, but to any attempt to analyse depiction by specifying the intended effect in the analysis of speaker meaning. Whatever effect is specified, it will be possible to write a sentence sincerely announcing the intention of the writer to induce that effect by means of recognition of that intention. That sentence would meet the conditions of the analysis, but it would fail to be a depiction. So to provide an analysis of depiction, the analysis of speaker meaning has to be combined with a feature distinctive of depiction not by specifying the intended effect in the analysis, but in some other way.

## 2.3 The salient feature in Grice's analysis

To see how resemblance and the analysis of speaker meaning can be combined to analyse depiction, consider the following two examples. First, suppose a shopkeeper antecedently knows that I want cigarettes. I pass the shopkeeper fifty dollars in order to induce him to give me cigarettes, by means of his antecedent recognition of my intention that he give me cigarettes. Second, suppose I pass the shopkeeper eleven dollars and fifty-five cents, the exact price of the brand I prefer, intending him to infer from the fact that I pass him that amount that I intend the money to induce him to give me those cigarettes by means of recognition of my intention.

Because in the first case the shopkeeper already knew that I wanted the cigarettes, it does not seem that by passing him the fifty dollars I meant that he should give me the cigarettes. But in the second case, because the shopkeeper inferred what I wanted, it does seem that I meant by the eleven dollars and fifty-five cents that I want the cigarettes (Grice, 1969, 94). To reflect this difference, the analysis should be altered to the following (Avramides, 1989, 47):

(7) A person means something by an utterance if and only if the person intends that:

   a. the utterance has a certain feature
   b. an audience recognise that the utterance has that feature
   c. the audience infer at least in part from the fact that the utterance has that feature that the person intends:
   d. that the utterance produce an effect in the audience
   e. and that that effect be produced at least in part by means of the audience's recognition of intentions (a)-(e).

So, for example, my passing the shopkeeper eleven dollars and fifty-five cents means he should give me the cigarettes because it has the feature of being exactly the price of my brand of cigarettes, and because the shopkeeper infers from that feature that I intend him to give me the cigarettes by means of recognition of my intention (see Harman (1974) for defence of the self-reflexivity in (e)).

In the case of linguistic representation, the feature from which the audience is intended to infer the speaker's intentions is the conventional meaning of the utterance or the fact that speakers have uttered it before with the same meaning. My utterance of 'it's raining', for example, means that it's raining because I intend you to infer from the conventional meaning of 'it's raining' in English that I intend to induce you to believe that it's raining by means of recognition of my intentions (Schiffer, 1972, 12). Convention connects words with what they represent by allowing audiences to infer the communicative intentions of speakers who conform to the convention.

But whereas words are connected to what they represent by convention, depictions are connected to what they represent by resemblance. So it's natural to mark this difference by inserting resemblance into the analysis of meaning in the same place that allows for the role of the conventional meanings of words, as follows:

(8) Something depicts another if and only if it is intended that:

    a. the former resembles the latter in a certain respect
    b. an audience recognise the former resembles the latter in that respect
    c. the audience infer at least in part from the fact the former resembles the latter in that respect that it is intended:
    d. that the former produce an effect in the audience
    e. and that that effect be produced at least in part by means of the audience's recognition of intentions (a)-(e).

This analysis is the result of specifying that resemblance is the feature of the picture from which audiences infer depicters' intentions, just as conventional meaning is the feature of linguistic utterances from which audiences infer speakers' intentions.

By specifying the role of resemblance in depictive representation, this analysis avoids the counterexamples to analysing depiction simply by conjoining representation with resemblance. The sentence 'this sentence is thirty-five letters long', for example, is not counted as a depiction of itself because, although it resembles and represents itself, the intentions of people who utter it to induce effects in their audiences by means of recognition of their intentions will normally be inferred not from the sentence's resemblance to itself, but from its conventional meaning in English. So the analysis captures the non-incidental role of resemblance in depictive representation.

Moreover, a counterexample to this analysis cannot be produced by a linguistic restatement of the relevant conditions. Even if I say 'I intend that this sentence resemble itself in shape, that you recognise this resemblance, and that you infer from this resemblance that I intend to induce you to believe that it's raining by means of recognition of my intention' I cannot be sincere because those inferences cannot be made from the sentence's resemblance to itself in shape and so I cannot rationally or successfully have the intentions I declare I have using that sentence. So the analysis avoids the counterexamples to the insufficiency of resemblance for representation.

It might be objected that analysing depiction in terms of intention reverses the correct order of discovery, since the intentions of a depiction's perpetrator are discovered from knowledge of what the depiction represents, rather than what it represents being discovered from knowledge of its perpetrator's intentions. Rather than discovering that the Mona Lisa represents Lisa, for example, by discovering that Leo intended to induce a certain effect in us by means of recognition of his intention, we discovered that Leo intended to induce this effect in us by means of recognition of his intention because we know that the Mona Lisa depicts Lisa.

This objection is only relevant if the analysis is intended as an epistemic reduction of depiction to intention. But the analysis isn't intended as an epistemic reduction of depiction to intention, so whether we discover what pictures represent by knowing their perpetrators' intentions or vice versa is irrelevant. The analysis is intended as a metaphysical reduction of depiction in terms of intention. But the analysis plausibly succeeds as a metaphysical reduction, since intention is plausibly metaphysically prior to depiction: intentions might have existed without depictions, but depictions could not have existed without intentions.

But the analysis is committed to an epistemic priority of resemblance over depiction, because it requires the communicative intentions of a depiction's perpetrator to be inferred from the resemblance of the depiction to what it represents, and this is open to question. It might be argued that the resemblance of hidden figures to what they represent, for example, is inferred from antecedent knowledge of what the figures represent, rather than what the figures represent being inferred from what they resemble (Lopes, 2005b, 167). If this is the case then – contrary to the analysis – there is no epistemic priority of resemblance over intention.

But although what hidden figures represent cannot be recognised immediately, this need not be because what they resemble is inferred from what they represent, since what hidden figures represent cannot be recognised immediately either. Moreover, it must be possible to recognise what hidden figures resemble independently of what they represent, since it would still be possible to recognise the resemblance of a figure to what it represents even if it ceased to represent that thing. It might be difficult, for example, to notice a figure hidden in the midst of a painting of clouds. But it must be possible, for the resemblance could still be pointed out even if the clouds were real.

Three clarifications. First, the analysis requires not merely that the picture is intended to resemble what it represents, but that it is intended to resemble what it represents in a certain respect. And the analysis requires not merely that the audience recognise that the picture resembles what it represents, but that they recognise that it resembles what it represents in this specific respect. For the Mona Lisa to depict Lisa, for example, the analysis requires that Leo had in mind a specific respect in which he intended the Mona Lisa to resemble Lisa. Moreover, it requires us to be able to recognise that the Mona Lisa resembles Lisa in this specific respect.

But it sometimes seems possible to recognise a resemblance without recognising the respect in which the resemblance obtains. It may be possible to recognise a similarity between two faces, for example, without being able to recognise the respect in which that similarity consists (Armstrong, 1978b, 98). And it may be possible to recognise a similarity between a portrait and the face it represents, without being able to recognise the respect in which the portrait and the face it represents are similar. If this is correct, then the portrait may depict the face without the artist or audience recognising in what respect it resembles the face, and so the analysis should be weakened.

However, the specific respect must be mentioned in the analysis since if the abundant conception of properties is a necessary truth, it's also a necessary truth that everything resembles everything, and so it's also a necessary truth that a picture resembles what it represents (if the picture and what it represents exist). In this case, the intention that a picture resembles what it represents would be problematic – it would be like having an intention that one plus one is two, or that bachelors are unmarried men. Moreover, the audience could easily recognise that the picture resembles what it represents, but it would be difficult for them to infer anything from this about the artist's intentions.

So if the sparse conception of properties is correct, then the analysis can be simplified and the counterexample above avoided by omitting to require that the resemblance be in a certain respect. But if on the other hand it's the abundant conception of properties which is correct, then the analysis cannot be simplified in this way, and the purported counterexample must be addressed head on. But this is not so much a problem for the analysis as a problem for the abundant conception of properties, for a proponent of the abundant conception of properties must argue that recognition of resemblance, unless it is vacuous, is always recognition of resemblance in a certain respect.

Second, though it contains the word "recognition", the analysis is not a version of the recognition theory of depiction. According to recognition theories, something depicts another only if the former causes (usually non-veridical) recognition of the latter. But according to analysis (8), something depicts another not only if it is intended that an audience recognise the latter itself, but only if it is intended that an audience recognise the *resemblance* of the former to the latter. And analysis (8) requires the recognition of the resemblance of the former to the latter be veridical. (See Newall (2011, 42-94) for an extremely helpful comparison of the recognition and resemblance theories.)

Third, the analysis leaves open the nature of the intended effect mentioned in clause (d). It is open to the proponent of experienced resemblance, for example, to hold that it is a necessary condition of depiction that experienced resemblance be the intended effect. But I'm doubtful that experienced resemblance or any other kind of experience is necessary for depiction, especially in view of my stipulation in the introduction that depiction may occur in any medium, and includes allegorical fiction. Moreover, if the intended effect in the analysis is allowed to be an action, belief, imagining or similar attitude, then the parallel with the analysis of speaker meaning is more perfect.

## 2.4 Abell's analysis of depiction

In arguing that depiction should be analysed in terms of resemblance and speaker meaning, I'm agreeing with Catharine Abell, according to whom something depicts an object O if "Its maker intended it to resemble O in a certain visible respect(s) and thus to bring O to viewers' minds, and intended that these resemblances have this effect in part because viewers recognise this intention ..." (Abell, 2009, 208). So the Mona Lisa depicts Lisa, according to Abell, because Leo intended the Mona Lisa to resemble Lisa in a visible respect and thus to bring Lisa to viewers' minds, in part because viewers recognise this intention.

The purpose of this section is to clarify the differences between Abell's analysis and my own. I agree with Abell about the sufficiency of the condition quoted in the last paragraph, which differs only superficially from analysis (8) in the last section. I also agree with Abell that there are counterexamples to the necessity of that condition and analysis (8). But I disagree with Abell about how to accommodate counterexamples to the necessity of her sufficient condition and analysis (8) and so also disagree with her about the final analysis of depiction. This section explains Abell's analysis and how I disagree with it. My own version will not be finalised until chapter nine.

The first issue I disagree with Abell about is how to address counterexamples to the necessity of an audience. It's possible to depict something without intending to induce an effect in an audience: it is possible, for example, to depict by doodling in margins, drawing preparatory sketches and tracing patterns in fogged-up glass, but not intend that the doodles, sketches or traces ever reach an audience other than oneself. In some of these cases, one can argue the intended audience of the doodle, sketch or tracing is simply the doodler, the sketcher or the tracer, but this response, I will argue in section 3.3, is not available in every case of this kind.

The second issue I disagree with Abell about is how to address counterexamples to the necessity of intention. Abell argues that an intention to depict, or to respond to a communication problem, is necessary for depiction (Abell, 2009, 205). Nevertheless, Abell argues that what an artist depicts may not be what the artist intends to depict. If, for example, a drawing inadvertently turns out to look more like a fat man than like a svelte man then, according to Abell, the drawing could turn out to depict a fat man even though it was intended to depict a svelte man (Abell, 2009, 194). In contrast, I'll argue in section 3.2 that there are no counterexamples to the necessity of intention.

To accommodate these possibilities, Abell argues that "Just as we are able to interpret sentences uttered without communicative intentions because they employ linguistic conventions with which we are familiar, we are able to interpret pictures produced without communicative intentions because they employ stylistic conventions with which we are familiar" (Abell, 2009, 204). So just as, for example, the sentences in my diary have meaning even though I don't intend them to reach an audience because of their conventional meaning in English, the doodles in my margins depict because they fall under certain stylistic conventions, which usually govern communication.

I have two objections to this response. First, it's possible to depict without intending to reach an audience or to conform to a stylistic convention. A painter, for example, may choose not to exhibit his or her paintings, precisely because the paintings are stylistically innovative and so don't conform to any stylistic conventions. Likewise a diarist, in the linguistic case, may write in non-literal language, the intended meaning of which isn't the conventional meaning of the words. To accommodate these cases, I will argue in section 3.3 that it is a necessary condition of depiction not that it induces an effect in an audience, but that it does so *if* it reaches an audience of a certain type.

Second, using convention to accommodate audienceless and unintentional depiction risks failing to distinguish between depiction and onomatopoeia. The word 'woof', for example, resembles but does not depict a dog's bark. But just as sentences now have their sentence meaning because of conventions arising from what they were used to speaker mean in the past, some onomatopoeic words have their meaning because of conventions arising from what they were used to depict in the past. So allowing that merely falling under stylistic conventions is sufficient for depiction risks including not only audienceless and unintended depiction, but also onomatopoeia.

However, Abell's appeal to convention may avoid this problem because falling under a stylistic convention, according to her analysis, is not quite sufficient for depiction. Instead, something depicts an object *O* if its maker produced the resemblance at issue "… and intended thereby to adhere to a stylistic convention extant in his or her community, characterized by resemblance in the respect(s) at issue, and thus bring *O* to viewers' minds" or else had "… the intention of responding to a communication problem to which a conventional solution is extant in his or her community, which is characterized by resemblance in the given respect(s)" (Abell, 2009, 204-205).

The first condition does exclude onomatopoeia, since though onomatopoeic words fall under stylistic conventions extant in their communities, they need not be intended to fall under these stylistic conventions. But the first condition also excludes depiction in the absence of an intended audience, since it requires the maker to intend to bring the object to viewer's minds, and unintentional depiction, since the maker must intend the resemblance at issue and intend thereby to adhere to the stylistic convention which is characterised by that resemblance. Abell's example of an inadvertent picture of a fat man, for example, does not satisfy the first condition.

The second includes depiction in the absence of an audience, since it doesn't require the maker to intend to bring the object to viewer's minds, and unintentional depiction, since makers may produce the resemblances at issue with the intention to respond to communication problems, while inadvertently producing a resemblance in the wrong respect. But in this case, onomatopoeia is included, since onomatopoeic utterances are intended to respond to communication problems to which conventional solutions are extant, and since those conventional solutions are characterised by resemblance in the respects which are responsible for explaining the origin of the onomatopoeia.

The Gricean program in the philosophy of language employs a strategy of divide and conquer by analysing speaker meaning in terms of intention, and sentence meaning in terms of convention and speaker meaning. By invoking conventions in the analysis of depiction, Abell hopes to employ a parallel strategy to respond to counterexamples to the necessity of intentions for depiction. In chapters four and five I will also argue for analysing some kinds of depiction in parallel with the analysis of sentence meaning – but I will deny that a convention which has its origin in resemblance is sufficient for depiction, and so exclude onomatopoeia.

The third issue I disagree with Abell about is how to respond to the problem posed by the intentionality of depiction. Three features of depiction are symptomatic of its intentionality. The first is the apparent possibility of depicting non-existents. The second is the possibility of depicting something without depicting anything in particular. The third symptom is the possibility of depictive misrepresentation. All three symptoms of the intentionality of depiction are problematic for the platitude that depiction is mediated by resemblance, but the difficulties are raised most strikingly by the problem of the depiction of non-existents.

Abell argues that depicting non-existents is possible because such depictions would resemble what they represent, if what they represent had existed. Although Santa's portrait, for example, does not actually resemble Santa, because Santa does not exist, it seems plausible that Santa's portrait would have resembled Santa if Santa had existed, because if Santa had existed, both he and his portrait would have shared the property of being partly red. In general, depictions of non-existents don't resemble what they represent, but they would have done if what they represent had existed, so the caveat appears to accommodate the depiction of non-existents (Abell, 2009, 212).

However, Santa may be depicted both as mostly red or as mostly green. But had he existed, he would have been either mostly red or mostly green, but not both. So either the depiction of Santa as mostly red or the depiction of Santa as mostly green would fail to resemble Santa in respect of colour, even if Santa had existed. In general, non-existent objects may be depicted as appearing in many different, often inconsistent, ways. If there is a fact of the matter about how the non-existent object would have looked, some depictions of it wouldn't have resembled that object; if there's no fact of the matter, then there's no fact of the matter about whether they'd resemble it or not.

Abell may argue that there are facts of the matter about how inexistent objects look, and that pictures which don't depict them as they would look are misrepresentations, the problem of which has to be solved differently. The problem of misrepresentation is that if a depiction misrepresents what it depicts in some respect, then it will fail to resemble what it represents in that respect. If a tree is depicted as blue, for example, then the depiction fails to resemble the tree in respect of colour. Likewise, if Santa is depicted as partly green instead of partly red, Abell may argue that this is possible for the same reason it is possible to depict a green tree as blue.

A picture misrepresents something as having a property, according to Abell, only if it resembles that thing or would if that thing existed and resembles things that have that property or would if they existed (Abell, 2009, 212). So, for example, it's possible for a picture to depictively misrepresent a green tree as blue, because the picture may resemble the tree in respect of shape and simultaneously resemble something blue in respect of colour. So as long as it's possible for a marked surface to simultaneously resemble a tree and blue things, it's likewise possible for the surface to depict the tree as blue, as long as the surface is marked with the relevant communicative intentions.

But this strategy cannot accommodate all examples of depictive misrepresentation, because some depictive misrepresentations don't resemble what they represent in any intended respect. Suppose, for example, that the police are completely misinformed about the appearance of a dangerous criminal. The police believe that the criminal is brunette, but he is blonde; the police believe he is bearded, but he is shaved; the police believe that he is tall, but in fact he is short; and so on (Kaplan, 1968, 198). If the police drew a wanted poster of this man, then it would resemble someone who is brunette, bearded, tall, and so on, but not resemble the man in any intended respect.

By invoking counterfactuals to address the problem of non-existents, Abell hopes to exploit the idea that although apparent depictions of non-existents don't resemble any actual thing, they may resemble a merely possible thing. In chapters eight and nine I will also argue for addressing the problems of depicting non-existents, depicting non-particulars and depictive misrepresentation by exploiting resemblances towards mere possibilia, but without invoking counterfactual conditionals. Chapters eight and nine will argue this approach is a general solution to the problem of intentionality, so there is no special problem for the platitude that depiction is mediated by resemblance.

So Abell and I agree that depiction should be analysed by resemblance in combination with communicative intentions, but disagree about how purported counterexamples to this analysis should be accommodated. In the case of counterexamples due to absence of the relevant intentions, I disagree with Abell's appeal to convention. In the case of counterexamples due to the depiction of inexistents and depictive misrepresentation, I disagree with Abell's appeal to resemblance in counterfactual respects and her claim that even a misrepresentation must resemble what it represents in at least one relevant respect. These disagreements are all about the details, not the spirit, of the analysis.

## 2.5 Conclusion

Resemblance in depictive representation is intended to enable audiences to infer the communicative intentions of a depiction's perpetrator. The Mona Lisa depicts Lisa, for example, because Leo intended audiences to infer from the fact that the Mona Lisa resembles Lisa that he intended an effect in them by means of recognition of his intentions. By specifying the non-incidental role of resemblance in depiction, this analysis avoids counterexamples to the sufficiency of resemblance for representation, and so supports the platitude that whereas descriptive representation is mediated by convention, depiction is mediated by resemblance.

By defining both depiction and description as kinds of intentional representation, the analysis also supports a strong analogy between depiction and description. Both depictions and descriptions, according to the analysis, depend for their meaning on the intentions of their perpetrators to induce effects in their audience, by means of recognition of these intentions. The difference is merely in the feature from which these intentions are inferred: in the case of description, they are inferred from the conventional meanings of words, whereas in the case of depiction, they are inferred from the resemblance of pictures to what they represent.

# 3. Depiction and Intention

Whereas the analysis of meaning in terms of intention is orthodoxy in the philosophy of language, it is highly controversial in the philosophy of art. So even if it is agreed that inserting resemblance into the analysis of speaker meaning in terms of intention escapes counterexamples to the sufficiency of resemblance for depiction, it's likely to be argued that defining depiction as a kind of intentional representation draws too close an analogy between depiction and description. Counterexamples to the necessity and sufficiency of communicative intentions for depiction, it might be argued, are just as threatening as those to the necessity and sufficiency of resemblance.

This chapter defends the analysis of depiction as a kind of intentional representation from this objection. The strategy is to argue that all counterexamples to applying the analysis of speaker meaning to depiction are also counterexamples to the analysis of speaker meaning simpliciter. And whichever revision or reply is available in defence of the analysis of speaker meaning simpliciter, the same revision or reply is available in defence of its application to depiction. So applying the analysis of speaker meaning to depiction supports not only the platitude that depiction is mediated by resemblance, but also a strong analogy between depiction and description.

The first section responds to objections to the necessity of intention for depiction. It argues there is no genuine counterexample to the necessity of intention for depiction. The second section addresses objections to the necessity of an audience. It argues that there are counterexamples to the necessity of an audience, but they can be addressed by a simple revision. The third section responds to counterexamples to the sufficiency of intention for depiction, which can also be accommodated by a simple revision. The fourth section addresses a counterexample based on the evidential use of photographs. The fifth section concludes.

http://dx.doi.org/10.11647/OBP.0046.03

Two clarifications. First, the correct analysis of intention is an extremely controversial topic, which it would be out of place to broach here. However, it can't be emphasised enough that the intentions relevant to what is meant or depicted are the *tacit* intentions which govern action, rather than explicitly formulated plans (Grice, 1957, 221-222). In some cases, the intentions involved in drawing or talking may be explicitly thought out in advance, but these cases are unusual. In ordinary cases, the intentions involved in drawing and talking are just as implicit and spontaneous as the intentions involved in driving or walking.

Second, a full defence of intentionalism in the philosophy of art would require a book length treatment (such as Paisley Livingston's (2005)). In this chapter, I will focus on issues which are to do with pictures in particular, rather than issues which are general to the philosophy of art. In particular, I will focus on issues which purport to establish a disanalogy between the analysis of speaker meaning and the analysis of depiction, such as counterexamples which suggest that the analysis of depiction ought to parallel the analysis of sentence meaning, or counterexamples which purport to establish that the analysis of depiction ought to parallel the analysis of natural meaning.

## 3.1 Objections to the necessity of intention

Suppose an ant is crawling on a patch of sand. As it crawls, it traces a line in the sand. By pure chance the line it traces curves and recrosses itself in such a way that it ends up looking like a recognizable caricature of Winston Churchill (Putnam, 1981, 1). In cases like this, it is tempting to say that the ant traces a depiction of Churchill, even though the ant does not intend to depict Churchill. But this temptation should be resisted, because in the absence of any intention on the part of the ant, or a connection to Churchill other than resemblance, the only explanation of how the line depicts him is its resemblance to him, and that is insufficient (Putnam, 1981, 1-2).

As it is for depiction, so it is for description. Suppose the ant is crawling on a patch of sand and, as it crawls, it traces a line which by pure chance has the same shape as the sentence 'Churchill wins' (Putnam, 1981, 2). The temptation to say that the ant means by 'Churchill wins' that Churchill wins should be resisted, because in the absence of any intention on the part of the ant, or another connection to Churchill's winning, the only explanation of how the 'Churchill wins' means Churchill wins is its conventional meaning in English, but that is insufficient to establish what the ant means by it, since the ant is not really writing in English.

Nevertheless, in the case of language the temptation to say that a sentence may mean something in the absence of an intention is explained by the fact that the sentence may have a conventional meaning in a language such as English. Likewise, in the case of depiction the temptation to say that a marking depicts something in the absence of an intention may be explained by the fact that the marking may have a standard meaning in a depictive symbol system. The line the ant traces, for example, may be a standard shape used for Churchill's caricature. I'll pursue this parallel in chapters four and five (but I will deny that the standards in the case of depiction are conventions).

Not every case in which it is tempting to say there is a depiction in the absence of an intention can be explained in this way. If the ant, for example, traces a line which by pure chance resembles the face of another politician, but one whose caricature has no standard shape, then there is nothing in virtue of which the line depicts the politician, and so it does not depict the politician at all. And although *Jabberwocky*, for example, has meaning in virtue of Carroll's (1871, 155-156) intentions, if an ant had traced lines of the same shape, there would have been neither intention nor convention in virtue of which the lines would have meant anything, and so they would have meant nothing.

The right response to these extreme cases is to deny anything is meant or depicted, on the grounds that in these extreme cases there is nothing in virtue of which anything could be meant or depicted. But in many other purported cases of depiction without intention, the right response is not to deny the presence of depiction, but to maintain the presence of intention. And in many purported cases of meaning without intention, the right response is likewise not to deny the presence of meaning, but to maintain the presence of intention. In particular, many common counterexamples can be addressed simply by a spirit of liberality about how the relevant intentions may arise.

Found objects, for example, may become depictions because of the intentions of their finders. An artist may display some found driftwood, for example, in a way so that the driftwood resembles a spade, an audience recognise that it resemble a spade, and infer from its resemblance to a spade that the artist intended a certain effect in them, by means of recognition of this intention (the example is adapted from Weitz (1956, 34)). Likewise, if driftwood on the beach is strewn by pure chance into the shape of a sentence which warns of an impending tsunami, I may nevertheless use the driftwood to warn you of a tsunami simply by leaving it in its place (Eaton, 1969, 166).

In these cases, the relevant intentions are of the finder instead of the maker. In similar cases, the relevant intentions may be neither of the finder or maker but of the curator who exhibits a painting or the chemist who develops a photograph. In the case of cinema, the relevant intentions need not be those of the director, but may equally well be those of the actors, writers and producers or, in some cases, an intention of the group which is not an intention of any of its individual members. And in the case of literature the relevant intentions need not be those of the author, but may equally well be those of the editor or publisher.

So far I have argued that every purported counterexample to the necessity of intention for depiction is either not an example in which intention is absent or else, in extreme cases, is not an example in which depiction is present since, in extreme cases, there is nothing in virtue of which depiction could be present, except resemblance, which isn't sufficient. But it is plausible that photography is a source of counterexamples which escapes this dilemma, because in the case of photography there is something other than resemblance in virtue of which depiction could be present, because in the case of photography there is a causal connection between photos and what they represent.

Suppose, for example, you photograph your shoe by unintentionally dropping your camera. You did not intend an audience to infer from the photograph's resemblance to your foot that you intended to achieve an effect in them by means of recognition of your intention. But intuitively the photograph depicts your foot. This counterexample, if successful, suggests that the analysis of depiction, or the analysis of photographic depiction, should parallel the analysis of natural instead of non-natural representation, in which case applying the analysis of speaker meaning to depiction is mistaken (see Walton (1984, 101-103) for discussion of a similar point).

But the same point seems to apply to meaning in general, including speaker meaning. Suppose, for example, a sleep-talking husband desires to divorce his wife, but doesn't intend to do so – his desire is overruled by countervailing desires. Yet despite this, his desire to divorce his wife may cause him to call out 'I divorce you' thrice in his sleep. In this case, because of the causal connection between the desire and the utterance of 'I divorce you', it is tempting to say that by uttering 'I divorce you' thrice the husband meant to divorce his wife, even though he didn't intend to divorce her. If this were correct, it would follow that intention is not necessary for speaker meaning.

As for many of the examples above, the right response to these cases isn't to deny the presence of depiction or speaker meaning, but to maintain the presence of intention. If I drop my camera and it accidentally photographs my foot, for example, then I may still form the intentions relevant for it to depict my foot afterwards, when I take the film to be developed or when I place it in my photo album. Similarly, if the husband's desire to divorce his wife causes him to utter 'I divorce you' thrice during sleep, one may argue that it did so by causing him to form in his sleep an intention to divorce her (albeit an intention he may regret or forget by the morning).

Another popular response to the photographic case, suggested by both Hopkins (1998, 77) and Abell (2005a), is to argue that the relevant intentions are present by arguing that it is not the intentions of the photographer which are important, but rather the intentions of the camera's manufacturers. This approach predicts that the photograph resulting from your camera being dropped is a photograph of your foot, because the camera's manufacturers intended that the photograph would resemble your foot if it were dropped in this manner. If this is right, then accidentally taken photographs are not unaccompanied by the relevant intentions after all.

But additional intentions aren't available in every case. Even if, for example, I drop my Polaroid camera and it accidentally photographs my foot and then automatically develops the photo, which nobody ever becomes aware of or forms intentions about, there is still a temptation to say that the photograph depicts my foot. Likewise, even though it is possible for the husband's desire to divorce his wife to cause him to form an intention in his sleep, it is not necessary – the desire may cause the utterance in all kinds of indirect and deviant ways. Moreover, the desire is not necessary to cause the utterance – it may be caused, for example, simply by a nightmare.

There are similar examples in which even the camera's manufacturer's intentions are absent. Suppose, for example, a camera is created accidentally by a random collision of materials in space, without the normal procedure of design and manufacturing, and thus without the intentions of designers or manufacturers. And suppose this camera happens to shoot photos at regular intervals, without anyone intending those photos to be shot. Just as photographs taken accidentally are intuitively depictions, photographs taken unintentionally by accidentally created cameras are also intuitively depictions. So appealing to the intentions of manufacturers isn't able to resolve the problem.

One possible, but misguided, response to this problem would be to split the analysis of depiction into two separate analyses: one of non-natural depiction, such as painting and drawing, and one of natural depiction, such as photographic depiction. The analysis of non-natural depiction would combine resemblance with the analysis of speaker meaning, whereas the analysis of photographic depiction would somehow combine resemblance with causation or indication. This proposal is a very intuitive one, but unfortunately it cannot succeed: the problem is that there is no non-incidental role for resemblance to play in natural representation.

Take, for example, footprints. Footprints naturally represent the feet of the animals that make them. Furthermore, footprints normally resemble the feet of the animals that make them, since they are normally a similar shape to the prints. If photographic depiction were to be analysed by combining causation and resemblance, then such an analysis would be bound to include footprints as well as photographs. But this seems to be the wrong result, since the resemblance between feet and prints is incidental to the representation between feet and prints: even had the prints not resembled the feet, they would still represent the feet merely in virtue of being caused by the feet.

So the correct response is to deny that accidentally taken photographs, in the absence of an analogy with sentence meaning and further intentions in their development and presentation, are depictions at all. While this is counterintuitive, it may nevertheless be conceded that the accidentally taken photograph is a natural representation of my foot, but due to the causal connection between the photograph and my foot, rather than because of the incidental resemblance between them. This concession softens the blow to intuition since, while not all accidentally taken photographs are classified as depictions, all are still rightly included as natural representations.

Most photographs are still classified as depictions even though some are not, since most photographs possess non-natural as well as natural meaning. A photograph of a person represents the person in two distinct ways: it depicts the person because its resemblance to the person is intended to allow audiences to infer the photographer's communicative intentions, and it also naturally represents the person because of the causal connection between it and the person. So photographs are a kind of depiction insofar as they are a kind of non-natural representation, but not insofar as they are a kind of natural representation.

The analogous problem for the analysis of meaning in general has the same solution. In the case, for example, of somniloquy which reveals something truly unintended about the speaker, the solution is to deny that somniloquy has non-natural meaning and to argue instead that it is really an instance of natural meaning: somniloquy is revealing, if it is revealing at all, merely due to a causal connection with the speaker's psychology. If, on the other hand, there is no such causal connection nor relevant intention present – whether in the case of depiction or description – then there are no grounds for attributing representational significance at all.

## 3.2 Objections to the necessity of an audience

The paradigm case of speaker meaning is communication: meaning something by an utterance, according to the analysis above, constitutively involves the presence of an audience. But it may be argued that depiction, although it may sometimes involve communication, is not primarily directed at audiences. People may depict by doodling in their margins, drawing preparatory sketches for paintings, or tracing patterns in fogged-up glass, without intending that their doodles, sketches or traces ever find an audience. So depiction in the absence of an audience seems to be a counterexample to the application of the analysis of speaker meaning to depiction.

But in fact examples of depiction in the absence of an audience reveal no disanalogy between depiction and speaker meaning. People may mean things by writing in diaries, doodling in margins or singing in the shower, without intending any witnesses to their writing, doodling or singing. So while the primary case of meaning involves communication between an utterer and a separate audience, this isn't always the case. Meaning something is possible in the absence of an audience, so the absence of an audience is a counterexample not just to the analysis of depiction, but to the analysis of speaker meaning in general (Grice, 1969, 112-115; Schiffer, 1972, 76-80).

For both analyses some purported counterexamples can be accommodated without revision simply by a spirit of inclusiveness about who counts as an audience. The intended audience of a preparatory sketch, for example, may be the sketcher at a later time. Similarly, the intended audience of doodling in margins may be the doodlers, who want to relieve their present boredom, singing in the shower may be intended for the enjoyment of the singer and a diary intended for the diarist. Once it is allowed that the perpetrator may also be the audience, many of the problematic examples of depiction or meaning in the absence of an audience disappear.

But not every example of depiction without an audience can be accommodated by this move. Imagine, for example, that a pirate is sure of not forgetting the location of his treasure and intends to recover it in his own lifetime, but leaves a treasure map for his heirs. The pirate does not intend the map to produce an effect in an audience, because he intends to find the treasure and destroy the map before his death. Nor does the pirate intend the map to produce a belief or other effect in himself, since he already possesses the relevant beliefs. Nevertheless, the map does depict the island on which the treasure is located.

But although the pirate does not intend the map to produce an effect in the audience, he does intend that if he were to die then the map would produce in his heirs knowledge of the treasure's whereabouts. That suggests that in order to accommodate this, the analysis should be amended to:

(9) Something depicts another if and only if it is intended that if the former reaches an audience of a certain type then:

    a. the former resembles the latter in a certain respect
    b. an audience recognise the former resembles the latter in that respect
    c. the audience infer at least in part from the fact the former resembles the latter in that respect that it is intended:
    d. that the former produce an effect in the audience
    e. and that that effect be produced at least in part by means of the audience's recognition of intentions (a)-(e).

So the treasure map depicts the treasure island because the pirate intends that if his heirs discover the map then they will infer from the resemblance of the map to the island that the treasure is hidden on the island.

It is obvious that the same amendment has to be made to the analysis of speaker meaning. If, for example, I leave a note for my mother in law on the chance that she may call by while I am out, then I do not straightforwardly intend to induce an effect in my mother in law, because I don't intend her to call while I am out. Nevertheless, I do intend that if my mother in law sees the note, then it will induce an effect in her by means of recognition of my intentions (Schiffer, 1972, 73-76). So the analysis of meaning requires the same amendment as the analysis of depiction.

Three clarifications. First, notice that the utterance or the depiction must not only reach an audience, but must reach an audience of a certain type. That's because, for many utterances and depictions the perpetrator does not intend his or her intentions to be recognised by every audience the utterance or depiction reaches: allegorical writers or painters, for example, intend their intentions to be recognised by the cognoscenti, but not by the censors. The cognoscenti belong to the intended type of audience, but the censors don't. Likewise, the intended type may be simply a specific person: lovers may intend their letters, for example, only for their beloved (Schiffer, 1972, 75).

Second, the condition that a depiction resembles what it represents in a certain respect occurs within the scope of a conditional, so the depiction need only resemble what it represents in that respect if the antecedent of the conditional is true and the depiction actually reaches an audience of the relevant type. However, it might be objected that resemblance in the relevant respect ought to be a necessary condition for depiction, so that the resemblance of a picture to what it represents in the relevant respect ought to occur regardless of whether or not the depiction reaches an audience of the relevant type.

But in fact it's correct that resemblance in the intended respect is not necessary for depiction. Consider, for example, a drawing in invisible ink. If the drawing does not reach an audience, and so the ink does not become visible, then the drawing will not resemble what it depicts in the intended visible respects (even if it does in unintended invisible respects). Nevertheless, even if the drawing does not reach an audience of the relevant type, it still depicts, since if it reached an audience of the relevant type, then the ink would become visible and the drawing would in turn come to resemble what it represents in the intended visible respects.

Third, the conditional in this analysis should not be interpreted as material, since if it is, the conditions of the analysis would be trivially met if the antecedent is intended to be false. Since the pirate, for example, intends the map not to reach his enemies, then in the sense of the material conditional he intends that if it reaches his enemies, then it resembles a blue moon, that his enemies recognise it resembles a blue moon, and that his enemies infer from this that he intended to induce an effect in them by means of recognition his intention. But of course, the treasure map does not depict a blue moon merely because the pirate intended it not to reach his enemies.

## 3.3 Objections to the sufficiency of intention

Suppose that a madman scribbles messily on a page. The madman has a mad belief that the scribble resembles a mountain landscape in Tibet and that an audience will infer from the resemblance of the scribble to the Tibetan landscape that he intends to induce in them beliefs about the Tibetan landscape by means of recognising his intentions. Despite meeting the conditions of the analysis of depiction in the last chapter, the scribble is not a depiction of the Tibetan landscape. The example shows that intending to depict something is not sufficient for successfully doing so. In other words, intention is not sufficient for depiction.

The example is important because it threatens to undermine the analogy drawn in the last chapter between depiction and speaker meaning. It suggests that since intending to depict something falls short of depicting that thing, depiction shouldn't be analysed in terms of intention, as speaker meaning is. Instead, it suggests that depiction should be analysed in analogy with sentence meaning. Since just as what a picture depicts is not merely what it is intended to depict, what a sentence means is not merely what it's intended to mean, analysing depiction in analogy with sentence meaning rather than speaker meaning would avoid the consequence that intention suffices for depiction.

But there's an analogous counterexample to the analysis of speaker meaning. Suppose a madman believes that 'gleeg gleeg gleeg' means in English that it's snowing in Tibet. The madman might utter 'gleeg gleeg gleeg' intending the utterance to induce the audience to believe that it's snowing in Tibet by means of recognition of that intention. But the madman's utterance of 'gleeg gleeg gleeg' is meaningless. So, although the madman's utterance meets the conditions of Grice's analysis of speaker meaning, it does not seem to mean that it's snowing in Tibet (Ziff, 1967, 5). Intending to mean something is equally insufficient for successfully doing so.

There is one response to these counterexamples that would break the analogy between depiction and speaker meaning. It might be granted that 'gleeg, gleeg, gleeg' in the example has the speaker meaning that it's snowing in Tibet, but denied that granting this is problematic on the grounds that granting it would not adversely affect the analysis of sentence meaning. This would be unproblematic if the only role of speaker meaning was in order to analyse sentence meaning as what a sentence conventionally speaker means, since that it's snowing in Tibet would not, even on this occasion, be what the sentence conventionally speaker means (Lycan, 2000, 108-109).

But the analysis of speaker meaning is not only required for the analysis of sentence meaning, but also for the analysis of the non-conventional meaning of utterances. Somebody may mean something by a grunt or gesture, for example, without that grunt or gesture having any conventional meaning. Similarly, somebody may mean by a metaphor or malapropism something other than the conventional meaning of the sentence uttered. If it were granted that the madman's utterance of 'gleeg, gleeg, gleeg' means it's snowing in Tibet, this would adversely affect the analysis of non-conventional meaning.

To avoid the problem, the analysis has to be altered to specify that the perpetrator's intentions be successful, so that mad utterances of sentences like 'gleeg, gleeg, gleeg' do not possess speaker meaning. Similarly, the analysis of depiction should be altered so that scribbles with deluded intentions are excluded, as follows:

(10) Something depicts another if and only if it is *successfully* intended that if the former reaches an audience of a certain type then:

    a. the former resembles the latter in a certain respect
    b. an audience recognise the former resembles the latter in that respect
    c. the audience infer at least in part from the fact the former resembles the latter in that respect that it is intended:
    d. that the former produce an effect in the audience
    e. and that that effect be produced at least in part by means of the audience's recognition of intentions (a)-(e).

So, for example, the Mona Lisa depicts Lisa because Leo intended successfully that his audience recognise that the Mona Lisa resembles Lisa in certain respects and infer from that that Leo wanted them to believe that Lisa smiles by means of recognition of his intentions.

Three clarifications. Firstly, the intention which analysis (10) requires is successful is only the intention which has wide scope over the right hand side of the analysis, and not the intention that is embedded in clause (c). So if the Mona Lisa depicts Lisa, for example, then if it reaches an audience it must resemble Lisa in a certain respect, the audience must recognise that it resembles Lisa in that respect, and they must infer from this that Leo intended them to believe that Lisa smiles by means of recognition of his intention. But they needn't in fact believe that Lisa smiles and if they do, they needn't do so because Leo intended them to, but may do so for some other reason.

Second, for an intention to be successful is in part for what is intended to occur. For my intention to score a goal to be successful, for example, is in part for me to score a goal. But for an intention to be successful it must also cause what is intended to occur. For my intention to score a goal to be successful, for example, it is not enough for the ball to ricochet into the goal because I trip. And for an intention to be successful it must also cause what is intended in the right sort of way. For my intention to score a goal to be successful, for example, it is not enough for it to cause nervousness, which causes me to trip, which causes the ball to ricochet into the goal.

It might be thought that these requirements are too strong. Suppose Apelles intends to depict the lather on a horse's mouth, and so intends his painting to resemble the lather in a certain respect. But the effect is difficult to obtain, so Apelles flings his sponge at the painting in frustration. As a result, the sponge so happens to mark the painting in such a way that it resembles the lather in exactly the respect Apelles intended and so, intuitively, the painting depicts the lather. Apelles' intention causes his frustration and his frustration causes the resemblance, so his intention causes the resemblance. But it is still unsuccessful, since it doesn't cause the resemblance in the right kind of way.

As for many of the examples above, the right response to this kind of objection isn't to deny the presence of depiction, but to maintain the presence of successful intention. Although Apelles' initial intention for the painting to resemble the lather in a certain respect was unsuccessful, he also formed a subsequent intention for the painting to resemble the lather in that same respect, which he enacted by not removing the effect or destroying the painting, and this subsequent intention was successful. Just as drift-wood may depict in virtue of the intentions of its finder instead of its maker, Apelles' painting depicts not in virtue of his creating it, but in virtue of his not effacing it.

Thirdly, it might be suggested that to avoid the problem, the analysis may merely be altered to specify that the perpetrator's intentions be rational. But requiring rational and not successful intentions would still fall short of sufficiency, because a rational intention may not produce any action at all. Suppose, for example, I have a rational intention to paint, during a weekend away, a watercolour of the view from my hotel window. But just as I pick up my paintbrush I'm interrupted by an emergency phone call. I leave never to return, so my intention to paint is unsuccessful. Although it was a rational intention, the blank paper I left on the easel depicts nothing.

So the example of unsuccessful intentions doesn't show that depiction is disanalogous to speaker meaning. Nevertheless, the suggestion that depiction should be analysed in analogy with sentence meaning is not misguided. Just as there's a distinction between the meaning of a sentence in a language and what a speaker uses that sentence to mean, there's a distinction between what a depiction represents in a symbol system and what it's used to represent by its perpetrator. This analogy between depiction and speaker meaning is taken up again in chapters four and five, which analyse depictive symbol systems in analogy with conventional language.

## 3.4 Objections to the necessity of reasons

There's still a residual problem connected with photographs. When a photograph is presented as evidence it is intended to produce a belief in its audience. But if so, then the photograph is usually intended to produce the belief by means of recognition of its causal connection to what it represents rather than by means of recognition of the intentions of its perpetrator. So applying the analysis of speaker meaning to the sense in which depiction is representational may still appear to incorrectly exclude photographs by ignoring the fact that photographic representation is more naturally assimilated to natural than to non-natural representation.

But an analogous problem arises in the analysis of speaker meaning simpliciter. Suppose I give you an argument proceeding from premises you already believe to a conclusion I intend to convince you of. Then I mean by uttering the words of the conclusion that the conclusion is true. But I don't intend you to believe the conclusion by means of recognising my intention that you believe it; rather, because I am offering an argument, I want you to believe the conclusion by means of inferring it from the premises (Schiffer,

1972, 42-43). The condition that effects be produced by means of recognition of intention excludes arguments as well as photographs.

All this suggests that both the analysis of depiction and of speaker meaning should be weakened so that the intended effect need merely be accompanied by, rather than produced by means of, recognition of intention. In the case of depiction:

> (11) Something depicts another if and only if it is intended successfully that if the former reaches an audience of a certain type then:
>
> a. the former resembles the latter in a certain respect
> b. the audience recognise the former resembles the latter in that respect
> c. the audience infer at least in part from the fact the former resembles the latter in that respect that it is intended:
> d. that the former produce an effect in the audience
> e. and the audience recognise intentions (a)-(e).

This analysis allows for the inclusion of photographs, because it requires only that the effect in the audience is intended to be produced somehow or other, rather than by means of recognition of intention.

But this weakening comes at the cost of the sufficiency of the analysis. Imagine, for example, I intend a brightly painted canvas to produce in you an epileptic fit. Further, imagine it's intended that the canvas resembles canvasses that I have used to cause you epileptic fits in the past (in respect of colour) and that you infer from this that I intend it to produce the fit and that I intend you to recognise my intentions. The case meets the conditions of the analysis, but it isn't an example of depiction, because of the non-rational nature of the intended effect (see Schiffer (1972, 55-56) for the analogous counterexample to the analysis of speaker meaning simpliciter).

The original analysis would have excluded this example, because although your recognition of my intention would accompany your epileptic fit, your fit would not be produced by means of recognition of my intention, because your recognition of my intention for you to have a fit would provide you with no reason to have one – your recognition of my intention for you to have a fit is no reason for you to comply. But, as the examples of photographs and arguments showed, requiring that the audience's recognition of the perpetrator's intention to induce the effect be the audience's reason for enjoying the effect makes the analysis too strong.

This suggests that the audience must be given some reason in order to enjoy the intended effect, but that that reason need not always be provided by the audience's recognition of the perpetrator's intention. In the case of depiction:

(12) Something depicts another if and only if it is intended successfully that if the former reaches an audience of a certain type then:

   a. the former resembles the latter in a certain respect
   b. the audience recognise the former resembles the latter in that respect
   c. the audience infer at least in part from the fact that the former resembles the latter in that respect that it is intended:
   d. that the former induce an effect in the audience
   e. that this effect be induced by means of providing a reason
   f. and that the audience recognise intentions (a)-(f).

This analysis excludes the case of the epileptic fit, because in that case I provide you with no reason to have a fit, but still includes the case of photographs, because their evidential connection to what they represent tends to provide a reason for believing what they represent (see Schiffer (1972, 57-58) for the analogous amendment to the analysis of meaning).

Advertising, which is frequently unreasonable, might appear problematic for the idea that meaning and depiction require the provision of reasons. The intended effect of an advertising photograph showing glamorous people smoking, for example, may be to induce the audience to smoke. But although the photograph depicts glamorous people smoking, and although the advertisers mean by the photograph that the audience should smoke, the photograph does not provide the audience with any reason which would justify their smoking, because glamour is not a reason to smoke. Moreover, the advertisers need not even intend to provide a reason which would justify smoking.

Advertisements are frequently not intended to provide audiences with a reason which would truly justify their action – or justifying reasons – but this is compatible with the analysis because they're always intended to provide audiences with reasons which would motivate and thereby explain their actions – or explanatory reasons (see Woods (1972, 189) for the distinction). The photograph of glamorous people smoking doesn't provide me with any justifying reason to smoke. But if the photograph leads me to believe smoking is a means for me to be glamorous, and I want to be glamorous, then the photograph might provide me a reason which would explain my smoking.

It is compatible with this response that some advertising is intended to merely cause its effects in the audience, without providing even an explanatory reason, so long as it is not the case that such advertisements mean or depict anything. To the extent that a subliminal advertisement for smoking, for example, is a purely causal explanation for my smoking, it's not counterintuitive to deny that the advertisement causes me to smoke, but neither depicts smoking nor means that I should smoke. The perpetration and interpretation of pictures is not merely a causal process such as sneezing or snoring, but a rational activity like walking and talking.

## 3.5 Conclusion

So although there are counterexamples to both the necessity and sufficiency of the analysis of depiction proposed in the last chapter, these are all counterexamples to the necessity and sufficiency of the analysis of speaker meaning simpliciter. The replies and revisions required to accommodate the counterexamples to the analysis of depiction exactly parallel the replies and revisions required to accommodate the counterexamples to the analysis of speaker meaning simpliciter. Counterexamples to the analysis support, rather than undermine, the extremely strong analogy between depiction and description.

# 4. Depiction and Convention

The analogy between depiction and description is usually argued to undermine rather than support the platitude that depiction is mediated by resemblance. From the claim that depiction and description are both kinds of symbol system Nelson Goodman, for example, draws the conclusion that "Almost any picture may represent almost anything; that is, given picture and object there is usually a system of representation, a plan of correlation, under which the picture represents that object" (Goodman, 1968, 38). Because they are both kinds of symbol systems, depiction and description, according to Goodman, are supposed to be equally arbitrary.

Defining depiction as a kind of symbol system is interesting because it develops an even closer analogy between depictive and descriptive representation. The moral that can be drawn from this chapter is that it's possible to maintain such a close analogy between depiction and description, while still maintaining the platitude that whereas words are connected to what they represent merely by arbitrary convention, pictures are connected to what they represent by resemblance. The insight behind defining depiction as a kind of symbol system can be accepted, while the consequence that depictive representation is arbitrary is rejected.

This chapter and the next also address the objection that depiction should be analysed in analogy with sentence meaning, rather than speaker meaning. This chapter argues that there is an exact analogy between the analysis of depictive symbol systems and the analysis of speaker meaning, except whereas the latter is arbitrary and mediated by convention, the former is non-arbitrary and mediated by resemblance. Nevertheless, it doesn't follows that depiction should be analysed in analogy with sentence meaning and not speaker meaning, because some depictions don't belong to depictive symbol systems, and depict only in virtue of their perpetrators' intentions.

http://dx.doi.org/10.11647/OBP.0046.04

The first section describes the tension between defining depiction as a kind of symbol system and the platitude that depiction is mediated by resemblance. The second section describes an analogous tension between the definition of a language and the platitude that description is mediated by convention. The third section describes an analysis of conventional language which resolves this tension. And the fourth section argues for an analogous analysis of depictive symbol systems which reconciles the analogy between depiction and description with the platitude that whereas description is mediated by convention, depiction is mediated by resemblance.

## 4.1 Goodman's definition of symbol systems

A symbol system is a set of characters correlated with a set of extensions (Goodman, 1968, 143). In the symbol system of Arabic numerals, for example, the characters are the numerals '1', '2', '3', '4', … and the extensions are the numbers one, two, three, four, … and so on. The symbol system correlates '1' with one, '2' with two, '3' with three, '4' with four, … and so on. Likewise, in the symbol system of traffic lights, for example, the characters are red, orange and green and the extensions are stop, slow and go. The symbol system correlates red with stop, orange with slow and green with go. Depiction, according to Goodman, is a kind of symbol system.

A correlation between a set of characters and a set of extensions is simply a function from the characters to the extensions. A function is a mapping between two sets: it delivers a member of the second set for every member of the first set. The function of doubling, for example, takes every member of the set of natural numbers to a member of the set of even numbers: it takes one to two, two to four, three to six, four to eight, … and so on. Every many-one mapping between two sets, no matter how arbitrary, is a function. There's a function, for example, which takes every letter of the alphabet to the number of the day of the month on which it was first written.

The advantage of defining symbol systems as functions from characters to extensions is that any symbol system can be fully specified by such a function. The symbol system of traffic lights, for example, is fully specified by the function that takes green to go, orange to slow and red to stop. Similarly the symbol system of Arabic numerals is fully specified by the function that takes '1' to one, '2' to two, '3' to three, '4' to four, … and so on. The same point applies to depictive symbol systems. The symbol system of chess diagrams, for example, is completely specified by the function which takes each chess diagram to the position it represents.

Since a function is any mapping, no matter how arbitrary, between two sets, the definition of symbol systems as functions from characters to extensions shows that any depiction may represent anything in some symbol system or other. There is a function from portraits to people, for example, that takes the Mona Lisa to Socrates, and so it follows that there is a symbol system in which the Mona Lisa represents Socrates. Just as words represent other things in other languages, pictures depict other things in other symbol systems, so what a depiction represents appears to depend not on what it resembles but only on its extension relative to a symbol system.

So if depiction is a kind of symbol system, then any depiction, just like any word, may represent any thing in some symbol system. Goodman draws the conclusion that depictive representation is like descriptive representation in being arbitrary. As he writes, "Descriptions are distinguished from depictions not through being more arbitrary ... for what describes in some symbol systems may depict in others. Resemblance disappears as a criterion of representation..." (Goodman, 1968, 230-231). So if, as Goodman claims, depiction is a kind of symbol system, then depictive representation appears to be both arbitrary and unmediated by resemblance.

But even if it follows from the definition of symbol systems that any picture may represent anything, it does not follow that any picture may depict anything, since the alternative symbol systems relative to which characters possess other extensions may lack the syntactic and semantic properties required for being depictive. So although, for example, there is a symbol system in which the Mona Lisa represents Socrates instead of Lisa, that symbol system may not be a depictive one, in which case the fact that there is a symbol system in which the Mona Lisa represents Socrates would not show that the Mona Lisa's depiction of Socrates is arbitrary.

Furthermore, there seems to be little obstacle in principle to combining Goodman's thesis that depiction is a kind of symbol system with the thesis that depictions resemble what they represent, or any other thesis which maintains that the relationship between depictions and what they represent is non-arbitrary. As Dominic Lopes writes, "The claim that pictures are symbols in this [Goodman's] sense is not incompatible with perceptual explanations of depiction. Nothing in the symbol model rules out pictures being correlated with, and standing for, their subjects because they resemble them..." (Lopes, 1996, 57).

The following analysis, for example, might be taken to reconcile defining depiction as a kind of symbol system with the platitude that depiction is mediated by resemblance:

(13) A symbol system is depictive if and only if every character in that symbol system resembles its extension.

So the symbol system of maps, for example, is supposed by this analysis to be depictive because every map resembles the region it represents in that symbol system. If this analysis is right, defining depiction as a kind of symbol system establishes neither that depiction is arbitrary nor that it's unmediated by resemblance.

But the following example shows that this analysis cannot be right. Often, letters of the alphabet are used to represent themselves, so that 'a' represents 'a', 'b' represents 'b', 'c' represents 'c', and so on. Since resemblance is reflexive, every letter in this symbol system resembles and represents itself, but it is intuitively not the case that every letter in the symbol system depicts itself, or that the symbol system described is depictive. The letters' resemblance to themselves is incidental to their representation of themselves: even if, for example, capital letters were used to represent lower case letters, the way in which the letters represent each other would be the same.

So reconciling defining depiction as a kind of symbol system with the platitude that depiction is mediated by resemblance is not straightforward. The following sections exploit an analogy between symbol systems and languages which shows how to resolve this problem. The role of resemblance in depictive symbol systems, I will argue, is analogous to the role of precedent in conventional language. This suggests an analysis of depictive symbol systems which supports a strong analogy between depiction and description and the platitude that whereas description is mediated by convention, depiction is mediated by resemblance.

## 4.2 Formal definition of languages

Just as a symbol system is a function from characters to extensions, a language is a function from sentences to truth-conditions (Lewis, 1975,

163). So 'snow is white' means in English that snow is white, for example, because English is a function from sentences to truth-conditions that takes the sentence 'snow is white' to the condition of snow's being white. Similarly, 'grass is green' in English means grass is green because 'grass is green' is taken by the function to the condition of grass' being green. This section describes the tension between this definition of a language and the platitude that description is mediated by convention.

The main advantage of defining languages as functions from sentences to truth-conditions, as for defining symbol systems as functions from characters to extensions, is that every language is fully specified by such a function. English, for example, is fully specified by the function that takes 'snow is white' to the condition of snow's being white, 'grass is green' to the condition of grass' being green, 'it's raining' to the condition of its being raining, ... and so on. Once the relevant function from sentences to truth-conditions is specified, there's no further question about what the sentences of the language specified by that function mean.

Since truth-conditions are the extensions of sentences and sentences are the characters of languages, this definition of languages is just a special case of the definition of symbol systems (Lopes, 1996, 59). So defining depiction as a kind of symbol system is closely analogous to defining languages as functions from sentences to truth-conditions. Although I'll argue below that depiction should not be defined as a kind of symbol system, I'll also argue that the strong analogy behind this definition is correct: depictive symbol systems are exactly analogous to conventional languages.

Just as there's a tension between the definition of depiction as a kind of symbol system and the platitude that depiction is mediated by resemblance, there's a tension between the definition of languages as functions from sentences to truth-conditions and the platitude that description is mediated by convention. The reason is that a function from sentences to truth-conditions necessarily takes the sentences it does to the truth-conditions it does: just as the function of doubling necessarily takes two to four, the function from English sentences to their truth-conditions, for example, necessarily takes 'snow is white' to the condition of snow's being white.

If sentences necessarily mean what they do in a language, then it appears convention could have no role in linking them to their meaning. If 'snow is white', for example, necessarily means in English that snow is white, then no convention is needed to determine that it does. If languages are functions from sentences to truth-conditions, having a convention that 'snow is white' means that snow is white in English is like having a convention to the effect that falling objects must accelerate at approximately ten metres per second per second: clearly, the acceleration of falling objects is independent of any convention which may purport to govern it.

But to conclude on these grounds that language is not mediated by convention would be obviously incorrect. This is because, while it is a matter of necessity rather than convention that 'snow is white' in English means that snow is white, it is contingent that English, or the language given by the function from English sentences to their truth-conditions, is a language of this island, and this is a fact which is plausibly mediated by convention. It's mistaken to infer from the fact that sentences necessarily mean what they do in a language that language is not mediated by convention.

In general, while the meaning of a sentence in a language is a matter of necessity, it's a contingent matter whether a language or function from sentences to truth-conditions is used by a population. So although it's a matter of necessity, for example, that 'snow is white' means snow is white in English, it's nonetheless an arbitrary matter that a language in which 'snow is white' means that snow is white is spoken on this island, rather than a different language in which it means that grass is green. Convention doesn't mediate the meaning of a sentence in a language, but it does mediate which languages amongst many a population uses (Lewis, 1975, 166-167).

The moral of this point is to distinguish between the study of languages in use and in the abstract. The study of languages in the abstract focuses on the study of languages as abstract mathematical objects such as functions from sentences to truth-conditions and investigates further questions about the structure of those objects. The study of language in use focuses, in contrast, on how those abstract mathematical objects are connected with concrete speech and interpretation. Convention is part of this latter study, because the role of convention is to determine which languages in the abstract are used in speech and interpretation (Lewis, 1969, 160-165; 1975).

Likewise, one should distinguish between symbol systems in the abstract and symbol systems in use. The fact that any depiction may depict anything in some symbol system or another is a mathematical fact about the nature of symbol systems in the abstract. Nothing follows from this about the nature of symbol systems in use, since it doesn't follow that the choice between which symbol systems in the abstract are adopted for use is an arbitrary one. So the platitude that depiction is mediated by resemblance should not be interpreted as a thesis about symbol systems in the abstract, but as a thesis about symbol systems in use.

So the platitude that whereas description is mediated by convention, depiction is mediated by resemblances suggests that resemblance is responsible for determining which symbol systems in the abstract are symbol systems in use. If this suggestion is right, then the difference between depictive and other symbol systems is not in the abstract mathematical syntactic and semantic properties of symbol systems, but in the way that depictive symbol systems are connected to the populations which use them. The following sections attempt to confirm this suggestion by providing an analysis of depictive symbol systems analogous to the analysis of conventional language.

## 4.3 Lewis' analysis of convention

This section describes the analysis of conventional language; the next adapts it to the analysis of depictive symbol systems. A convention is a rationally self-perpetuating regularity in behaviour. Driving on the left, for example, is a convention in Australia because there is a regularity of driving on the left in Australia and because the existence of this regularity provides Australian drivers with a reason for continuing to drive on the left. Driving on the right is a convention in Europe because there is a regularity of driving on the right in Europe, and the existence of this regularity gives European drivers a rational reason for continuing to drive on the right.

To have a convention of driving on the left it must be, firstly, that there is a regularity of driving on the left and, secondly, that drivers are aware that there is a regularity of driving on the left and, thirdly, that drivers have a reason to drive on the left on condition that the others do. If any of these conditions failed then the regularity of driving on the left would not be rationally self-perpetuating: drivers would not continue driving on the left in the first case because it would not be better to do so, in the second case because they would not know that it was better to do so and in the third case because others driving on the left would not give them any reason to do so.

This suggests convention may be analysed as follows (Lewis, 1969, 58):

(14) A regularity in the behaviour of a group is a convention if and only if:

    a. everyone conforms to that regularity
    b. everyone expects everyone else to conform to that regularity
    c. and everyone has reason to conform on condition that everyone else conforms.

Driving on the left is a convention in Australia, for example, because everybody drives on the left, everybody expects everybody else to drive on the left, and everybody has reason to drive on the left if everybody else drives on the left.

Three amendments. First, imagine that everyone drives on the left because they expect others to and because everybody has reason to drive on the same side as others. However, nobody believes that others drive on the left for these reasons: rather everyone believes that others drive on the left merely out of habit or because driving on the left is more scenic. The regularity of driving on the left is not a convention for avoiding collision in this population, because members of the population would continue driving on the left even though they believe others may not care about collision (Lewis, 1969, 59).

To avoid this problem the analysis should be altered to reflect that everyone must be aware the conditions of the analysis are fulfilled. According to this amendment:

(15) A regularity in the behaviour of a group is a convention if and only if:

    a. everyone conforms to that regularity
    b. everyone has reason to conform on condition that everyone else conforms
    c. and everyone believes (a)-(c).

So, for example, driving on the left is a convention in Australia because everybody drives on the left, everybody prefers to drive on the left given that everybody else drives on the left and because everybody believes that everybody else conforms to the regularity for these three reasons.

Second, the condition that everyone has reason to conform on condition that others do is supposed to capture the cooperativeness of convention, since it's because of their common interests that everyone has reason to conform to the same regularity in conventional activities. Driving on the left in Australia is a convention, for example, because everybody has a common interest in driving on the same side, and this common interest gives them a reason to conform to the regularity of driving on the left if others do. In general, all convention arises from common interests (Lewis, 1969, 69).

But the conditions of the analysis may be met even when common interests are absent. Imagine an office in which everyone hopes to be promoted by working harder than their colleagues. A regularity of hard work obtains in this office, everybody in the office has reason to conform to this regularity of hard work on condition that everyone else does, and everybody in the office is aware of these three facts. But hard work is not a convention of the office, because there's no common interest in everybody working hard. In contrast, since everyone in the office is interested in promotion, their interests are best served by everyone else slacking off.

To avoid this problem the analysis should be amended to reflect that everybody has a common interest in conformity to the regularity. According to this amendment (Lewis, 1975, 165):

(16) A regularity in the behaviour of a group is a convention if and only if:

    a. everyone conforms to that regularity
    b. everyone has reason to conform on condition that everyone else conforms
    c. everyone prefers everyone to conform, on condition that most do
    d. and everyone believes (a)-(d).

So driving on the left, for example, is a convention since everyone prefers everyone to drive on the left on condition that most drive on the left, since driving on the left on condition that most do reduces crashes, and everyone prefers not to crash.

Third, the condition that everybody has reason to conform because others do is supposed to capture the arbitrariness of convention, since everyone is supposed to conform to the regularity for no other reason than that others do. The convention of driving on the left, for example, is supposed to be arbitrary because nobody has much reason to drive on the left except the fact that others drive on the left. The regularity of driving on the left is no better than the regularity of driving on the right, which everyone would happily adopt were it adopted by others.

But this condition is not sufficient to capture arbitrariness. Suppose, for example, that it's a regularity in our behaviour to meet for coffee once a week, on Fridays. We only like to drink coffee together, so that I have reason to go to the café on Friday only if you go to the café on Friday and both of us prefer to go if the other does. And suppose we're both aware of all this. Nevertheless, our regularity of meeting at the café on Fridays may not be chosen arbitrarily, because on Friday the café offers a heavy discount. Our regularity of meeting for coffee on Fridays meets the conditions of the analysis, but it is not a convention.

To avoid this problem the analysis has to be amended to reflect that the option chosen is a matter of indifference. According to this amendment (Lewis, 1969, 76):

(17) A regularity in the behaviour of a group is a convention if and only if:

    a. everyone conforms to that regularity
    b. everyone has reason to conform on condition that everyone else conforms
    c. there is an alternative regularity which everyone would have had reason to conform to if others had conformed to it
    d. everyone prefers everyone to conform, on condition that most do
    e. and everyone believes (a)-(e).

So, for example, driving on the left would not be a convention if it weren't for the existence of the option of driving on the right, which everyone else would have reason to do if others did.

Since conventions are regularities in behaviour, the analysis of convention doesn't apply directly to functions from sentences to truth-conditions, but only to a regularity in behaviour concerning those functions. David Lewis (1969, 177) suggests that the relevant regularity is truthfulness in a language, which consists in sometimes uttering sentences of the language, while trying not to utter sentences of the language which are false in that language. Being truthful in English, for example, consists in sometimes uttering sentences such as 'snow is white', while trying to abstain from uttering sentences such as 'the moon is blue cheese' if the moon is not blue cheese.

This suggests that a language is used if and only if there's a convention of truthfulness in that language. Together with the analysis of convention, this leads to following analysis of conventional language (Lewis, 1969, 177; 1975, 167-168):

(18) A group has a convention of using a language if and only if there is a regularity in the group such that:

    a. everyone is truthful in that language
    b. everyone has reason to be truthful in that language on condition that everyone else is truthful in that language

c. there is an alternative regularity of truthfulness in another language which everyone would have reason to conform to if others did
d. everyone prefers everyone to conform to a regularity of truthfulness in that language on condition that most do
e. and everyone believes (a)-(e).

English, for example, is a language spoken by English speakers since English speakers are truthful in English, English speakers expect all other English speakers to be truthful in English, and all English speakers prefer to be truthful in English given that everybody else is.

## 4.4 Analysis of depictive symbol systems

It's a platitude that whereas words are connected to what they represent merely by arbitrary conventions, pictures are connected to what they represent by resemblance. That suggests that the role of resemblance in depictive representation is analogous to the role of convention in descriptive representation, so that instead of simply stating that depictive symbol systems are those whose characters resemble their extensions, depictive symbol systems may be defined by substituting symbol systems for languages and resemblance for arbitrariness in the analysis of conventional language.

Arbitrariness is ensured in the analysis of convention by the second condition, which ensures that the population conforms to the regularity for no other reason than that other members of the population conform to it, and the third condition, which ensures that there are other regularities which all members would have preferred to conform to had others done so. So to adapt the analysis of the conventions governing linguistic representation in order to provide an analysis of depictive symbol systems, these two conditions ought to be altered.

The second condition of the analysis captures the arbitrariness of linguistic conventions by specifying that which language the members of a population have reason to use depends on which language other members of that population choose to use, rather than any feature of the language independent of the choices of others (Lewis, 1969, 70). To provide an analysis of depictive symbol systems this condition should be amended to include resemblance, because the resemblance of a symbol system's characters to their extensions in that symbol system provides an additional reason for its use.

The third condition of the analysis further ensures the arbitrariness of linguistic conventions by specifying that there must be an alternative to the regularity members of the population actually conform to which would serve their purposes just as well. Since the relationship between depictions and what they represent is not arbitrary, this condition becomes unnecessary and should be dropped: although there may be alternative regularities which would serve just as well, there need not be such alternatives in order for the use of a symbol system to count as depictive.

This suggests the following analysis of depictive symbol systems:

(19) A symbol system is depictive if and only if there is a regularity of truthfulness in that symbol system such that:

a. everyone is truthful in that symbol system
b. everyone has reason to be truthful in that symbol system, since its characters resemble their extensions
c. everyone prefers everyone to conform to a regularity of truthfulness in that symbol system on condition that most do
d. everyone believes (a)-(d).

So, for example, the symbol system of maps is depictive because everybody uses them, everybody expects everybody to use them, everybody has reason to do this because maps resemble what they represent, rather than simply because everybody else uses them, and everybody is aware that these conditions obtain.

By specifying the role of resemblance in depictive symbol systems, this analysis avoids counterexamples to simply defining depictive symbol systems as those whose characters resemble their extensions. The symbol system of using letters to represent themselves, for example, is not counted as depictive because although all the characters in that symbol system resemble their extensions, it is not for this reason that this symbol system is preferred over others as a method of representing the letters: the alternative of using capital to represent lower case letters, for example, would serve equally well.

Furthermore, the analysis shows that it does not follow from depiction being a kind of symbol system that the relationship between depictions and what they represent is merely arbitrary. While it is true that there are always other symbol systems in which the same pictures would have different extensions, which symbol system is selected for use in communication is not arbitrary but depends on the resemblance between the characters and extensions of that system just as, while it is true that sentences have their meaning in English necessarily, linguistic meaning is not a matter of necessity since which language is spoken depends on arbitrary conventions.

Whereas the analysis of depiction in the previous two chapters paralleled the analysis of speaker meaning in terms of intention, the analysis of depictive symbol systems in this chapter parallels the analysis of sentence meaning in terms of convention, and so accommodates the possibility of depiction without intention. Just as a person uttering a sentence whose meaning in a language they do not know might accidentally utter a sentence which means something they don't intend, a person who doesn't know that the top of a map, for example, represents north may accidentally depict the orientation of a nation in a way which they don't intend.

In chapter two, I said that using convention to accommodate unintentional depiction risks failing to distinguish between depiction and onomatopoeia. The word 'woof', for example, resembles but does not depict a dog's bark. But just as sentences now have their sentence meaning because of conventions arising from what they were used to speaker mean in the past, onomatopoeic words now have their meaning because of conventions arising from what they were used to depict in the past. The word 'woof', for example, represents a dog's bark due to a convention, which arose because 'woof' was used to depict a dog's bark in the past.

Though the analysis of depictive symbol systems in this chapter parallels the analysis of sentence meaning in terms of convention, it can still distinguish between depiction and onomatopoeia. Although there are symbol systems in use in which 'woof', for example, represents a dog's bark, these symbol systems are not depictive but merely conventional, since the reason for being truthful in those symbol systems is no longer because the characters in the symbol system resemble what they represent, but is now merely because others are truthful in that symbol system. In other words, use of those symbol systems is no longer mediated by resemblance, but merely by convention.

Two clarifications. First, the definition of truthfulness in a language cannot be straightforwardly applied to symbol systems, since symbol systems are functions from characters to extensions rather than truth-conditions and extensions need not be true or false. One cannot be truthful in the symbol system of Arabic numerals, for example, since the extensions of the numerals in the system are numbers, which exist or not rather than obtaining or being true or false. Similarly, if the extensions of chess diagrams are chess positions, one cannot be truthful in the symbol system of chess diagrams, because chess positions cannot be true or false.

The solution is to observe that depiction is of states of affairs as well as objects. The Mona Lisa, for example, does not merely depict Lisa but also the state of affairs of Lisa smiling. Similarly, depictions resemble states of affairs as well as objects: the Mona Lisa does not merely resemble Lisa (the object), but the Mona Lisa's having certain properties also resembles Lisa's smiling (the state of affairs). So the difficulty can be overcome by applying the analysis first towards the depiction of states of affairs and then stipulating that something depicts an object if and only if it depicts a state of affairs of that object's having a property (see section 8.4).

Second, both the analysis of conventional language and of depictive symbol systems have to be altered to accommodate non-assertoric utterances. The sentences 'the door is closed' and 'shut the door', for example, have the same truth-condition. But their meanings in English are different, since the first is an indicative and the second is an imperative. The solution is to redefine languages as functions from sentences to ordered pairs of moods and truth-conditions. English, for example, is a function taking 'the door is shut' to the ordered pair of the indicative mood and the door's being shut and 'shut the door' to the ordered pair of the imperative mood and the door's being shut.

As a result of this revision, the definition of truthfulness in a language also has to be revised. Truthfulness, according to the revision, is sometimes uttering sentences of the language in the indicative mood while abstaining from uttering indicative sentences which are false in the language and trying to make true in the language sentences of the language addressed to one in the imperative mood, if those sentences are uttered by the appropriate agent – such as someone in authority, someone one can trust or whom one wants to please (Lewis, 1969, 184). Analogous revisions are required to accommodate other moods, depending on the usual force of the mood.

The analysis of depictive symbol systems requires less revision, since the definition of symbol systems need not be altered to include moods. This is because, while some pictures are intended to produce beliefs and others actions, this difference is not marked in the syntactic structure of the pictures in the way that the intended force of the utterance of a sentence is marked using the mood of the sentence. Differences in mood are syntactic differences between sentences used as prima facie markers of the intended force of a sentence, but there are not usually corresponding syntactic differences between depictions.

There is no difference corresponding to mood, since there is no syntactic difference at all, between, for example, the picture of a Lego castle on the front of the Lego box which tells you how the Lego will look when it is built and the picture of the Lego castle contained in the Lego instructions which tells you where to put the final bricks to complete the castle. Although the picture on the front of the box – like 'the door is shut' – is designed to induce belief and the picture in the instructions – like 'shut the door' – is designed to induce action, this difference in force is not marked by any syntactic difference in mood between the pictures.

Nevertheless, the fact that some depictions are used to produce action rather than belief does require a revision of the definition of truthfulness used in the analysis of depictive symbol systems. The definition of truthfulness says that someone is truthful in a symbol system if and only if they sometimes perpetrate characters in that symbol system while abstaining from perpetrating characters in the symbol system when the state of affairs they represent does not obtain. This definition only accommodated depictions intended to induce belief: Lego instructions which tell you where to put the bricks, for example, are not perpetrated only when the bricks are already arranged.

So the definition of truthfulness in a symbol system has to be revised. Truthfulness in a symbol system, according to the revision, is sometimes perpetrating characters of the symbol system while trying to abstain from perpetrating characters of the symbol system which represent states of affairs which don't obtain or else trying to bring about the state of affairs the character represents, if the character is perpetrated by an appropriate agent (further problems involving truthfulness are addressed in the next chapter). So, for example, a picture of Lego may be perpetrated both if the Lego is arranged in a certain way or if it is to be arranged in that way.

## 4.5 Conclusion

There are two kinds of philosophy of language, which address two different kinds of question. The first kind is descriptive: it answers questions about what kinds of syntax and semantics our languages have. Answers to these descriptive questions include, for example, the definition of a language as a function from sentences to truth-conditions. The second kind is foundational: it answers questions about what makes it the case that our languages have the syntax and semantics that they do. Answers to these foundational questions include, for example, the thesis that language is mediated by convention (Lewis, 1969, 204; Stalnaker, 1984, 32-35; 1997, 166-168).

Correspondingly, there are two kinds of question about the nature of depiction: descriptive questions about the syntax and semantics of pictures and foundational questions about what makes it the case that depictions have the syntax and semantics they do. The descriptive questions include, for example, the question of whether the semantics of depiction is compositional or the content of a picture is a state of affairs. The foundational questions include, for example, the questions of whether depiction is mediated by resemblance, and of how what a depiction represents is dependent on its perpetrators' intentions.

According to the platitude that depiction is mediated by resemblance the difference between depiction and other kinds of representation is a foundational issue about what makes it the case that depictions represent what they do. An important alternative is that the difference between depiction and other kinds of representation is a descriptive issue concerning the descriptive syntactic and semantic properties of symbol systems. As Goodman, for example, writes: "... whether a denoting symbol is representational [depictive] depends not upon whether it resembles what it denotes but upon its own relationships to other symbols in a given system" (Goodman, 1968, 226).

Which symbol systems in the abstract are symbol systems in use is not a descriptive question about the syntactic and semantic properties that symbol systems actually use, but a foundational question about what makes it the case that we use certain symbol systems rather than others. English, for example, is a symbol system in use rather than merely a symbol system in the abstract because we have a convention of speaking and writing in English. So even if depiction is to be defined as a kind of symbol system, this definition must still address foundational questions about what makes it the case that our symbol systems have the syntactic and semantic properties that they do.

In terms of the distinction drawn at the beginning of this section, questions about the definition of depiction are not descriptive questions about the syntax and semantics of pictures, but foundational questions about how depiction is mediated. As Kulvicki writes "… one appealing direction in which to proceed is to claim that facts about us … contribute to determining which representational systems are pictorial … After all, a merely structural analysis of representational systems must fail to take into account how and by whom such representational systems are used …" (Kulvicki, 2006, 42). If a symbol system is depictive, it is so because of the way in which we use it.

# 5. Symbol Systems

It's often argued that the theory of language ought to be subsumed by a general theory of representation, of which language is merely one kind. Ferdinand de Saussure, for example, writes "A language is a system of signs expressing ideas, and hence comparable to writing, the deaf-and-dumb alphabet, symbolic rites, forms of politeness, military signals, and so on. It is simply the most important of such systems. It is therefore possible to conceive of a science which ... would investigate the nature of signs and the laws governing them" (Saussure, 1972, 15). Language, according to Saussure, is merely a special case of representation in general.

In a similar vein, Charles Peirce writes, "...there are three kinds of representations. 1st Those whose relations to their objects is mere community in some quality, and these representations may be termed *Likenesses*. 2nd Those whose relations to their objects consists in a correspondence in fact, and these may be termed *Indices* or *Signs*. 3rd Those the grounds of whose relation to their objects is an imputed character, which are the same as *general signs*, and these may be termed *Symbols*" (Peirce, 1868, 7). However, Peirce continues "... the rules of logic ... have no immediate application to likenesses or indices, because no arguments can be constructed from these alone" (Peirce, 1868, 7).

Lack of success has led to pessimism. Gilbert Harman, for example, writes "... there is no ordinary sense of the word 'mean' in which a picture of a man means a man or means that man. This suggests that Peirce's theory of signs would comprise at least three rather different subjects: a theory of intended meaning, a theory of evidence, and a theory of pictorial depiction. There is no reason to suppose these three theories would have any principles in common" (Harman, 1977, 214). Language, according to Harman, has little in common with other kinds of representation, so the study of language cannot be subsumed under a study of representation in general.

http://dx.doi.org/10.11647/OBP.0046.05

The last chapter argued for an analysis of depictive symbol systems analogous to the analysis of languages in use. But not all symbol systems are depictive or descriptive: as well as languages and pictures, there are, for example, traffic lights, musical scores, graphs and dewy decimal numbers. This suggests that the analyses of depictive and descriptive symbol systems are special cases of an analysis of symbol systems in use in general. This chapter argues that a symbol system is in use in a group if and only if the group conforms, has reason to conform and prefers others to conform if most do to a regularity of speaker meaning in the symbol system, and if they believe all this.

The first section addresses some objections to the necessity and sufficiency of Lewis' analysis of languages in use, and argues for replacing regularities of truthfulness with regularities of speaker meaning. The second section argues for a generalisation of this analysis and the analysis of depictive symbol systems which drops the clauses which are unique to each while retaining the clauses which are common to both. The third section uses this analysis to argue that not all depictions belong to symbol systems in use, and so depiction is not a kind of symbol system. The fourth section addresses an objection concerning non-literal language, and the fifth concludes.

## 5.1 Analysis of conventional language

A language is used by a population, according to Lewis' original analysis (1969, 177), if and only if there's a convention of truthfulness in that language in that population or, in other words, if and only if there's a convention of sometimes uttering sentences of the language in the indicative mood while trying to abstain from uttering indicative sentences which are false in the language, and trying to make true in the language sentences of the language addressed to one in the imperative mood, if those sentences are uttered by an appropriate agent – such as someone in authority, someone one can trust or someone whom one wants to please (Lewis, 1969, 184).

But there are counterexamples to both the necessity and sufficiency of Lewis' original analysis. The analysis is not necessary because a population of inveterate liars may have a language of use in which there is no regularity of truthfulness, since although they often utter sentences of their language, they never do so while trying to abstain from uttering sentences of their language which are false, but actively try to say sentences which are false, and although imperatives in their language are addressed to them by appropriate agents, they never try to make those imperatives true, but go out of their way to try to make them false (Lewis, 1969, 195; 1975, 182).

The analysis is not sufficient because every conventional regularity of behaviour in a population can be redescribed as a conventional regularity of truthfulness in some language in the population. If garbage is conventionally collected on Tuesday, for example, there's a conventional regularity of truthfulness in the language in which collecting garbage is an indicative sentence meaning that it's Tuesday, since people sometimes collect garbage but abstain from collecting garbage when it's not Tuesday. But the language in which collecting garbage means that it's Tuesday is obviously not a language in use (Schiffer, 1993, 233).

Liars have a language of use in which they are not truthful and garbage collectors are truthful in a language which is not their language of use, because garbage collectors do not mean anything by collecting garbage whereas liars mean something by lying. This suggests that languages in use should be defined, not in terms of conventional regularities of truthfulness in a language, but in terms of conventional regularities of speaker meaning in a language (Schiffer, 1993, 233). In other words, this suggests the original plan of analysing speaker meaning directly in terms of intention, and sentence meaning jointly in terms of convention and speaker meaning.

A regularity of speaker meaning in a language, is a regularity of uttering sentences in the language only if they mean what the speaker means by uttering them (Schiffer, 1987, 252). In other words, speaker meaning in a language is uttering sentences in the language approximately only if one intends an audience to believe, make it the case, imagine or have some other attitude towards the truth-condition of the sentence in the language, by means of recognition of one's intention. A regularity of speaker meaning in English, for example, is a regularity of uttering 'the door is shut' only if one means the door is shut, 'shut the door' only if one means shut the door ... and so on.

So a language is used by a group, according to this suggestion, if and only if there's a conventional regularity of speaker meaning in the language, or a convention of uttering sentences in the language only if they mean what their speaker means by uttering them. English, for example, is supposed to be our language of use because we have a convention of speaker meaning in English or, in other words, a convention of uttering English sentences only if their meaning in English is what we mean by uttering them: we utter 'the door is shut' only if we mean that the door is shut, 'shut the door' only when we mean the door to be shut, ... and so on.

One clarification. The conditional in this analysis shouldn't be interpreted as material, since if it were, the conditions of the analysis would be trivially met if the antecedent of the conditional is false. The convention of silence during the eleventh minute of the eleventh hour of the eleventh month, for example, would count as a convention of speaking every language at that time, since by not uttering sentences of any language, speakers utter those sentences only if they speaker mean what the sentences mean in the language. But the convention of silence during the eleventh minute of the eleventh hour of the eleventh month is obviously not a convention of speaking any language.

## 5.2 Analysis of symbol systems in use

The natural generalisation of this analysis of language in use to symbol systems is: a symbol system is in use if and only if there's a convention of speaker meaning in that symbol system, where speaker meaning in a symbol system is perpetrating characters of the symbol system only if they represent a state of affairs their perpetrator speaker means by perpetrating them. Traffic lights, for example, are in use because there's a convention of speaker meaning in the symbol system of traffic lights: the lights are red only if we are meant to stop, green only if we are meant to go and orange only if we are meant to be careful.

This analysis accommodates many depictive symbol systems without amendment (Bennett, 1974; Novitz, 1977). Maps, for example, are a symbol system in use since there's a regularity of speaker meaning in the symbol system of maps, there's reason to conform to this regularity if others do, there's an alternative regularity – speaker meaning in the symbol system in which the bottom instead of the top of a map represents north – which there would be reason to conform to if others conformed to it, others are preferred to conform to this regularity if most do, and it's believed that all these conditions obtain. In other words, maps are used in virtue of a convention of speaker meaning.

But depiction is still a counterexample to the necessity of this analysis, because some depictive symbol systems are not mediated by convention, even in part. The symbol system of colour charts, for example, in which colour samples are used to represent colour shades, is a symbol system in use. But the regularity of speaker meaning in the symbol system of colour charts is not conventional, because there's not an alternative regularity which we would have reason to conform to if others did: the symbol system in which samples are the same colour as the shades they represent is the only symbol system which allows the represented shade to be seen by looking at the sample.

Globes, for example, also seem to belong to a regularity of meaning in a symbol system which lacks any equally good alternatives. Mercator projections, for instance, are not as good as globes because they inevitably distort the Earth's shape by making the poles seem larger than they actually are; other systems of projection produce other distortions. Any globe, of course, could be replaced by a larger or smaller globe, but that replacement would not amount to a change in the symbol system being used but just to another representation in the same system. So depictions and depictive symbol systems need not conform to the analysis of convention (Lopes, 1996, 132-135).

Depiction is not the only illustration of the point that not all symbol systems in use are mediated by convention. Imagine, for example, a species incapable of learning, which knows the grammar and vocabulary of its language innately. For this species, there's no alternative language in which a regularity of speaker meaning would be preferred if it were preferred by others, because everyone in the population prefers to speak the only language they know. In this case, the species' language of use is mediated not by convention, but by psychological necessity (Peacocke, 1976, 169). Human language is mediated by convention, but this is contingent, and not a matter of necessity.

The fact not all symbol systems are mediated by convention might be taken to suggest that symbol systems should be analysed in terms of any, instead of only conventional, regularities of speaker meaning, as follows: a symbol system is in use if and only if there is a regularity of speaker meaning in that symbol system. So the symbol system of traffic lights, for example, is supposed to be in use just because there's a regularity of speaker meaning in the symbol system of traffic lights or, in other words, merely because the lights are red only if we're meant to stop, green only if we're meant to go and orange only if we're meant to be careful.

If this analysis were sufficient, then every depiction would belong to a symbol system in use, because there is a regularity of speaker meaning in the symbol system defined by the function which takes every depiction to the state of affairs its audience is intended to believe, imagine, bring about ... or so on, by means of recognition of this intention. Because Leo intended the Mona Lisa, for example, to induce in us the belief that Lisa smiles by means of recognition of his intention, Leo conformed to a regularity of speaker meaning in a symbol system which takes the Mona Lisa to the state of affairs of Lisa's smiling.

But this analysis entails that every depiction belongs to a symbol system in use only because it entails every arbitrary function from utterances to what is meant by them is a symbol system in use. There's a regularity of speaker meaning, for example, in the language defined by the function taking English sentences to what English speakers mean by them and German sentences to what German speakers mean by them, since English speakers utter 'it's raining' and 'es regnet' only if it's raining, 'snow is white' and 'schnee ist weiß' only if snow is white, ... and so on for all English and German sentences.

But the function taking English sentences to what English speakers mean by them and German sentences to what German speakers mean by them obviously isn't a language in use, because the fact that there's a regularity of speaker meaning in this language is simply a by-product of the fact that there's a regularity of speaker meaning in English and also a regularity of speaker meaning in German. In general, it's not sufficient for a symbol system in the abstract to be a symbol system in use that there's a regularity of speaker meaning in that symbol system, because that regularity might simply be a by-product of the use of other symbol systems or disparate acts of communication.

This suggests dropping from the analysis of symbol systems of use not the analysis of convention as a whole, but just those parts of the analysis of convention which entail that choice of symbol system is arbitrary, leading to the following analysis:

(20) A symbol system is in use in a group if and only if everyone in the group:

    a. perpetrates characters of the symbol system only if they speaker mean what the characters represent in the symbol system
    b. has reason to perpetrate characters of the symbol system only if they speaker mean what the characters represent in the symbol system
    c. prefers other members of the group to perpetrate characters of the symbol system only if they speaker mean what the characters represent in the symbol system, on condition that most do
    d. and everyone in the group believes (a)-(d).

Traffic lights, for example, are in use because the lights are red only if we're meant to stop, green only if we're meant to go and orange only if we're meant to be careful, there's reason to conform to this regularity, conformity is preferred if most conform, and all this is believed.

This analysis generalises both the analysis of conventional language and the analysis of depictive symbol systems by retaining the clauses common to both while dropping the clauses which are unique to each. In particular, while it's still required that there be a reason for conforming to a regularity of speaker meaning in a symbol system, it's not required that this reason be precedent or the conformity of others as is required by the analysis of conventional language or that the reason be resemblance of characters to their extensions, as in the analysis of depictive symbol systems. An innately known language, for example, may be spoken simply because of psychological necessity.

Requiring that everyone in the group has reason to conform to the regularity, without specifying what kind of reason, may seem redundant, since if the group conforms to a regularity, it seems they must have reason to conform to that regularity. But this is not the case, since the explanation of a group's conformity to a regularity may be brutely causal, rather than rational. If the explanation of a group's conformity to a regularity of speaker meaning in a symbol system is brutely causal, rather than rational, then even if everyone in the group prefers others to conform on condition that most do, and everyone believes all this, the symbol system is not used by the group.

Suppose, for example, there's a group of people who sneeze only if they pronounce a certain sentence which tickles their noses and which they use to mean that it's raining. Then there's a regularity in the group of uttering sentences of a language in which sneezing means that it's raining only if they speaker mean what the sentence means in that language. If everyone in the group is proud of any eccentricity they all happen to have, then they prefer the others to conform to this regularity if most do. And they might all believe all this. Even so, a language in which sneezing means it's raining is not their language of use, since they don't conform to the regularity for a reason, but merely because of a physiological accident (Peacocke, 1976, 176).

Since the requirement that everyone in the group prefer others to conform if most do is merely inherited from the analysis of convention, it may not seem necessary. But this is not the case, since the use of a symbol system in a group, like the adoption of a convention, requires coinciding interest: just as a group adopts a convention because they have a common interest in some end which is furthered by the adoption of a common pattern of behaviour, a group adopts a symbol system for use because they have a common interest in communication about a certain subject matter, which is furthered by the adoption of a common symbol system.

Suppose, for example, that the members of an automobile club conform to a regularity of driving vintage cars only if they mean that they are wealthy, that they have reason to conform to this regularity because they're prepared to risk the expense of denting their vintage cars only if they mean that they are wealthy, and that everyone in the club believes all this, but they don't prefer other members of the club to drive vintage cars only if they mean that they're rich, because they don't mind other members' cars being dinted. Since the regularity is not adopted in response to a common interest, the club doesn't use a symbol system in which driving vintage cars represents wealth.

## 5.3 Depiction outside of symbol systems

Whether depiction should be defined as a kind of symbol system is hard to adjudicate: since there is a function which takes every depiction to what it represents, it's trivially true that every depiction belongs to a symbol system in the abstract. The distinction between symbol systems in the abstract and in use makes adjudicating this question easier, because whereas it's trivial that every depiction belongs to a symbol system in the abstract, it's non-trivial whether every depiction belongs to a symbol system in use. The analysis defended in the last section shows not all depictions belong to symbol systems in use, and so depiction should not be analysed as a kind of symbol system.

The function taking English sentences to what English speakers mean by them and German sentences to what German speakers mean by them isn't a symbol system in use, according to this analysis, since though English speakers conform to a regularity of uttering sentences in this language only if they mean what the sentences mean in the language, not all English speakers believe this. Although it's true that people utter 'es regnet' only if it's raining and 'schnee ist weiß' only if snow is white, for example, most English speakers don't believe this – as far as they know, 'es regnet' is uttered only if it's sunny and 'schnee ist weiß' only if snow is black.

For the same reason, this analysis does not entail that every depiction belongs to a symbol system in use. Although there's a regularity of perpetrating depictions only if the perpetrator speaker means what the depiction represents, this is not believed by all perpetrators of depictions, so condition (d) isn't met by the function which takes each depiction to what it represents. Not everyone believes *Nude Descending a Staircase*, for example, is perpetrated only if it's meant that a nude is descending a staircase – as far as people unfamiliar with cubism believe, *Nude Descending a Staircase* may only be perpetrated if several knights in armour are filing down a staircase.

So the symbol system defined by the function which takes each depiction to the state of affairs it represents is not a symbol system in use. But this doesn't show that not all depictions belong to symbol systems in use, because though there's no single symbol system in use to which every depiction belongs, it may be true that all depictions belong to some symbol system in use or another, but that different depictions belong to different symbol systems in use. Whereas the Mona Lisa, for example, may belong to a symbol system in use of renaissance painting, *Nude Descending a Staircase* may belong to a symbol system in use of cubist painting.

But even if everyone in a group believes there's a regularity of speaker meaning in a symbol system, the symbol system may not be in use if they don't prefer others to conform to a regularity of speaker meaning in that symbol system if most do. Cubist painting, for example, may not be a symbol system in use because cubists may not prefer other cubists to conform to a regularity of speaker meaning in that system on condition that most do. If Marcel, for example, prefers his paintings to be original, then he might not prefer that others perpetrate *Nude Descending a Staircase* only if they mean that a nude is descending a staircase but may prefer them, less originally, to perpetrate it only if they mean that knights in armour are filing down a staircase.

Moreover, because some depicters don't believe that there are regularities of speaker meaning in any symbol system, their depictions don't conform to any regularity of speaker meaning which meets condition (d). It is probable, for example, that the first person to depict something did not believe in any other instance of speaker meaning, in which case the person did not believe in a regularity of speaker meaning in any symbol system. So even though the first depicter conformed to regularities of speaker meaning in many symbol systems, not everyone believed in any of these regularities, because the first depicter believed in none of them.

It might be objected that single occurrences are degenerate regularities, so that even if only one depiction were ever perpetrated, there'd be a regularity of speaker meaning in a symbol system defined by the function taking that depiction to the state of affairs its audiences is intended to believe, imagine, bring about ... or so on by means of recognition of intention, constituted by the single act of speaker meaning that state of affairs by perpetrating that depiction. In this case, then even the first depicter would have believed he or she conformed to a regularity of speaker meaning in a symbol system, simply in virtue of believing that he or she meant something by the depiction.

But if single occurrences were degenerate regularities, then even a single behavioural occurrence could count as conventional. If, for example, both of us go to a party in the hope that the other will, there's another party on the same night we would have been equally happy to go to, both of us prefer to go to the same party as the other, and both of us are aware of all this, then our going to this party would count as a convention, even if we never go to another party our whole lives long. Since single occurrences of this kind are intuitively not conventions, single occurrences should not be regarded as degenerate regularities in the analyses of convention or depictive symbol systems.

## 5.4 Meaning outside conventional language

The argument just given that not all depictions belong to symbol systems in use might be thought to prove too much, on the grounds that a similar argument undermines the analysis of languages in use. The problem arises because there's in fact no regularity of uttering English sentences only if one means what the sentence means in English, because English sentences are often uttered loosely, when their meaning in English merely approximates what one means by them, and non-literally, when their meaning in English is not what one means by them. If I utter 'John is a fine friend' ironically, for example, then I mean not that John is a fine friend, but that he's a false friend.

One response to this problem is to agree that there is no regularity of speaker meaning in literal English, but argue instead that there is a regularity of speaker meaning in a more complex language, which consists of a function that takes English sentences and contexts to their non-literal rather than their literal truth-conditions or meanings. The function which defines this language would take the sentence 'John is a fine friend' in contexts in which it's uttered ironically to the truth-condition of John's being a false friend, 'Juliet is the sun' in contexts in which it's uttered metaphorically to the truth-condition of Juliet's being pretty, ... and so on (Lewis, 1975, 183).

But this response to the problem is incorrect, because although there is a regularity of speaker meaning in the language defined by the function taking English sentences and contexts to their non-literal truth-conditions or meanings which English speakers have reason to conform to, this function may not meet the third and fourth conditions of the analysis of being a symbol system in use: it may be that not everyone prefers others to conform to a regularity of speaker meaning in this language if most do and it may be that not everyone believes everyone conforms to a regularity of speaker meaning in this language, even though everyone does conform to it.

If, for example, we all spoke non-literally in order to show off our cleverness by the aptness of our metaphors, then although we would all conform to a regularity of speaker meaning in the language defined by the function taking English sentences in contexts to their non-literal truth-conditions, we would not prefer others to conform to a regularity of speaker meaning in that language: we would prefer others to conform to a regularity of speaker meaning in literal English, in order that the cleverness of our own speech be more impressive in comparison. In this case, the regularity of speaker meaning in non-literal English wouldn't meet clause (c) of the analysis.

Moreover, it's possible we conform to a regularity of speaker meaning in non-literal English, without believing that we conform to a regularity of speaker meaning in non-literal English. It might be that we utter 'Juliet is the sun', for example, only if Juliet is pretty, but that each time we utter 'Juliet is the sun', we believe that we don't conform to a regularity of speaker meaning in non-literal English because we believe that that 'Juliet is the sun' is uttered on all other occasions only if Juliet is the sun. In this case, non-literal English is not our language in use, because it does not meet clause (d) of the analysis of symbol systems in use.

If the correct response to this were to weaken clauses (c) and (d) of the analysis, that would undermine the argument that not all depictions belong to symbol systems in use, which relied on those clauses. But the correct response is to weaken the analysis to reflect that speakers may utter a sentence of their language not only if they mean by it what it means in their language, but also if they mean by it something non-literal, which the audience is intended to infer from its literal meaning. Although 'Juliet is the sun', for example, is not uttered only if it's meant that Juliet is the sun, what is meant by 'Juliet is the sun' is inferred from the fact that it means Juliet is the sun in English.

A language in the abstract is a language in use, according to this suggestion, if and only if there's a convention of taking utterances of sentences in the language as prima facie evidence that the utterer means what they mean in the language. English is our language in use, for example, because there's a convention of taking utterances of 'it's raining' as prima facie evidence the utterer means it's raining and utterances of 'Juliet is the sun' as prima facie evidence that the utterer means that Juliet is the sun. In the latter case, this prima facie evidence is outweighed, and allows the audience instead to infer that the speaker means that Juliet is pretty (Peacocke, 1976, 172).

In general, this leads to the following analysis of symbol systems in use:

(21) A symbol system is in use in a group if and only if everyone in the group:

a. takes perpetrations of characters of the symbol system as prima facie evidence that the perpetrator means what the characters represent in the symbol system
b. has reason to take perpetrations of characters of the symbol system as prima facie evidence that the perpetrator means what the characters represent in the symbol system
c. prefers other members of the group to take perpetrations of characters of the symbol system as prima facie evidence that the perpetrator means what the characters represent in the symbol system, on condition that most do
d. and everyone in the group believes (a)-(d).

Traffic lights, for example, are in use because red lights are prima facie evidence that we're meant to stop, green lights are prima facie evidence that we're meant to go and orange lights are prima facie evidence that we're meant to be careful.

## 5.5 Conclusion

So a symbol system is in use in a group if and only if there's a regularity of taking the perpetration of a character in that symbol system to be prima facie evidence that the perpetrator means what it represents, everyone in the group has reason to conform to that regularity, everyone prefers everyone to conform to that regularity on condition that most do and everyone believes all this. Traffic lights, for example, are in use because there's a conventional regularity of taking red lights as prima facie evidence that we're meant to stop, green lights as prima facie evidence that we're meant to go and orange lights as prima facie evidence that we're meant to be careful.

It follows from this analysis that since not all depictions belong to symbol systems in use, depiction should not be defined as a kind of symbol system. Though perpetrating a picture is prima facie evidence that the perpetrator means what it represents in some symbol system, this is not sufficient for the picture to belong to a symbol system in use because it may not be the case that others are preferred to conform to that regularity on condition that most do and it may not be the case that it's believed that those regularities obtain. Depictive symbol systems are an important, but not the only, kind of depiction.

It might be objected that this conclusion – that depiction is not a kind of symbol system – undermines the analogy between depiction and language, since the analysis of languages in use encompasses all of the phenomena it's expected to, whereas the analysis of depictive symbol systems does not. While languages, for example, have their depictive analogues in maps, chess diagrams and other symbol systems, it may seem that depictions which don't belong to symbol systems lack linguistic cousins, so that the analogy between depiction and description is not as close as the analogy between languages and depictive symbol systems originally seemed to suggest.

But this objection would be incorrect. Just as some depictions fall under the analysis of depictive symbol systems and others do not, some spoken and written utterances belong to languages whereas others fall outside it. If somebody calls out loudly in alarm, for example, then, whilst their call trivially belongs to some language in the abstract or another, whether it falls under the analysis of languages in use will depend on the preferences, reasons and beliefs of the speaker and their population. Spoken and written utterances of this kind – instances of speaker meaning without sentence meaning – are analogous to depictions not belonging to depictive symbol systems.

Just as there is a distinction between the meaning of sentences in a language of use and what speakers mean by their utterances, there's a distinction between the extensions of depictions in a depictive symbol system and what perpetrators represent by perpetrating depictions. The analysis of languages in use is an analysis of the meaning of sentences in a population's language of use, which is why it excludes examples of speaker meaning in the absence of a language, such as shouts of alarms or ad hoc gestures. By paralleling this analysis, the definition of depictive symbol systems captures the aspect of depiction which is analogous to sentence meaning.

# 6. Depiction and Composition

Language has compositional structure. The meaning of 'Theaetetus flies' for example depends on the meaning of 'Theaetetus', the meaning of 'flies' and the order in which they are concatenated. In general, the meaning of a sentence depends on the meanings and arrangement of its parts. In contrast, depiction is supposed to lack compositional structure. The Mona Lisa for example is supposed not to be divisible into parts in the way that 'Theaetetus flies' is divisible into 'Theaetetus' and 'flies'. In general, what a picture represents is supposed not to depend on what its parts represent in the way that what a sentence means is supposed to depend on what its parts mean.

Despite the platitudinousness of this observation, a sense in which what is represented by pictures doesn't depend on what is represented by their parts is difficult to discern. The Mona Lisa represents Lisa, for example, in part because parts of the Mona Lisa represent parts of Lisa; if it's left and right halves didn't represent her left and right halves, for example, then it as a whole wouldn't have represented her as a whole. If there's a sense in which what pictures represent does not depend on what their parts represent in the way that the meaning of sentences does depend on what their parts mean, that sense cannot simply be that pictures do not have representational parts.

So the supposed disanalogy between depiction and description is not that pictures do not have representational parts, but that the division of a picture into representational parts is arbitrary in a way that the division of a sentence into representational parts is not. The meaning of 'Theaetetus flies' depends on the meaning of 'Theaetetus' and of 'flies' in a way that what the Mona Lisa represents doesn't depend on what its left and right halves represent, for example, because the division of 'Theaetetus flies' into

'Theaetetus' and 'flies' is natural in a way that the division of the Mona Lisa into its left and right halves is arbitrary.

This disanalogy between depiction and description is constantly cited in the literature. Roger Scruton, for example, claims "there seems to be no way in which we can divide [a] painting into grammatically significant parts – no way in which we can provide a syntax which isolates those parts of the painting that have a particular semantic role" (Scruton, 1983, 107). Likewise, David Braddon-Mitchell and Frank Jackson write "there is no preferred way of dividing [a] map into basic representational units. There are many jigsaw puzzles you might make out of the map, but no one would have a claim to have pieces that were all and only the most basic units" (Braddon-Mitchell and Jackson, 1996, 180).

Similarly, Jerry Fodor writes "Iconic representations ... have no canonical decomposition; which is to say they have no canonical structure; which is to say that, however they are sliced, there's no distinction between their canonical parts and their mere parts" (Fodor, 2008, 174). Even Roberto Casati and Achille Varzi, who are sympathetic to an extremely close analogy between depiction and description, ask "Suppose you have a uniformly coloured map region: is it composed of its left and right halves or is it composed of its top and bottom halves?" (Casati and Varzi, 1999, 191). Despite this consensus, I'll argue that this disanalogy is illusory: depiction is compositional in the same sense description is.

The refrain that the division of a picture into representational parts is arbitrary echoes an earlier refrain from the philosophy of language, according to which the division of sentences into meaningful parts is equally arbitrary. Almost exactly the same point is raised by Willard Quine, for example, about language when he writes "... suppose again a language for which we have two extensionally equivalent systems of grammar ... According to one of these systems, the immediate constituents of a certain sentence are 'AB' and 'C'; according to the other system they are 'A' and 'BC'. ... which is right?" (Quine, 1970, 392).

But whereas this point is still widely accepted in the philosophy of pictures, it's now rarely accepted in the philosophy of language. As Fodor, for example, writes in the same passage quoted above "....'John', 'Mary', and 'loves Mary' are among the constituents of [John loves Mary] ... But 'John loves' isn't, and nor is 'John ... Mary'" (Fodor, 2008, 172-173). If Fodor is right about this, there must be a way to decide between theories of English which agree about its sentences but disagree about their division into meaningful parts. That there is is supposedly uncontroversial: "Further details are available upon application at your local department of linguistics" (Fodor, 2008, 172).

Further details, I argue, do show there is a way to decide between competing theories of a language which agree about its sentences but disagree about their division into meaningful parts – a theory according to which the meaningful parts of 'John loves Mary' include 'loves Mary' but not 'John loves', for example, meets constraints that a theory according to which the meaningful parts include 'John loves' but not 'loves Mary' do not. But the same constraints which must be met for a theory of meaning for a language to properly reflect its structure, I shall argue, also reveal that there are non-arbitrary divisions of pictures into their representational parts.

I'll consider three constraints on theories of representation – the finite axiomatization constraint, the mirror constraint and the structural constraint – and argue that only the structural constraint ensures that a theory of representation reveals how and whether what a representation is of depends on what is represented by its parts. Neither the finite axiomatization constraint nor the mirror constraint entail that theories of representation for depictive symbol systems should be compositional, but – I'll argue – the structural constraint does. Language has compositional structure. Pictures have compositional structure of the same kind.

Two clarifications. First, it's often argued that pictures cannot have a compositional semantics on the grounds that they do not have a compositional grammar. Scruton, for example, writes "While there may be repertoires and conventions in painting, there is nothing approaching a grammar as we understand it" (Scruton, 1983, 107). And Flint Schier writes "Pictures, by contrast, have no grammatical rules, natural or conventional" (Schier, 1986, 66). But whether or not pictures have compositional grammar, I will argue in the last section, turns on the same kind of consideration as whether or not they have compositional semantics, so the question cannot be resolved so quickly.

Second, I will focus on two highly simplified examples – chess diagrams and maps. The example of chess diagrams is intended to simply and uncontroversially illustrate the thesis, whereas the example of maps extends the argument to a more controversial case – one that is taken as paradigmatically non-language-like (Braddon-Mitchell and Jackson, 1996, 180; Lewis, 1994, 310). Just as semantics for natural languages begin with simplified fragments of those languages, semantics for pictures must begin with simplified fragments of depictive symbol systems (Casati and Varzi, 1999, 187). But it is hoped that the arguments generalise in principle to other kinds of depiction.

## 6.1 Theories of representation

A theory of meaning for a language is a theory which entails, for each sentence in the language, a statement of the meaning of that sentence (Davidson, 1967, 22). A theory of meaning for English, for example, should entail statements such as that 'snow is white' in English means that snow is white and that 'grass is green' in English means that grass is green. Likewise, a theory of meaning for German should entail statements such as that 'es regnet' in German means that it's raining and that 'schnee ist weiß' in German means that snow is white. If a theory of meaning for a language is adequate, it should reveal the structure of sentences in the language.

In general, a theory of representation for a symbol system is a theory which entails, for each character in the symbol system, a statement about what that character represents. A theory of representation for the symbol system of Arabic numerals, for example, should entail statements such as that '1' represents one, that '2' represents two, that '3' represents three, ... and so on. Likewise, a theory of representation for the symbol system of traffic lights should entail that red represents stop, that orange represents slow and that green represents go. If a theory of representation for a symbol system is adequate, it should reveal the structure of that symbol system.

A theory of representation is compositional if and only if the statement of what each character represents is derived from axioms which state the contribution of the parts of the character, and the significance of their arrangement. The statement that 'snow melts' in English means that snow melts, for example, might be derived in a compositional theory of English from an axiom stating that 'snow' refers to snow and an axiom stating that a referring term followed by 'melts' means the referent of that term melts. Likewise, in a compositional theory of representation for chess diagrams, the theorems which state what each diagram represents might be derived from axioms stating what the two colours, six figurines and sixty-four squares represent.

So just as a theory of meaning may reveal the structure of a language, a theory of representation may reveal the structure of a depictive symbol system. According to the compositional theory of representation for maps proposed by Roberto Casati and Achille Varzi, for example, what a map represents depends compositionally on what its atomic map stages represent, which in turn depends compositionally on what its colours and regions represent. If this theory of representation for maps were adequate, then – like a theory of meaning for a language – it would reveal that the structure of maps – like the structure of language – is compositional.

A map stage, according to Casati and Varzi (1999, 192), is any colouring of a map's regions. A map stage is atomic if and only if it colours all and only the regions of a single shade (1999, 192). If, for example, the whole of the region representing France is coloured purple, then the colouring of that region is an atomic map stage. In contrast, if the region representing Vichy France is coloured purple, and the region representing occupied France is coloured red, then the red and purple colouring of the region representing France is not an atomic map stage. And if the region representing the British Empire is coloured pink, then this colouring is also an atomic map stage.

An atomic map stage is true, according to the theory, if and only if (a) it colours a region of the map which represents a region of the world which has the property represented by its colour and (b) the region of the world represented by the rest of the map does not have that property (Casati and Varzi, 1999, 194; Rescorla (2009) defends (b) whereas Blumson (2012, 427-430) and Bronner (forthcoming) argue it should be dropped). So the maximal blue colouring of the world map, for example, is true if and only if the region it colours represents a region covered by ocean, and the rest of the map represents a region which does not have the property of being covered by ocean.

A map, according to the theory, is true if and only if all its atomic map stages are true (Casati and Varzi, 1999, 195). So the world map, for example, is true if and only if its maximal green and blue colourings are both true. Casati and Varzi's theory reveals compositional structure in the symbol system of maps: map regions are like names referring to world regions, colours are like predicates representing properties, atomic map stages are like atomic sentences predicating properties of regions, and whole maps are like complex sentences conjoining atomic map stages. So the structure of maps, according to the theory, is closely analogous to the structure of language.

One clarification. Strictly speaking, Casati and Varzi's theory is not a theory of representation which entails, for each map, a statement of what that map represents but a theory of truth which entails, for each map, a statement of the truth-conditions of that map. The theory entails that the world map, for example, is true if and only if the region represented by its blue part is covered by ocean and the region represented by its green part is covered by land, but not that the world map represents that the region represented by its blue part is covered by ocean and the region represented by its green part is covered by land.

An interpretive theory of truth is one in which 'is true if and only if' in its theorems can be correctly replaced by 'represents that' (Davies, 1981a, 34). A theory which entails that 'snow is white' is true if and only if snow is white and the earth moves, for example, is not interpretive, because 'snow is white' does not represent that snow is white and the earth moves. So if a theory of truth is interpretive, one should not be able to infer from 'snow is white' is true if and only if snow is white that 'snow is white' is true if and only if snow is white and the earth moves. As long as a theory of truth is interpretive, it may serve as a theory of representation.

If Casati and Varzi's theory of truth for maps is interpretive, then from its statements about the truth-conditions of maps one can infer statements about what those maps represent. So as long as one is not able to infer from, for example, the fact that the world map is true if and only if the region its blue part represents is ocean and the region its green part represents is land that the world map is true if and only if the region its blue part represents is ocean, the region its green part represents is land and the earth moves, one may infer that the world map represents that the region its blue part represents is ocean and the region its green part represents is land.

One objection. It might be argued that because some pictures cannot be finitely paraphrased, what they represent can't be stated, so that no theory of representation could entail statements about what those pictures represent. A theory which entailed, for example, simply that a photograph of a cup on a table represents that a cup is on the table would be incomplete, since the photograph would also have to represent that the cup is smaller than the table, whiter than the table, curvier than the table, ... and so on. So although it may be possible to construct theories of representation for some symbol systems such as maps, this may not be possible in general.

This objection can be avoided in two ways. First, a theory may completely specify what a picture that can't be finitely paraphrased represents if it is allowed to entail an infinite number of statements about what that picture represents. A theory of representation could entail, for example, an infinite number of theorems which combine to state that the photograph of the cup on the table represents that the cup is smaller than the table, whiter than the table, curvier than the table, … and so on. Even if what a picture represents cannot be paraphrased by a single sentence, it may be paraphrased by an infinite number of sentences.

Second, a statement of what a picture represents may be made using that very picture, just as what a sentence means may be stated by using that very sentence. So instead of entailing a theorem which states in English what is represented by a photograph of a cup, a theory of representation may entail a theorem of the form: \_\_\_\_\_ represents \_\_\_\_\_, where the second blank is replaced by the picture of the cup, and the first is replaced by a picture of that picture (framed, instead of in quotes). Since the picture itself is used in the statement of what it represents, it cannot fail to be an accurate paraphrase, and no problem is posed by it's being unparaphrasable in English.

## 6.2 The finite axiomatization constraint

Just as a theory of meaning for a language should reveal how and whether the meanings of sentences in that language depend on the meanings of their parts, a theory of representation for a symbol system should reveal whether and how what its characters represent depends on what their parts represent. A theory of representation for chess diagrams, for example, should reveal whether and how what diagrams represent depends on what's represented by the figurines and their arrangement and a theory of representation for maps should reveal whether and how what maps represent depends on what their parts represent.

But a theory of meaning for a language may entail what each sentence in the language means without revealing how or whether the meanings of sentences depend on the meanings of their parts. A theory of meaning for English, for example, might simply list an infinite number of axioms which state separately the meaning of each English sentence (Davidson, 1970, 56). Likewise, a theory of representation for pictures might simply list an infinite number of axioms of the form: \_\_\_\_\_ represents \_\_\_\_\_, where the second blank is replaced by each picture, and the first by a picture of that picture (framed, instead of in quotes).

It's sometimes suggested that to exclude trivial theories of meaning or representation of this kind which fail to reveal the structure of a language or symbol system, they should be constrained to a finite number of axioms (Davidson, 1970, 56). Since, for example, both the theory of meaning for English which simply lists an infinite number of axioms which state separately the meaning of each English sentence and the theory of representation for pictures which simply lists a separate axiom which states what is represented by each picture both possess an infinite number of axioms, both are rightly excluded by imposing this constraint.

The finite axiomatization constraint reveals a lacuna in Casati and Varzi's theory of representation for maps. To entail a statement of what each map represents, the theory must entail statements about what each atomic map stage represents. And to entail what each atomic map stage represents, the theory should entail what property each colour represents and what world region each map region which is coloured by an atomic stage represents. The natural way to do so is to add an axiom for each colour stating which property it represents and an axiom for each map region coloured by an atomic map stage stating which world region it represents.

To entail what's represented by the world map, for example, four axioms could be added: an axiom stating that green represents the property of being covered by land, an axiom stating that blue represents the property of being covered by ocean, an axiom stating which part of the world the blue coloured part of the map represents and an axiom stating which part of the world the green coloured part of the map represents. The theory would then entail that the world map represents that the region represented by its blue part is covered by ocean and the region represented by its green part is covered by land.

If maps use only a finite number of colours, then only a finite number of axioms will be required to state which property each colour represents. But since every difference in shape, size and location is a different region, there's an infinite number of regions which atomic map stages may colour, so an infinite number of axioms would have to be added to state which world region each map region which may be coloured by an atomic map stage represents. If this were the case, then Casati and Varzi's theory would not meet the finite axiomatization constraint, despite being a compositional theory which states what maps represent in terms of what their parts represent.

Perhaps with this problem in mind, Casati and Varzi suggest two constraints on which map regions represent which world regions. First, a map region is part of another if and only if the world region the former represents is part of the world region the latter represents (Casati and Varzi,

1999, 194). So the part representing France, for example, must be a part of the part representing Europe. Second, one map region is connected to another if and only if the world region the former represents is connected to the world region the latter represents (Casati and Varzi, 1999, 194). So the part representing Italy, for example, must be connected to the part representing France.

But these constraints don't resolve the problem, because they don't entail which regions of the map represent which regions of the world, but only which regions of the map represent which regions of the world given which other regions of the map represent which other regions of the world. The first constraint entails, for example, that a map represents the world if and only if its halves represent the hemispheres, but not that it does represent the world nor that its halves do represent the hemispheres. Likewise, the second constraint entails that the parts representing Italy and France are connected, but not which represents which.

Despite revealing a lacuna in Casati and Varzi's theory, the finite axiomatization constraint does not ensure that a theory of representation for a symbol system reveals how or whether what its characters represent depends on what their parts represent. A theory of meaning for English might, for example, have a single axiom consisting of an infinitely long conjunction, the conjuncts of which are separate statements, for each English sentence, of what that sentence means. Such a theory would be finitely axiomatised, but still fail to reveal how or whether the meanings of English sentences depend on the meanings of their parts (Davies, 1981a, 61).

Likewise, a theory of representation for pictures might have a single axiom consisting of an infinitely long conjunction, the conjuncts of which are separate statements of the form: _____ represents _____, where the second blank is replaced by each picture, and the first by a picture of that picture (framed, instead of in quotes). Such a theory would be finitely axiomatised, but would still fail to reveal whether and how what pictures represent depends on what their parts represent. So a theory of representation for a symbol system may meet the finite axiomatization constraint, without revealing the structure of that symbol system or whether it is compositional.

Excluding infinitely long conjunctions as well as infinitely many axioms does not resolve the problem. Substitutional quantification, for example, can be used to state a theory of meaning for English whose only axiom is: $(\prod \phi)$ '$\phi$' in English means that $\phi$ (Davies, 1981a, 62). Likewise, a theory of representation for pictures could be given by a single axiom which states that all statements of the form ____ represents ____, where the second blank is replaced by each picture, and the first by a picture of that picture (framed), are true. Both theories are finitely axiomatised, but don't reveal how or whether what complexes represent depends on what their parts represent.

Infinitary conjunction and substitutional quantification raise controversial issues, but the same point can be made by considering finite languages and symbol systems. Take, for example, a language with just ten names and ten predicates. The finite axiomatization constraint cannot be used to decide between a theory of meaning for this language with one hundred distinct axioms which state the meaning of each sentence separately, and a theory of meaning with just twenty axioms which state the contribution made by each name and each predicate to the meaning of sentences which contain them (Evans, 1981, 326-328).

Likewise, since there is only a finite number of positions in chess, the finite axiomatization constraint cannot decide between a theory of representation for chess diagrams with a large but finite list of axioms which state what each diagram represents separately, or a smaller number of axioms which state the contribution made by each figurine to what is represented by the diagrams which contain them. So a theory of representation for a symbol system may meet the finite axiomatization constraint, without revealing whether or how what the characters of that symbol system represent depends on what is represented by their parts.

## 6.3 The mirror constraint

The failure of the finite axiomatization constraint to favour a twenty over a hundred axiom theory of meaning for a language with just ten names and ten predicates is often taken to motivate imposing a constraint according to which a theory of meaning for a language, or of representation for a symbol system, should mirror the structure of the ability of interpreters to understand it. According to this mirror constraint, the axioms of a theory which entail what $s_1...s_n$ represent should entail what $s$ represents if and only if people with the ability to understand what $s_1...s_n$ represent can understand what $s$ represents without further training (Davies, 1983, 15).

Since, for example, people with the ability to understand what 'John is happy' and 'Harry is sad' mean can understand what 'John is sad' means without further training, the mirror constraint entails that the axioms of a theory of meaning which entail what 'John is happy' and

'Harry is sad' mean should also entail what 'John is sad' means. So in the case of the language with just ten names and ten predicates, the mirror constraint favours a theory of meaning with just twenty axioms stating the contribution made by each name and each predicate over the theory of meaning with one hundred distinct axioms which state the meaning of each sentence separately.

Likewise, since people with the ability to understand the chess diagram illustrating the opening position can understand a diagram illustrating any other position, the mirror constraint entails that the axioms of a theory of representation for chess diagrams which entail what the diagram of the opening position represents should also entail what is represented by the diagrams illustrating every other position. So the mirror constraint favours a theory which states the contribution made by each figurine to what is represented by the diagrams which contain them over a theory with a large but finite list of axioms which state what each diagram represents separately.

It might be suggested that people with the ability to understand one picture can understand any picture without further training (Schier, 1986, 43). In this case, the mirror constraint would favour a theory of representation for pictures with a single axiom, such as the theory consisting of an infinitely long conjunction, the conjuncts of which are separate statements of what each picture represents or a theory of representation for pictures with a single axiom which states that all statements of the form _____ represents _____, where the second blank is replaced by each picture and the first by a picture of that picture (framed, instead of in quotes), are true.

But two qualifications are required to the suggestion that people with the ability to understand one picture can understand any picture without further training. First, one may have the ability to understand one picture, without being able to understand pictures in other styles or symbol systems (Schier, 1986, 46-48). Someone with the ability to understand chess diagrams, for example, may be unaware of the conventions governing contour lines and thus be unable to understand topographical maps. And someone with the ability to understand impressionist paintings, for example, may still lack the familiarity required to understand cubist paintings.

If it's true that people with the ability to understand a picture can understand every picture in the same symbol system without further training, then the mirror constraint would favour separate single axiom theories of representation for each symbol system. For the symbol system of chess diagrams, for example, the mirror constraint might favour a theory of representation consisting of a long but finite conjunction, the conjuncts of which are separate statements of what each chess diagram represents. So even in this case, the mirror constraint would still favour non-compositional theories of representation for depictive symbol systems.

Second, one may have the ability to understand a picture, without having the ability to understand every picture in the same symbol system, because some pictures in the symbol system depict things one lacks the ability to recognise (Schier, 1986, 44). If you don't have the ability to recognise armadillos, for example, then you may not be able to understand a picture of an armadillo either, even if you have the ability to understand other pictures in the same symbol system. So it's not the case that people with the ability to understand a picture can understand every picture in the same symbol system, and the mirror constraint may not favour single axiom theories.

If people with the ability to understand a picture have the ability to understand any picture in the same symbol system which depicts something they're able to recognise, the mirror constraint will sometimes favour compositional theories. If one's able to recognise a chess piece, for example, one's able to understand the figurine which represents that piece. And if one understands one chess diagram, one can understand other chess diagrams which contain only figurines one understands without further training. So the mirror constraint would favour a theory which states what diagrams represent in terms of the contribution of each figurine.

But if people with the ability to understand a picture can understand any picture in the same symbol system which depicts something they're able to recognise, the mirror constraint will not always favour compositional theories. If one is able to recognise the sex of chickens, for example, and one understands a picture of a female chick, one may be able to understand a picture of a male chick in the same symbol system with no further training. This may be true even if the picture of the male and of the female chick have no parts in common, because the two pictures differ in their shape, colour and other representational properties.

In this case, the mirror constraint wouldn't favour a compositional theory with axioms which entail a statement of what is represented by the picture of the female chick and a statement of what is represented by the male chick by stating the contribution of the common parts of those pictures, because those pictures have no parts in common. In general, the mirror constraint does not always favour compositional theories, because sometimes people with the ability to understand some pictures are able to understand another picture in the same symbol system which represent things they can recognise without further training, even if none of the pictures have parts in common.

However, the mirror constraint is not the appropriate constraint to impose on theories of representation, since if a language is spoken by a psychologically unusual population, a theory which meets the mirror constraint may nevertheless fail to reveal how, or whether, the language is structured. If the language with just ten names and ten predicates, for example, were spoken by a dim-witted population who had to learn the meaning of each sentence in the language individually, then the mirror constraint would favour the hundred axiom theory which states what each sentence means over the twenty axiom theory which states the contribution of each name and predicate.

Similarly, if a language were spoken by a population which was so wired-up that familiarity with any one sentence of the language triggered knowledge of every sentence of the language, then the mirror constraint would favour a theory of meaning for that language such as that with a single long conjunction, the conjuncts of which are separate statements of the meaning of each sentence. So the mirror constraint favours theories of representation which reflect the psychology of a symbol system's users over theories of representation which reveal whether, and how, what its characters represent depends on what their parts represent.

## 6.4 The structural constraint

The failure of the finite axiomatization constraint and the mirror constraint to favour structure revealing theories motivates the imposition of a structural constraint, according to which the axioms of a theory which entail what $s_1...s_n$ represent entail what $s$ represents if and only if what $s$ represents can be inferred by rational inductive means from what $s_1...s_n$ represent. The axioms of a theory of meaning which entail what 'John loves Mary' means, for example, should entail what 'Mary loves John' means because its possible to infer what 'Mary loves John' means from what 'John loves Mary' means by rational inductive means (Davies, 1981a, 56).

The structural constraint favours theories of meaning which reveal how and whether the meanings of sentences in a language depend on the meanings of their parts, even when those languages are spoken by psychologically unusual populations. Since the inference from what

'John is sad' and 'Harry is happy' mean to what 'John is happy' means is inductively strong, for example, the structural constraint favours a theory of meaning with separate axioms stating the contribution made by 'John', 'Harry', 'is sad' and 'is happy' to the meaning of sentences containing them, so the structural constraint favours compositional theories of meaning for languages.

Likewise, since it's possible to go by rational inductive means from knowledge of what the chess diagram of the opening position represents to knowledge of what any other chess diagram represents, the structural constraint entails that the axioms of a theory of representation which entail what the opening position represents should also entail what is represented by any other chess diagram. So the structural constraint favours a compositional theory of representation for chess diagrams, with axioms which state the contribution of each figurine to what's represented by the diagrams which contain them, over non-compositional theories.

If people with the ability to understand a picture can understand any picture in the same symbol system which depicts something they're able to recognise, the structural constraint will not cease to favour compositional theories, because this ability is not explained by the possibility of going by rational inductive means from knowledge of what a picture represents to knowledge of what other pictures represent. Rather, this ability is explained by unusual features of the psychology of picture interpreters: for example, by the thesis that the ability to understand a picture of a thing is underlain by just the ability to recognise the thing and competence in the picture's symbol system.

If one is able to recognise the sex of chickens, for example, and one understands a picture of a female chick, one may be able to understand a picture of a male chick in the same symbol system with no further training, even if the pictures of the male and of the female chick have no parts in common. But because one does not proceed from understanding the picture of the female chick to understanding the picture of the male chick by rational inductive means, the structural constraint doesn't favour a theory the axioms of which which entail what the picture of the female chick represents entail what the picture of the male chick represents, but may favour a compositional theory.

It might be objected that in going from knowledge of what a picture represents to knowledge of what another picture in the same symbol system of something one's able to recognise represents, one does proceed by rational inductive means, since if a picture engages one's ability to recognise something, it probably depicts that thing. If one knows, for example, what a picture of a female chick represents and has the ability to sex chickens, and if that ability is engaged by a picture in the same symbol system as the picture of the female chick, then one would be rational to infer that the picture which engages one's ability to recognise a male chick depicts a male chick.

However, the phrase "rational inductive means" in the structural constraint should not be construed to allow bringing to bear general knowledge, such as the knowledge that pictures which engage one's ability to recognise something probably depict that thing. Etymological knowledge, for example, would trivialise the constraint (Davies, 1981b, 141): if one knows what 'chickens roost' means, for example, then knowledge of etymology would allow one to infer what 'chooks roost' means, but the axioms of a theory which entail what 'chickens roost' means should not entail what 'chooks roost' means, since different axioms should state the contributions of 'chicken' and 'chook'.

The structural constraint also reveals the lacuna in Casati and Varzi's theory of maps revealed by the finite axiomatization constraint. If an axiom for each colour stating which property it represents and an axiom for each map region coloured by an atomic map stage stating which world region it represents is added to the theory, then the axioms which entail what some maps represent also entail what other maps composed of the same atomic map stages represent. The axioms which entail what the world map represents, for example, also entail what is represented by the map of just the ocean and what is represented by the map of just the land.

But it's also possible to proceed by rational inductive means from knowing what a map represents to knowing what other maps composed of different atomic map stages represent. If slightly more of the world map were coloured blue, for example, then its atomic map stages would be colourings of different regions, so the axioms stating what the world map represents would not entail what this slightly different map represents. But it'd be possible to proceed by rational inductive means from knowing what the world map represents to knowing what the slightly different map represents, so the structural constraint entails the same axioms should entail what both represent.

So the structural constraint favours not a theory of representation for maps which has axioms which state which world regions are represented by map regions coloured by atomic map stages, but a theory of representation for maps which states which map regions represent which world regions using a coordinate system. Since a coordinate system would entail what every point on the map represents, it would accommodate the fact that if one understands what the world map represents, one can go by rational inductive means to understanding what a map slightly more of which is coloured blue represents – that slightly more of the world is covered by ocean.

Braddon-Mitchell and Jackson (1996, 180) argue maps lack compositional structure because "there is no natural *minimum* unit of truth-assessable representation in the case of maps ... part of a map that stands for a city itself stands for part of that city." In the same vein, Roger Scruton writes that "... the parts themselves are understood in *precisely the same way*; that is, they too have parts, each of which is potentially divisible into significant components, and so on ad infinitum" (Scruton, 1983, 107) and Gregory Currie writes that "There are no atoms of meaning for cinematic images; every temporal and spatial part of the image is meaningful ..." (Currie, 1995, 130).

But a theory of representation for maps which states which map regions represent which regions of the world using a coordinate system would accommodate the point that all the parts of maps are representational, while still revealing the compositional structure of maps. And a theory of representation for maps which states which map regions represent which world regions using a coordinate system isn't arbitrary but is forced upon us by the constraint that the axioms of a theory which entail what $s_1...s_n$ represent entail what $s$ represents if and only if what $s$ represents can be inferred by rational inductive means from what $s_1...s_n$ represent.

## 6.5 Conclusion

I've considered three constraints on theories of representation – the finite axiomatization constraint, the mirror constraint and the structural constraint – and argued that only the structural constraint ensures that a theory of representation for a symbol system reveals whether and how what the characters of that symbol system represent depends on what their parts represent. The finite axiomatization constraint does not ensure that a theory of representation reveals whether or how what the characters of a symbol system represent depends on what their parts represent, because it can be met trivially by theories with only a single axiom.

The mirror constraint does not ensure that a theory of representation for a symbol system reveals whether or how what its characters represent depends on what their parts represent, since if the symbol system is used by idiosyncratic people, the theory will reflect their idiosyncratic psychology instead of the actual structure of characters in the symbol system. If the psychology of depictive representation is different from the psychology of descriptive representation, then theories of representation for depictive symbol systems conforming to the mirror constraint would reflect these differences, instead of revealing whether and how depiction is compositional.

The structural constraint does suggest that a theory of representation for a symbol system reveals whether and how what its characters represent depends on what their parts represent. And just as theories of meaning which conform to the structural constraint reveal that the meanings of sentences depend on the meanings of their parts, theories of representation which conform to the structural constraint reveal that what pictures represent depends on what their parts represent, since one may proceed by rational inductive means from knowing what some pictures represent to knowing what other pictures composed of the same parts represent.

The same considerations drawn on above to support the thesis that pictures have compositional semantics support the thesis that they have compositional grammar. Just as, for example, there is both a twenty axiom and a one hundred axiom theory of meaning for the one hundred sentence language, there is a grammar for that language with ten names and ten predicates as its basic expressions and another grammar with all one hundred sentences as its basic expressions. The former grammar and not the latter reveals the grammatical structure of the language, since only the former meets the grammatical analogue of the structural constraint (Davies, 1981b, 158).

Likewise, there is a grammar for chess diagrams which lists every diagram as a basic expression and another grammar for chess diagrams which takes figurines and squares as basic expressions. The latter grammar and not the former reveals the grammatical structure of chess diagrams, because only the latter meets the grammatical analogue of the structural constraint. So the idea that pictures lack compositional grammar can't be used to argue they lack compositional semantics, because the same considerations which support the thesis that they have compositional semantics support the thesis that have compositional grammar as well.

# 7. Interpreting Images

Just as it's possible to understand novel sentences without having heard them before, it's possible to understand novel pictures without having seen them before. But these possibilities are traditionally supposed to have very different explanations (Schier, 1986, 43-84; Currie, 1995, 79-136): whereas the possibility of understanding novel sentences is supposed to be explained by their compositional structure, the possibility of understanding novel depictions is supposed not to be. The last chapter argued that depictions have compositional structure; this chapter considers the further question of whether their compositional structure explains our ability to understand them.

Just as how – and whether – the meanings of sentences in a language depends on the meanings of their parts is revealed by the construction of a theory of meaning for the language, whether – and how – what depictions represent depends on what their parts represent is revealed by the construction of a theory of representation for their symbol system. But it's a further question how – and whether – tacit knowledge of a theory of meaning for a language explains the ability of speakers of that language to understand it. Likewise, it's a further question whether – and how – the ability to understand novel depictions is explained by tacit knowledge of a theory of representation.

So although it might be conceded that depictions and descriptions are alike in having compositional structure, it might still be argued that there is an important disanalogy between them, because the ability to understand novel sentences is explained by tacit knowledge of a compositional theory of meaning for their language, but the ability to understand novel depictions is not explained by tacit knowledge of a compositional theory of representation. This chapter argues against this disanalogy: the ability to

http://dx.doi.org/10.11647/OBP.0046.07

*118  Resemblance and Representation*

understand some, but not all, novel depictions and some, but not all, novel sentences is explained by tacit knowledge of a compositional theory.

Just as it's common to distinguish the Gricean program in the philosophy of language from the Sellarsian program, it's also common to distinguish the Gricean program in the philosophy of language, which elucidates meaning in terms of intention, from the Davidsonian program, which elucidates meaning in a language in terms of a theory of meaning or truth for that language. But unlike the Gricean and Sellarsian programs, the Gricean and Davidsonian programs are compatible, since whereas the Gricean program pursues the foundational question of what it is for a population to speak a certain language, the construction of a theory of meaning for a language pursues the descriptive question of what the sentences in a language mean.

So this chapter also bridges the Gricean program pursued in chapters two to five with the variation of the Davidsonian program pursued in chapter six. In chapters four and five it was assumed that interpreters have knowledge or beliefs about what characters in a symbol system mean. In other words, it was assumed interpreters tacitly know or believe a theory of representation for the symbol systems they use. So by elucidating the sense in which interpreters tacitly know theories of meaning or representation and explaining how it is possible to antecedently know what novel characters in a symbol system represent, this chapter also fills a lacuna in chapters four and five.

The first section describes how tacit knowledge of a compositional theory of meaning explains the ability to understand some novel sentences. The second section argues that the ability to understand some novel depictions is likewise explained by tacit knowledge of a compositional theory of representation for their symbol system. The third section agrees that the ability to understand some novel depictions is not explained by tacit knowledge of a compositional theory. But the fourth section argues that this is no disanalogy, because the ability to understand some novel sentences isn't explained by tacit knowledge of a compositional theory either.

## 7.1 Compositionality and language understanding

According to the simplest conception of tacit knowledge, tacitly knowing a theory is simply being disposed to judge in accordance with its theorems. Tacitly knowing the theory of representation for traffic lights, for example, is being disposed to judge that red represents stop, that orange represents slow and that green represents go. Tacitly knowing a theory of meaning for English, according to this conception, is just being disposed to judge that 'snow is white' in English means that snow is white, that 'grass is green' in English means that grass is green, ... and so on for each English sentence. And tacitly knowing a theory of representation for chess diagrams is being disposed to judge, for each diagram, which position it represents.

If this conception is correct, then if there is a compositional theory of representation for a symbol system, competent interpreters tacitly know that theory, since they are disposed to judge in accordance with its theorems. If there is a compositional theory of representation for pictures, for example, then it would follow trivially that I tacitly know that theory, simply because I'm disposed to judge that my portrait represents me, that the Mona Lisa represents Lisa, ... and so on for each picture. So according to this conception, if there is a compositional theory of representation for pictures, then everybody who has the ability to understand pictures tacitly knows that compositional theory.

But because it doesn't distinguish between tacit knowledge of compositional and non-compositional theories, the simplest conception is inadequate. Take, for example, a language with just one hundred sentences, composed of ten names and ten predicates. A compositional theory of meaning for the language might have a separate axiom for each name and predicate, and so twenty axioms in total, whereas a non-compositional theory of meaning for the language might have separate axioms for each sentence, and so one hundred axioms in total. Intuitively, the possibility of understanding novel sentences in the language could be explained by tacit knowledge of the compositional theory, but not tacit knowledge of the non-compositional theory (Evans, 1981, 327).

But since the non-compositional theory of meaning with one hundred axioms and the compositional theory of meaning with just twenty axioms have all the same theorems, being disposed to judge in accordance with the theorems of the compositional theory is being disposed to judge in accordance with the theorems of the non-compositional theory. So the simplest conception of tacit knowledge can't distinguish between tacit knowledge of the compositional theory and tacit knowledge of the non-compositional theory (Evans, 1981, 327). Likewise, the simplest conception of tacit knowledge can't distinguish tacitly knowing a compositional theory of representation for pictures from simply having the ability to understand pictures.

So tacitly knowing a theory of representation for a symbol system is not merely being disposed to judge in accordance with its theorems. Instead, tacitly knowing a theory of representation for a symbol system requires possession of a distinct disposition to judge what its characters represent corresponding to each axiom of the theory (Evans, 1981, 328). Tacitly knowing the hundred axiom theory of meaning for a one hundred sentence language, for example, requires possessing a distinct disposition, for each of the hundred sentences, to judge what that sentence means. But tacitly knowing the twenty axiom theory merely requires possessing a distinct disposition, for each name and predicate, to judge what the sentences composed of that name or predicate mean.

If, for example, the language contained the expressions 'John', 'Harry', 'is happy', and 'is sad', then the hundred axiom theory would have four distinct axioms which state what sentences composed of those expressions mean. They would state that 'John is happy' means John is happy, that 'John is sad' means John is sad, that 'Harry is happy' means Harry is happy and that 'Harry is sad' means Harry is sad. So tacitly knowing the one hundred axiom theory requires possessing four distinct dispositions corresponding to each of these four axioms: a disposition to judge that 'John is happy' means John is happy, that 'John is sad' means John is sad, that 'Harry is happy' means Harry is happy, and that 'Harry is sad' means Harry is sad.

In contrast, someone who tacitly knows the twenty axiom theory would have four interlocking dispositions, corresponding to the four axioms for the expressions 'John', 'Harry', 'is happy' and 'is sad'. The axiom that 'John' refers to John, for example, would correspond to the disposition to judge, when it's tacitly known that a predicate following a name means the referent of that name has a certain property, that 'John' followed by that predicate means that John has that property. And the axiom that 'is sad' following a name means that the referent of that name has the property of being sad, for example, would correspond to a disposition to judge, when it's tacitly known what a name refers to, that 'is sad' following that name means that its referent is sad.

Two clarifications. First, to properly distinguish between tacit knowledge of theories with different axioms, the dispositions involved must be "full-blooded" (Evans, 1981, 329), since in a weak-blooded sense the dispositions corresponding to the hundred axiom theory also confer the dispositions corresponding to the twenty axiom theory. If one tacitly knows the hundred axiom theory, for example, one is disposed to judge that 'John' prefixed to a predicate means that John has the property represented by that predicate, in the sense that one is disposed to judge that 'John is sad' means that John is sad, 'John is happy' means that John is happy, ... and so on. So in a weak-blooded sense, tacit knowledge of the one theory is still tacit knowledge of the other.

So the possession of a distinct disposition corresponding to each axiom cannot merely require a tendency to judge in accordance with those axioms, but requires that a single state figures in the causal explanation of each of the judgements corresponding to the theorems those axioms entail (Evans, 1981, 30). To possess a full-blooded disposition to judge, for example, that 'John' prefixed to a predicate means that John has the property represented by that predicate, requires a single state to figure in the causal explanation of the judgements that 'John is sad' means that John is sad, that 'John is happy' means that John is happy, ... and so on for the other eight sentences which prefix 'John' to a predicate.

Second, one might be worried that vicious circularity is involved in the inter-definition of the dispositions corresponding to the axioms for names and predicates (Wright, 1986, 233). The disposition corresponding to the axiom that 'John' refers to John, for example, is defined partly in terms of tacit knowledge of the axioms which state that predicates followed by names mean that the referent of the names have a certain property. And the disposition corresponding to the axiom that 'sad' following a name means that the referent of the name has the property of being sad, for example, is defined partly in terms of tacit knowledge of the axioms which state what names refer to. In case this circularity is vicious, it's desirable to circumvent it.

This suggests a theory of representation is tacitly known if and only if whenever the axioms of a theory which entail what $s_1...s_n$ represent also entail what $s$ represents, the states figuring in the causal explanation of judgements of what $s_1...s_n$ represent jointly suffice to causally explain a judgement of what $s$ represents (Davies, 1987, 446-447). If the twenty axiom theory is tacitly known, for example, then because the axioms entailing what 'Harry is sad' and 'John is happy' mean entail what 'Harry is happy' and 'John is sad' mean, the states which causally explain judgements of what 'Harry is sad' and 'John is happy' mean also suffice to causally explain judgements of what 'Harry is happy' and 'John is sad' mean.

Tacit knowledge of the twenty axiom theory explains the ability to understand some novel sentences, since if one judges, for example, that 'Harry is sad' means that Harry is sad and that 'John is happy' means that

John is happy by tacitly knowing the twenty axiom theory, then the states which causally explain these judgements will also suffice to explain one's judgement that 'Harry is happy' means that Harry is happy, even if 'Harry is happy' has not previously appeared. But tacit knowledge of the hundred axiom theory doesn't explain the ability to understand novel sentences, since then the judgement of what each sentence means is causally explained by a separate state, which never suffices to causally explain any other judgement.

In general, tacit knowledge of a compositional theory of meaning explains the ability to understand some novel sentences, since if a compositional theory of meaning for the language of those sentences is tacitly known, then states which causally explain judgements about what some sentences of the language mean will suffice to causally explain judgements about what some novel sentences of the language composed of the same parts mean. If English speakers tacitly know a compositional theory of meaning for English, for example, then the states causally explaining their judgement that 'John loves Mary' means John loves Mary might also explain their judgement of what the novel sentence 'Mary loves John' means.

## 7.2 Compositionality and understanding pictures

If this analysis of tacit knowledge is correct, then whether interpreters tacitly know the compositional theory of representation for a depictive symbol system is not trivial, since it might not be the case that the axioms of the compositional theory which entail what some of the pictures represent entail what another picture represents whenever the states which causally explain judgements of what the former represent suffice to explain judgements of what the latter represent. Nevertheless, this section argues that the ability to understand some novel depictions is explained by tacit knowledge of a compositional theory of representation for their symbol system, even according to the more demanding analysis of tacit knowledge just outlined.

It's a non-trivial question, for example, whether the ability to understand novel chess diagrams is explained by tacit knowledge of a compositional theory of representation for their symbol system, because this depends on whether or not the states responsible for causally explaining what chess diagrams represent suffice to causally explain what other chess diagrams composed of the same parts represent. If judgements about what's represented by diagrams containing the figurine representing the knight, for example, don't all have a common causal explanation, then a theory of representation with an axiom stating what that figurine represents is not tacitly known by interpreters of the diagrams.

But tacit knowledge of the compositional theory for chess diagrams does explain the ability to understand novel chess diagrams. Because the axioms of the compositional theory which entail what some chess diagrams represent entail what chess diagrams composed of the same parts represent, and because someone able to understand some chess diagrams has the ability to understand what other diagrams composed of the same parts represent, whenever the axioms of the compositional theory which entail what some chess diagrams represent entail what other chess diagrams represents, the states figuring in the causal explanation of judgements of what the former represent suffice to causally explain judgements of what the latter represent.

If one can understand the diagram of an endgame position with a pawn and two kings, for example, then one is able to understand the diagram of every endgame position with a pawn and two kings. So the states which figure in the causal explanation of judgements of what the diagram of the endgame position with a pawn and two kings represents should suffice to causally explain judgements of what the diagram of every endgame position with a pawn and two kings represent. And so since the axioms of the compositional theory which entail what the diagram of the endgame position with a pawn and two kings represents entail what the diagram of every endgame position with a pawn and two kings represents, one tacitly knows the compositional theory.

Similarly, the ability to understand some novel maps is explained by tacit knowledge of a compositional theory of representation for their symbol system. If one is able to understand a page of one's street directory, for example, then one's able to understand any other page of one's street directory on which only the same symbols occur. So the states figuring in the causal explanation of judgements of what that page represents should suffice to causally explain judgements of what the other pages represent. And so since the axioms of a compositional theory which entail what the page represents should also entail what the other pages composed of the same parts represent, one tacitly knows that compositional theory.

Maps and chess diagrams are especially clear illustrations of this phenomenon, but they are controversial examples of depiction. But many other examples, while less simple, are paradigmatic examples of depiction. Imagine, for example, two successive panels of a graphic novel, depicting the same scene first illuminated, but then in darkness. In the first panel, one sees the villain clearly. But in the second, one sees only the whites of his eyes and his maniacal grin, which are depicted by the same white parts as in the first panel. If one can understand the first panel, one can understand the second panel, because one already understands its parts.

Since if one can understand the first panel, one can understand the second panel, the states which suffice to causally explain one's judgement of what is represented by the first panel also suffice to causally explain one's judgement of what is represented by the second panel. And so since the axioms of a compositional theory of representation which entail what the first panel represents also entail, by stating what is contributed by the white parts, what the second panel represents, the causal explanation of one's judgements of what the panels represent corresponds to the derivational structure of the compositional theory, and the theory is tacitly known. Any kind of picture placed in sequence – such as tapestries, friezes or films – could furnish similar examples.

In general, whether compositional theories of meaning for depictive symbol systems are tacitly known is not trivial, since it depends on whether or not the causal structure of interpretive judgements corresponds to the derivational structure of a theory. But in many cases, if one is able to understand a picture, one is able to understand what other pictures composed of the same parts represent. In these cases, the states which suffice to causally explain one's judgement of what the picture represents should also suffice to causally explain one's judgements of what the others represent. And since axioms of a compositional theory entailing what that picture represents entail what pictures composed of the same parts represent, the compositional theory is tacitly known.

It might be objected that the correspondence between the derivational structure of the compositional theory of representation for chess diagrams and the causal structure of interpretive judgements about chess diagrams does not establish that the theory is tacitly known, since the correspondence may simply be a coincidence or the result of an unusual psychological structure. It's often suggested, for example, that the ability to understand novel pictures is explained by the ability to recognise its subject face to face – one can understand a novel picture of a horse, for example, because one can recognise a horse (Schier, 1986, 43-55). That these abilities mirror the structure of a compositional theory may just be an odd coincidence.

If, for example, someone has one hundred brain compartments in which an explicit representation of each axiom of the hundred axiom theory of meaning for the hundred sentence language is stored, then intuitively he or she tacitly knows only the hundred axiom theory. But suppose the hundred compartments are arranged by coincidence in ten columns and ten rows, with all the axioms stating the meaning of sentences composed of the same name in the same row, and all the axioms stating the meaning of sentences composed of the same predicate in the same column, and that nutrients flow to the compartments through the rows and columns (Davies, 1987, 451). Then intuitively, he or she still only knows the hundred axiom theory.

But if nutrient flow through a row is closed, then the ability to understand sentences composed of one of the names will be compromised. If nutrient flow throw a column is closed, then the ability to understand sentences composed of one of the predicates will be compromised. So the states figuring in the causal explanation of judgements of what sentences composed of some of the names and predicates mean jointly suffice to causally explain judgements of what other sentences composed of the same names and predicates mean and it follows from the analysis above – contrary to intuition – that the person tacitly knows the twenty axiom theory.

The states figuring in the causal explanation of the judgements that, for example, 'Harry is sad' means Harry is sad and 'John is happy' means John is happy include nutrient flow's being open in the row which stores sentences containing 'Harry' and nutrient flow's being open in the column storing sentences containing 'is happy'. And these states suffice to causally explain the judgement that 'Harry is happy' means that Harry is happy. This corresponds to the derivational structure of the theory, since the axioms entailing that 'Harry is sad' means Harry is sad and 'John is happy' means John is happy suffice to entail that 'Harry is happy' means Harry is happy.

To avoid merely accidental coincidence between the derivational structure of a theory and the causal structure of interpretive judgements, the analysis of tacit knowledge should be revised as follows: A theory of representation is tacitly known if and only if whenever the axioms of a theory which entail what $s_1...s_n$ represent also entail what $s$ represents, the states figuring in the causal explanation of judgements of what $s_1...s_n$ represent jointly suffice to causally explain the judgement of what $s$ represents and also, together with revision to judgements of what $s$ represents, explain corresponding revision in judgements about what $s_1,..., s_n$ represent (Davies, 1987, 457).

Explicit representation of each axiom of the hundred axiom theory in one hundred brain compartments arranged by coincidence in ten columns and rows, for example, does not constitute tacit knowledge of the twenty axiom theory, because although this causal structure corresponds to the derivational structure of the twenty axiom theory, revisions to judgements about what some of the sentences represent don't explain corresponding revisions in what the other sentences represent. Since the information about what each sentence means is stored in a separate compartment, revision to that information doesn't involve revision to any other information.

But the correspondence between the derivational structure of the compositional theory for chess diagrams and the causal structure of interpretive judgements about them is not a coincidence in this sense, because revision to judgements of what some of the diagrams represent does explain corresponding revision in judgements about what some others represent. If one revises one's judgement about which figurine represents the king in one diagram, for example, then one will revise one's judgement about which figurine represents the king in all diagrams. So the compositional and not the listiform theory of representation for chess diagrams is still tacitly known.

## 7.3 Understanding pictures without compositionality

So the ability to understand some novel pictures – such as novel chess diagrams – is explained by tacit knowledge of a compositional theory of representation for their symbol system, since the structure of causal explanations of the ability to understand some novel pictures mirrors the derivational structure of the compositional theory for their symbol system. Nevertheless, this section agrees that the ability to understand some novel pictures isn't explained by tacit knowledge of a compositional theory, because the structure of causal explanations of the ability to understand some novel pictures doesn't mirror the derivational structure of a compositional theory for their symbol system.

The ability to understand some novel pictures can't be explained by tacit knowledge of a compositional theory because their parts are also novel. It's possible to recognise that "My Drawing Number One" from *The Little Prince* (Saint-Exupéry, 1943, 6), for example, depicts a hat, even on its first appearance. But this cannot be explained by tacit knowledge of a compositional theory, because a disposition corresponding to an axiom which states, for example, that its lower part represents a brim or an axiom which states, for example, that its upper part represents a crown could not have been acquired from previous appearances of its upper and lower parts, since on the first appearance of "My Drawing Number One" its upper and lower parts were appearing for the first time too.

The problem is not that the interpreter doesn't tacitly know a compositional theory of representation for the picture. The interpreter does know a compositional theory, since just as an axiom which entails that the top part represents a crown and an axiom which entails that the bottom part represents the brim would also entail that the whole picture represents a hat, the states which suffice to causally explain the judgement that the top part represents a crown and the judgement that the bottom part represents the brim would also suffice to causally explain the judgement that the whole represents the hat and also, together with revision to judgements of what the whole represents, explain corresponding revisions in judgements about what the two parts represent.

But the interpreter's tacit knowledge of a compositional theory of representation for the symbol system of the picture doesn't explain the interpreter's ability to understand it on its first appearance, since the interpreter's ability to judge that the top represents a crown and that the bottom part represents a brim also requires explanation, because the bottom and top part of the picture are also appearing for the first time. So rather than the interpreter's antecedent tacit knowledge of what the top and bottom parts represent explaining the interpreter's judgement of what the whole represents, tacit knowledge of what the parts represent is acquired simultaneously. What the parts represent was tacitly known, but not before seeing the picture.

Moreover, the possibility of understanding some novel pictures whose parts are not novel can't be explained by tacit knowledge of a compositional theory, because their parts don't represent what they did on previous appearances. It's possible to recognise even on its first appearance that "My Drawing Number Two" from *The Little Prince* (Saint-Exupéry, 1943, 6) depicts a boa constrictor swallowing an elephant. But tacit knowledge of a compositional theory could not explain this, since a disposition which corresponds to an axiom stating that the outer part represents a boa constrictor could not have been acquired from the outer part's previous appearance, because although the outer part did appear previously, when it did so it depicted a hat.

The problem is not that the interpreter doesn't tacitly know a compositional theory of representation for the picture. The interpreter does know a compositional theory, since just as an axiom which entails that the outer part represents a boa constrictor and an axiom which entails that the inner part represents an elephant might entail that the whole represents a boa constrictor swallowing an elephant, the states which suffice to causally explain the judgement that the outer part represents a boa constrictor and the judgement that the inner part represents an elephant would also suffice to causally explain the judgement that the whole picture represents a boa constrictor swallowing an elephant.

But the interpreter's tacit knowledge of a compositional theory of representation for the symbol system of the picture doesn't explain the interpreter's ability to understand it on its first appearance, since the interpreter's ability to judge that the outer part represents a boa constrictor also requires explanation, since the outer part represented a hat on its previous appearance, and so the interpreter should have been expected to judge that the outer part represents a hat. So rather than the interpreter's antecedent tacit knowledge of what the outer part represents explaining his or her judgement of what the whole represents, tacit knowledge of what the whole picture, outer part and inner part represent was acquired simultaneously. What the parts represent was tacitly known, but not in advance of seeing the picture.

It might be objected that just as the fact that the referents of indexicals such as 'I', 'now' and 'here' vary from context to context doesn't show that the possibility of understanding sentences composed of them is not explained by pre-existing tacit knowledge of a compositional theory of meaning (Kaplan, 1989), the fact that what is represented by some parts of pictures varies from context to context doesn't show that the ability to understand those pictures isn't explained by antecedent tacit knowledge of a compositional theory of representation. Perhaps the variation in what picture parts represent may be accommodated in just the same way as the variation in what indexicals refer to (Abell (2005b, 193) has an excellent discussion of this issue).

To accommodate indexicals, a theory of meaning for a language should entail what each sentence in the language means not simpliciter, but relative to a time, place and individual (Davidson, 1967, 34). A theory of meaning for English, for example, shouldn't entail simply that 'I am tired' in English means that I am tired, since 'I am tired' spoken by somebody else doesn't mean that I am tired. Instead, the theory should entail that 'I am tired' spoken by a person at a time and place means that that person is tired at that time and place. Similarly, the theory should entail that 'I am here now' spoken by a person at a place and time means that that person is at that place at that time.

To entail statements of what each sentence in a language means relative to a time, place and individual, the axioms of the theory of meaning for a language should be similarly modified. A theory of meaning for English should not, for example, have an axiom stating that 'I' refers to me, since 'I' spoken by someone else does not refer to me. Instead, the theory should have an axiom stating that 'I' spoken by a person at a time and place refers to that person. Similarly, the theory should have an axiom stating that 'now' spoken by a person at a time and place refers to that time and that 'here' spoken by a person at a time and place refers to that place. In combination with an axiom for 'am', these axioms entail the appropriate theorem for 'I am here now'.

So although the referents of indexicals vary from context to context, the possibility of understanding novel sentences containing them is still explained by tacit knowledge of a theory of meaning which entails what each sentence means relative to a context. English interpreters, for example, may tacitly know a theory of meaning with the axiom stating that 'I' spoken by a person at a time and place refers to that person, because they are disposed to judge, when they tacitly know that a predicate represents a certain property, that 'I' prefixed to that predicate by a person at a time and place means that that person has that property. They are disposed to judge, for example, that 'I am happy' spoken by Harry means that Harry is happy.

Likewise, it might be argued that the possibility of understanding novel depictions is explained by tacit knowledge of a compositional theory of representation which entails statements of what pictures represent relative to people, times and places, even when their parts don't represent what they did on previous occasions. Tacitly knowing a theory with an axiom stating in which contexts the irregular shape above represents a hat, in which contexts it represents a boa constrictor and in which contexts it represents something else, for example, would explain the ability to understand the picture of the boa constrictor swallowing the elephant on its first appearance, as long as tacit knowledge of the axiom were antecedently acquired.

But even if there are compositional theories of representation with axioms stating what is represented by the parts of pictures relative to each context in which they occur, it's implausible that interpreters of pictures tacitly know these theories, because it's implausible they have distinct dispositions corresponding to these axioms. It's not plausible, for example, that anyone has a distinct disposition to judge that the shape above, when it appears alone, represents a hat but, when they tacitly know what is represented by a shape that it surrounds, that it represents a boa constrictor swallowing the thing represented by the shape that it surrounds – it's more plausible that there are two distinct dispositions corresponding to the two judgements.

Moreover, even if a single state corresponding to tacit knowledge of an axiom stating the contribution of the irregular shape figured in the causal explanation of both the judgement of what the picture of the hat represents and the judgement of what the picture of the boa constrictor swallowing an elephant represents, it would not follow from the analysis above that this state constitutes tacit knowledge of such an axiom, since that state together with revision to judgements about what the picture of the hat represents would not explain corresponding revisions to judgements about what the picture of the boa constrictor swallowing the elephant represents.

So the ability to understand some novel pictures is not explained by antecedent tacit knowledge of a compositional theory of representation for their symbol system. If the ability to understand all novel sentences were explained by antecedent tacit knowledge of a compositional theory of meaning for their language, this would be an important disanalogy between depiction and description. However, the next section argues that the ability to understand some novel sentences isn't explained by pre-existing tacit knowledge of a compositional theory of meaning for their language either. If this is right, the purported disanalogy between depiction and description in this respect is merely an illusion.

## 7.4 Understanding language without compositionality

So the ability to understand some novel pictures – those with novel parts and parts which don't represent what they did on previous occasions – is not explained by tacit knowledge of a theory of representation for their symbol system, since dispositions corresponding to the axioms of such a theory could not have been acquired from previous appearances of the parts. Nevertheless, this section argues that this is no disanalogy between depiction and description, because the ability to understand some novel sentences – those with novel parts and parts which don't mean what they did previously – isn't explained by tacit knowledge of a compositional theory either, for the same reasons that the ability to understand some novel pictures isn't.

Even though many of its words, such as 'mimsy', 'vorpal', 'chortled', 'frumious' and 'beamish' were novel, most of *Jabberwocky* (Carroll, 1871, 155), for example, could be understood the first time it was read, but tacitly knowing a compositional theory of meaning could not explain this possibility. The disposition corresponding to an axiom stating that 'chortled' suffixed to a referring term means that the referent of that term laughed, for example, could not have being acquired from a previous appearance of the word 'chortled', since it had never previously appeared. But it was still possible to understand 'he chortled in his joy' (Davidson, 1986, 90). Likewise, it was possible to understand 'O frabjous day', even though 'frabjous' had not appeared before.

The problem is not that the interpreter doesn't tacitly know a compositional theory which entails what 'he chortled' means. The interpreter does know a compositional theory which entails what 'he chortled' means, because just as the axioms of a compositional theory which entail what 'she chortled' and 'he is happy' mean, for example, suffice to entail what 'he chortled' means, the states which causally explain the judgement of what 'she chortled' and the judgement of what 'he is happy' means suffice to causally explain the judgement of what 'he chortled' means and, together with revisions to judgements of what 'he chortled' means, suffice to causally explain corresponding revision in judgements to what 'she chortled' and 'he is happy' mean.

But the interpreter's tacit knowledge of a compositional theory which entails what 'he chortled' means doesn't explain the interpreter's ability to understand 'he chortled' on its first appearance, because the interpreter's ability to judge what 'she chortled' means also requires explanation, since 'she chortled' might not have appeared previously either. So rather than the interpreter's antecedent tacit knowledge of what 'she chortled' and 'he is happy' mean explaining the interpreter's judgement of what 'he chortled' means, tacit knowledge of what 'she chortled' and 'he chortled' mean is acquired simultaneously. What the parts represent is tacitly known, but not in advance of hearing the sentence.

Because 'chortled' is a portmanteau word derived from 'snorted' and 'chuckled', it might be objected that the ability to understand what 'he chortled' means on its first appearance is explained by tacit knowledge of a compositional theory of meaning with axioms which entail what 'he snorted', 'he chuckled' and 'he chortled' mean by stating the contribution of 'ch...l', '...ort' and '...ed'. But the states figuring in the causal explanation of judgements of what 'he snorted' and 'he chuckled' mean do not suffice to causally explain the judgement of what 'he chortled' means, since a causal explanation must also involve knowledge that 'chortled' is a portmanteau of 'snorted' and 'chuckled' (see Davies, 1981b, 140-141) for discussion of a similar point).

Just as the possibility of understanding novel sentences whose parts are also novel cannot be explained by pre-existing tacit knowledge of a compositional theory, nor can the possibility of understanding some novel sentences the parts of which aren't novel, but don't mean what they did on previous appearances. Dispositions acquired from previous appearances of the parts of these sentences would correspond to axioms that state what the parts meant previously, instead of to axioms that state what they mean currently. Since manifestations of these dispositions would result in false judgements about the meaning of novel sentences, they wouldn't explain the ability to understand those novel sentences.

The ability to understand a novel utterance of 'the ATM swallowed my card', for example, is not explained by tacit knowledge of a compositional theory of meaning, since the disposition acquired from previous appearances of 'swallowed' would correspond to an axiom stating that 'swallowed' between two referring terms means that the referent of the first term swallowed the referent of the second term, and result in the judgement that 'the ATM swallowed my card' means the automatic transaction machine literally swallowed my card, rather than the more appropriate judgement that 'the ATM swallowed my card' means simply that the automatic transaction machine retained my card (Recanati, 2004, 26).

Similarly, it's possible to understand the intended meaning of malapropisms such as 'we need a few laughs to break up the monogamy', 'lead the way and we'll precede', or 'we're all cremated equal', even though 'monogamy', 'precede' and 'cremated' are not used with their usual meanings in these sentences (Davidson, 1986, 90). But these possibilities can't be explained by antecedent tacit knowledge of a compositional theory of meaning entailing what the malapropisms are being used to mean, because tacit knowledge of an antecedently known theory would lead to the judgement, for example, that 'we need a few laughs to break up the monogamy' literally means that we need a few laughs to break up the monogamy.

The problem is not that the interpreter doesn't tacitly know a compositional theory which entails what these sentences mean. The interpreter does know a compositional theory which entails what the sentences mean, since just as axioms of a compositional theory which entail what 'lead the way and we'll precede' means, for example, suffice to entail what 'precede and we'll lead the way' means, the states which causally explain the judgement of what 'lead the way and we'll precede' means suffice to causally explain the judgement of what 'precede and we'll lead the way' means and, together with revisions to judgements of what the former means, suffice to causally explain corresponding revision in judgements to what the latter means.

But the interpreter's tacit knowledge of a compositional theory which entails what the sentences mean does not explain the interpreter's ability to understand them on their first appearance, because the interpreter's ability to judge what the sentences mean also requires explanation, since their parts are not appearing with the meanings they had previously. So rather than the interpreter's antecedent tacit knowledge of what 'we'll precede' means on this occasion explaining the interpreter's judgement of what 'lead the way and we'll precede' means on this occasion, tacit knowledge of what both 'we'll precede' and 'lead the way and we'll precede' mean on this occasion is acquired simultaneously.

Finally, the ability to judge whether a novel utterance of 'my horse is winning' means that the horse I bet on is winning, for example, may not be explained by antecedent tacit knowledge of a compositional theory of meaning, since on previous appearances of 'my horse' it may have referred to the horse I own, or ride, or like, or eat ... and so on, but not to the horse I bet on. In this case, the axioms which entail 'my horse is neglected' means that the horse I own is neglected, for example, would not entail that 'my horse is winning' means that the horse I bet on is winning, but would entail that 'my horse is winning' means that the horse I own is winning. So tacit knowledge of a compositional theory does not explain the ability to understand ambiguous sentences.

Two objections. First, it might be that the examples of metaphor and malapropism do not show that tacit knowledge of a compositional theory of meaning doesn't explain the ability to understand some sentences, but only that it doesn't explain the ability to understand what speakers mean by using those sentences. In the case of metaphor, for example, tacitly knowing a theory of meaning can explain the ability to form the judgement that the sentence 'the ATM swallowed my card' means that the

ATM literally swallowed my card, which in turn may enable an interpreter to infer that what I meant by uttering 'the ATM swallowed my card' on a particular occasion is that the ATM retained my card (since, of course, ATMs cannot really swallow things).

In contrast, it might be argued that in the case of depiction there's nothing analogous to sentence meaning, the ability to understand which could always be explained by tacit knowledge of a compositional theory of meaning. It's not the case, for example, that the irregular shape above standardly represents a hat, that interpreters are able to judge on its second appearance that it standardly represents a hat, but that they are then able to infer from this that on this occasion its perpetrator is instead using it to represent a boa constrictor. On the contrary, neither its representation of a hat nor of a boa constrictor is particularly standard (although chapters four and five argued that there's no disanalogy between depiction and description even in this respect).

But it's false even in the case of language that tacitly knowing a theory of meaning explains the ability to understand the sentence meaning of all novel sentences, since it's sometimes possible to understand even the sentence meaning of a novel sentence without tacitly knowing a theory of meaning for its language. It may be possible to understand what the sentence 'and you in Grecian tires are painted new', for example, means by first inferring what Shakespeare meant by it, and then proceeding to figure out from this that the meaning of the sentence is that the addressee is painted new in Grecian clothes (Davidson, 1986, 92). So the points above apply to sentence meaning just as well as they do to speaker meaning.

Second, it may be objected that ambiguity does not show that the ability to understand some novel sentences is not explained by tacit knowledge of a compositional theory, since the ability to understand ambiguous sentences can be explained by tacit knowledge of compositional theories of meaning which explicitly distinguish between the senses of ambiguous expressions, and which are tacitly known. The fact that 'bank' is ambiguous between river bank or financial bank, for example, doesn't show that the possibility of understanding novel sentences containing 'bank' is not explained in part by tacit knowledge of a compositional theory of meaning, because interpreters tacitly know the two disambiguations of 'bank' in advance (Currie, 1995, 125).

To accommodate ambiguity, a theory of meaning for a language should possess a distinct theorem for each ambiguous expression (Larson and

Segal, 1995, 46). A theory of meaning for English, for example, shouldn't entail simply that 'the bank is open' means that the bank is open, since this theory doesn't state unambiguously what 'the bank is open' means. Instead the theory of meaning for English should entail two theorems: one stating that ˈthe bank$_1$ is openˈ means that the river bank is open and one that the ˈthe bank$_2$ is openˈ means that the financial bank is open, where the two subscripts mark the two different senses of 'bank'. In general, a theory of meaning should entail a distinct theorem for each disambiguation of a sentence.

To entail distinct theorems for lexically ambiguous sentences, a theory of meaning for a language should include distinct axioms for their lexically ambiguous primitives. So the theory of meaning for English should not, for example, have a single axiom stating that 'the bank' refers to the bank, since this axiom doesn't unambiguously state the contribution of 'the bank' to sentences which contain it. Instead a theory of meaning for English should have two axioms, one stating that ˈthe bank$_1$ˈ refers to the river bank and one stating that ˈthe bank$_2$ˈ refers to the financial bank, where the two different senses of 'the bank' are again marked by the two subscripts ('the bank' isn't really a primitive or referring term, but this complication isn't important here).

It's plausible that the ability to understand many ambiguous sentences is explained by tacit knowledge of compositional theories of meaning of this kind. Corresponding to the distinct axioms stating that ˈthe bank$_1$ˈ refers to the river bank and that ˈthe bank$_2$ˈ refers to the financial bank are two distinct dispositions, one to judge that sentences containing ˈthe bank$_1$ˈ are about the river bank and one to judge that sentences containing ˈthe bank$_2$ˈ are about financial banks. Which disposition manifests itself in the interpretation of a particular utterance containing 'the bank' depends on further factors. But it's plausible that dispositions corresponding to these axioms are tacitly known, prior to hearing 'bank' in any novel sentence one understands.

But it's not plausible that the ability to understand every novel ambiguous sentence is explained by tacit knowledge of a compositional theory of meaning of this kind. In order for a tacitly known theory to explain the ability to understand novel sentences composed of 'my horse', for example, it would require axioms (or rather theorems derived from axioms for 'horse' and the various senses of 'my') stating that ˈmy$_1$ horseˈ refers to the horse I own, ˈmy$_2$ horseˈ refers to the horse I ride, ˈmy$_3$ horseˈ

refers to the horse I like, ˊmy$_4$ horseˋ refers to the horse I eat, ˊmy$_5$ horseˋ refers to the horse I bet on, ... and so on. Even if their number is finite, it's implausible that anyone has in advance distinct dispositions corresponding to all these axioms (Currie's, (1995, 125) defence of the disanalogy involves denying this point).

So just as the possibility of understanding some novel pictures isn't explained by tacit knowledge of a compositional theory of representation for their symbol system, the possibility of understanding some novel sentences isn't explained by tacit knowledge of a compositional theory of meaning for their language. And just as the ability to understand some novel sentences is explained by tacit knowledge of a compositional theory of meaning for their language, the ability to understand some novel pictures is explained by tacit knowledge of a compositional theory of representation for their symbol system. Insofar as tacitly knowing a compositional theory explains the ability to understand novel sentences, it explains the ability to understand novel pictures too.

## 7.5 Conclusion

I have argued that insofar as the ability to understand novel sentences is explained by tacit knowledge of a compositional theory for their language, the ability to understand novel pictures is likewise explained by tacit knowledge of a compositional theory of representation for their symbol system. I did this by arguing that just as the possibility of understanding some, but not all, novel sentences is explained by tacit knowledge of a compositional theory of meaning for their language, the possibility of understanding some, but not all, novel pictures is explained by tacit knowledge of a compositional theory of representation for their symbol systems. This exact parallel between the two theses supports an extremely strong analogy between depiction and description.

Inevitably, much of what I have said about the philosophy of language in this chapter is extremely controversial, and many readers will want to disagree with it. Whereas, for example, I said above that the various different senses of 'my horse is winning' stem from an ambiguity in the word 'my', many philosophers of language may argue that the various different sense of 'my horse is winning' stem from contextual dependence in the meaning of 'my'. The reference of 'my horse' in a particular context, according to this view, depends not only on who is the speaker in that context, but also on the relevant sense of possession which is at issue in the context – perhaps legal ownership in some contexts, but mere familiarity in others.

Other philosophers of language may wish to argue that 'my horse' is unambiguous on the grounds that it refers to the horse the speaker possesses in some unspecific sense. The sentence meaning of 'my horse is winning', according to this view, is simply that a horse the speaker possesses in some unspecific sense is winning. Utterances of 'my horse is winning' on particular occasions, of course, will tend to convey that a horse the speaker possesses in some more specific sense – perhaps legal ownership on some occasions, and mere familiarity on others – is winning. But more specific implications like these may be merely a matter of speaker meaning, not sentence meaning. If this is the case, there is no reason to conclude that 'my horse' is ambiguous.

But insofar as points of this kind undermine the thesis that the ability to understand some novel sentences isn't explained by tacit knowledge of a compositional theory of meaning for their language, analogous points undermine the thesis that the ability to understand some novel pictures isn't explained by tacit knowledge of a compositional theory of representation for their symbol system. Just as admitting ambiguity in some sentences can be avoided by treating them as context-dependent, admitting ambiguity in some pictures can be avoided by treating them as context-dependent too. How best to treat any particular case is bound to be controversial. But I hope to have shown that the same kinds of consideration are relevant for both pictures and language.

Likewise, just as admitting ambiguity in some sentences might be avoided by arguing that they have an extremely thin sentence meaning, from which their thicker speaker meaning may be inferred, admitting ambiguity in some pictures can be avoided by arguing that they have an analogous bare-bones content, which may be fleshed-out in an analogous way (see Kulvicki (2006, 159-169) for an approach of this kind). Just as one might argue that the sentence meaning of 'my horse is winning', for example, is simply that the horse I possess in some unspecific sense is winning, one may argue that the hat shape discussed above depicts neither a hat nor a boa constrictor, but just an unspecific thing of a particular shape.

So although much of what I have said about the philosophy of language and pictures in this chapter is inevitably very controversial, I would like to emphasise again that the main point I have put forward is that there is a very close analogy between depiction and description with respect to compositionality. The considerations which support the thesis that the ability to understand some, but not all, novel sentences is explained by tacit knowledge of a compositional theory equally support the thesis that the possibility of understanding some, but not all, novel pictures is explained by tacit knowledge of a compositional theory. In this respect, depictions and descriptions are exactly alike, and the differences between them must be sought elsewhere.

# 8. Intentionality and Inexistence

The intentionality of depiction is often cited as a reason for denying the platitude that depiction is mediated by resemblance. This chapter argues that the apparent problem posed by the intentionality of depiction for the platitude that depiction is mediated by resemblance is really a manifestation of the more general problem of intentionality. The best solution to the problem is to analyse representation in general and depiction in particular as primarily relations towards states of affairs, rather than objects. This solution, it's argued, supports both the analogy between depiction and other kinds of representation and the platitude that depiction is mediated by resemblance.

Three features of depiction are symptomatic of its intentionality. The first symptom is the apparent possibility of depicting non-existents. The second symptom is the possibility of depicting something without depicting anything in particular. The third symptom is the possibility of depictive misrepresentation: it is possible to depict Tolstoy as a child, for example, even if Tolstoy is not a child. All three symptoms of the intentionality of depiction are problematic for the platitude that depiction is mediated by resemblance, but the difficulties are raised most strikingly by the problem of the depiction of non-existents.

The problem of the depiction of non-existents can be appreciated by considering the following trilemma, which consists of three theses which are individually plausible, but jointly inconsistent:

(1) All depictions resemble what they represent
(2) Resemblance is a relation between existents
(3) Some depictions represent non-existents

The first two theses imply that depictions only represent existents, but this is incompatible with the third thesis, that some depictions represent non-existents.

The first thesis, that all depictions resemble what they represent, is plausible because it's suggested by the platitude that depiction is mediated by resemblance. Since the Mona Lisa's representation of Lisa, for example, is mediated by resemblance, it seems to follow that the Mona Lisa must resemble Lisa. Similarly, if Holmes' portrait's representation of Holmes is mediated by resemblance, it seems to follow that Holmes' portrait must resemble Holmes. (Abstract painting, which may seem like an obvious counterexample, is not classified as depiction because it is intuitively not the same kind of representation as figurative painting.)

The second thesis, that resemblance is a relation between existents, is plausible because it follows from the analysis of resemblance as a relation obtaining between things if and only if they share properties. Peas in a pod, for example, resemble each other because they share the properties of greenness, roundness and yuckiness. Since non-existents do not have properties, it follows that resemblance is a relation between existents. Peas, for example, cannot be green without existing, so only existent peas can resemble each other in respect of greenness. Similarly, since Santa cannot be red without existing, Santa's portrait cannot resemble Santa in respect of being red unless Santa exists.

The third thesis, that some depictions represent non-existents, is supported by intuitive examples. The most obvious example is depiction of fiction: Holmes does not exist, but *The Adventures of Sherlock Holmes* contains illustrations which depict Holmes. But examples are not confined to depiction of fiction: it's possible to depict things which are thought to exist, but in fact do not. For example, Vulcan, the planet hypothesised to be the cause of perturbations in the orbit of Mercury, does not exist, but there are depictions of Vulcan. Those that were produced when Vulcan was really thought to exist are no more fiction than depictions of the other nine planets, since the mere discovery that a depiction is not veridical is not sufficient to make it fictional.

Two other problems arise from the intentionality of depiction. The first is the problem of depicting non-particulars. It arises from the fact that it seems possible to depict something without depicting something in particular, but impossible to resemble something without resembling something in particular. A picture may depict a horse, for example, without depicting Phar Lap, Bucephalus, Incitatus or any other particular horse. But a picture cannot resemble a horse without resembling a particular horse, since a picture cannot share a property with horses in general, but only with particular horses such as Phar Lap, Bucephalus and Incitatus. Correctly resolving the trilemma concerning the depiction of non-existents should resolve this problem too.

The second is the problem of depictive misrepresentation. Suppose, for example, that the police are completely misinformed about the appearance of a dangerous criminal. The police believe that the criminal is brunette, but he is blonde; the police believe he is bearded, but he is shaved; the police believe that he is tall, but in fact he is short; and so on. If the police draw a wanted poster of this man, then it would resemble someone who is brunette, bearded, tall, and so on, and so would not resemble the criminal in the relevant respects. But despite failing to resemble the criminal, the drawing would still succeed in representing him (Kaplan, 1968, 198). Resolving the trilemma concerning the depiction of non-existents should resolve this problem too.

The first section considers Robert Hopkins' proposal to deny that all depictions resemble what they represent by analysing depiction in terms of experienced rather than genuine resemblance. The second considers Nelson Goodman's proposal to reject the platitude that depiction is mediated by resemblance on the grounds that depiction, unlike resemblance, is not unequivocally relational. The third section considers the possibility of denying the thesis that resemblance is a relation between existents by postulating non-existent objects. The fourth argues for denying the thesis that some depictions represent non-existent objects by arguing that depiction is a relation towards states of affairs.

## 8.1 Analysing depiction in intentional terms

It's possible to resolve the trilemma of depicting non-existents by denying the first thesis, that all depictions resemble what they represent, without denying the platitude that depiction is mediated by resemblance. To see how this is possible, recall that resemblance is obviously insufficient for depiction. Everything resembles itself, for example, but not everything is a depiction of itself. To provide for sufficiency, analyses of depiction usually combine resemblance with various intentional attitudes such as beliefs, intentions or experiences. Given that resemblance is not a sufficient condition for depiction, it's not implausible to suggest that resemblance need not be a necessary condition for depiction either.

Hopkins (1994; 1998, 94-121), for example, proposes exploiting this gap by analysing depiction in terms of experienced resemblance, in order to deny the first thesis of the trilemma without denying the platitude. This suggests the analysis:

(22)   Something depicts another if and only if the former is intended to induce the former to be experienced as resembling the latter by means of recognition of this intention.

So the Mona Lisa, for example, is supposed to depict Lisa because Leo intended it to be experienced as resembling Lisa, by means of recognition of his intention.

By embedding resemblance within the context of experience, this analysis retains the platitude that depiction is mediated by resemblance but avoids the consequence that resemblance is a necessary condition of depiction. Just as, for example, having an experience of Santa does not entail that Santa exists, having an experience which represents a picture as resembling Santa in some respect does not entail that the picture genuinely resembles Santa in that respect. More generally, although it is impossible for a picture to resemble something that doesn't exist, it is possible for a picture to be experienced as resembling something which doesn't exist.

As well as the depiction of non-existents, Hopkins' proposal appears to resolve the problems of depicting non-particulars and of depictive misrepresentation. Although, for example, it is not possible to resemble a horse without resembling Phar Lap, Bucephalus, Incitatus or some horse in particular, it is possible to experience a picture as resembling a horse without experiencing it as resembling any particular horse. In general, although it is not possible to resemble something without resembling something in particular, it is possible to experience a picture as resembling something without experiencing it as resembling anything in particular, since it is possible in general to experience something without experiencing something in particular.

Similarly, the proposal appears to resolve the problem of depictive misrepresentation. Even if the police, for example, produced a wanted poster of a criminal which, due to misinformation, failed to resemble the criminal in the relevant respects, the wanted poster may still be experienced as resembling the criminal in those respects. Since, in general, experiences are capable of misrepresentation, it is possible to experience pictures as resembling what they represent even when they in fact fail to do so. So analysing depiction in terms of experienced resemblance and dropping the thesis that all depictions resemble what they represent appears to reconcile the intentionality of depiction with the platitude that it is mediated by resemblance.

But there are two problems with the proposal. The first is that analysing depiction in terms of experienced resemblance only accommodates the possibility of depicting non-existents at the cost of entailing that experiences of these depictions are not veridical, even under optimal conditions. Take, for example, Santa's portrait. According to the analysis, Santa's portrait is experienced as having the property of resembling Santa. But since Santa does not exist, Santa's portrait cannot genuinely have the property of resembling Santa. It follows that experiences of Santa's portrait as resembling Santa are not veridical, even when they are accompanied by perfect lighting, clear eyesight and full knowledge that Santa does not exist.

The second problem is that by analysing depiction in terms of experience the analysis trades one kind of intentionality for another equally problematic kind. Experiences of non-existents, or hallucinations, are just as puzzling as depictions of non-existents, since it is plausible both that experiences are relations towards what is experienced and that relations cannot obtain towards non-existents. My seeing an apple, for example, seems to be a relation between me and the apple, but my hallucinating an apple cannot be such a relation, since in the case of hallucination there is no real apple for me to be related to. By trading the problem of depicting non-existents for the problem of hallucination, the proposal merely shifts the bump in the rug.

The force of this objection may be brought out by considering the proposal's mirror image. One solution to the problem of hallucination is to analyse experiences as relations to inner pictures or mental images. My hallucination of an apple, for example, could be construed as an unproblematic relation between me and an inner picture of an apple, instead of being construed as a problematic relation between myself and a non-existent apple. The problem of the experience of non-existents would then be replaced by the problem of the depiction of non-existents. But this replacement would produce no progress, because the problem of the depiction of non-existents is just as puzzling as the problem of hallucination. Trading the problem of depicting non-existents with the problem of hallucination is equally unilluminating.

The moral of this objection is that the problems of depicting non-existents, depicting non-particulars and depictive misrepresentation are really manifestations of the more general problem of intentionality. This means that an adequate solution to the problems cannot presuppose a solution to the problem of intentionality. Instead, an adequate solution to the specific problems concerning depiction should be part of a broader solution to the problem of intentionality in general. Resolving the problem in the specific case of depiction involves showing how the solution to the problem of intentionality in the general case is consistent with the platitude that depiction is mediated by resemblance.

The force of the objection may also be brought out by analogy with the analysis of meaning. The analysis of meaning is part of a reduction of all intentionality – mental and linguistic – to the purely physical. That reduction can be undertaken in two steps: the first step is to reduce linguistic representation to mental representation via the analyses of speaker and sentence meaning and the second step is to reduce mental representation to the physical via some other analysis, in terms of indication or causation. The reduction is successful only if the second stage – analysing mental representation in terms of the physical – makes no use of intentional notions.

The difficulty that arises for the analysis of meaning from this requirement may be appreciated by considering the following analysis of assertion, which introduces the variable '$p$' to make the quantification in the analysis explicit: a person asserts that $p$ by an utterance if and only if the person intends the utterance to produce the belief that $p$ in the audience by means of recognition of that intention. So, for example, I assert that it's raining by uttering the sentence 'it's raining' if and only if I intend someone to believe that it's raining by means of recognition of my intention (Schiffer, 1987, 13).

The difficulty for the reductive project involves specifying the domain which the variable '$p$' ranges over, and this involves specifying what belief is a relation towards. One not implausible candidate is that belief is a relation towards internal sentences and that '$p$' in the analysis of assertion ranges over these sentences. But if that is the correct proposal then the analysis of assertion, and the analysis of meaning of which it is an instance, cannot do the work required for it to be a part of a reduction of all intentionality to the purely physical (Schiffer, 1987, 13-17).

So for the reductive project to succeed, some other account of what '$p$' ranges over has to be given. As I argue below, for example, belief and intentionality in general may have to be construed as relations towards propositions or states of affairs, rather than towards inner sentences. But if this is the correct solution in the case of belief, then the analysis indicates that it is also the correct solution in the case of meaning, since the left hand side of the analysis must now be understood as expressing a three-place relation between people, utterances and propositions.

Analogous points apply to exploiting the analysis of depiction in terms of intentions and resemblance or experienced resemblance in order to resolve the trilemma by denying its first thesis. This would amount to an attempt to reduce the depictive representation of non-existents to the mental representation of non-existents. But this reduction can only be successful if it can be shown that mental representation of non-existents does not tacitly involve depictive representation. If the mental representation of non-existents doesn't tacitly involve depictive representation, whatever the correct solution is in the case of mental representation should apply to depiction directly.

## 8.2 Denying depiction is relational

Another way to motivate resolving the trilemma by denying its first thesis is to deny the platitude that depiction is mediated by resemblance on the grounds that depiction, unlike resemblance, is not unequivocally relational. Nelson Goodman, for example, writes "What tends to mislead us is that such locutions as 'picture of' and 'represents' have the appearance of mannerly two-place predicates and can sometimes be so interpreted. But 'picture of Pickwick' and 'represents a unicorn' are better considered unbreakable one-place predicates..." (Goodman, 1968, 21-22). Depiction, according to Goodman, is not always a relation between existents, because it is not always a relation at all.

One clarification. A one-place predicate is a sentence with one name removed, a two-place predicate is a sentence with two names removed ... and so on. So the predicate 'depicts Lisa', for example, is a one-place predicate, because it results from removing 'the Mona Lisa' from 'the Mona Lisa depicts Lisa', whereas 'depicts' is a two-place predicate, since it results from removing both 'the Mona Lisa' and 'Lisa' from the sentence 'the Mona Lisa depicts Lisa'. So Goodman doesn't deny there is a sense of 'depicts' in which it's a two-place predicate which expresses the relation of depiction. He just denies that every occurrence of 'depicts' expresses this relation.

In particular, the predicate 'depicts Pegasus', according to Goodman, is unbreakable – one cannot, according to Goodman, remove the name 'Pegasus' from the one-place predicate 'depicts Pegasus' to form the two-place predicate 'depicts'. This is because, according to Goodman, 'Pegasus' is not a genuine name in this context – the grammar of the predicate 'depicts Pegasus', according to Goodman, is in fact like the grammar of the predicate 'is weather beaten', which does not express a relation of being beaten towards the weather, but rather expresses the property of having suffered a particular kind of beating – namely, a weather beating.

So Goodman tries to resolve the problem of depicting non-existents by denying that the apparent depiction of non-existents is a relation towards anything at all. Predicates like 'depicts Santa', 'depicts Pegasus' and 'depicts a dragon', according to Goodman, do not express relations towards Santa, Pegasus or dragons. Rather, according to Goodman, predicates such as 'depicts Santa', 'depicts Pegasus' and 'depicts a dragon' merely classify depictions into various categories – the categories of Santa depiction, Pegasus depiction and dragon depiction. The appearance that there must be a relation towards what is depicted, according to Goodman, is merely a grammatical illusion.

Likewise, the depiction of non-particulars, according to Goodman, is not depiction in the relational sense. Predicates such as 'depicts a horse', according to Goodman, are ambiguous. In one sense 'depicts a horse' expresses a relation towards a horse, and in this sense there is a particular horse which the relation is towards. But there is another sense, according to Goodman, in which 'depicts a horse' does not express a relation towards a horse, but merely classifies something as a horse depiction. In this sense, according to Goodman, there need not be any particular horse it is a depiction of – the appearance that there must be is merely a grammatical illusion.

Similarly, the proposal appears to resolve the problem of depictive misrepresentation. According to Goodman, predicates such as 'depicts a bearded criminal', for example, are ambiguous. In one sense, 'depicts a bearded criminal' expresses a relation towards a bearded criminal, and in this sense what is depicted must be as it is represented. But in another sense, 'depicts a bearded criminal' is an unbreakable one-place predicate, and in this sense it does not imply that what is depicted must be as it is represented, since if a picture satisfies 'depicts a bearded criminal' in the non-relational sense, it does not follow that there is a bearded criminal which the picture depicts.

Misrepresentation, according to Goodman, occurs when there is a mismatch between the relational two-place and the non-relational one-place predicates which apply to a picture. A wanted poster produced by misinformed police, for example, misrepresents a blonde clean-shaven criminal as bearded and brunette since it satisfies the predicate 'depicts a blonde clean-shaven criminal' in the two-place relational sense but satisfies the predicate 'depicts a bearded brunette criminal' in a non-relational one-place sense. But the Mona Lisa depicts Lisa accurately, according to Goodman, because it satisfies 'depicts a smiling woman' both in its relational and non-relational senses.

As well as appearing to resolve these problems, the proposal is an improvement on analysing depiction in terms of experienced resemblance, because it does not merely shift the bump in the rug, but instead appears to form part of a solution to the general problem of intentionality. In the case of experience, for example, it may be argued that 'is an experience of an apple' is ambiguous between a relational and a non-relational sense. When I see a real apple, I would have an experience in the relational sense, whereas when I hallucinate an apple, my experience is of an apple merely because it falls under the unbreakable predicate 'is an experience of an apple'.

So far, Goodman's proposal hasn't provided a resolution to the trilemma, because he hasn't said which of its theses must be rejected. But it's clear that Goodman takes his account to motivate rejecting the first thesis. For example, he writes that "... the copy theory of representation takes a further beating here; for where a representation does not represent anything there can be no question of resemblance to what it represents" (Goodman, 1968, 25). Since, according to Goodman, depiction is unlike resemblance because resemblance but not depiction is always relational, depictions cannot always resemble what they represent. By denying that depiction is unequivocally relational, Goodman appears able to motivate resolving the trilemma by denying its first thesis.

But although Goodman appears to offer a compelling motivation for denying the platitude that depiction is mediated by resemblance, the proposal with which he replaces it is highly unsatisfactory. While it is obvious that certain pictures and representations fall under certain predicates, it seems that the reason pictures and representations fall under these predicates is because of the things they represent. Pegasus' portrait and 'Pegasus', for example, both fall under the predicate 'is a Pegasus representation', but the explanation of this ought to be that there is something which both Pegasus' portrait and Pegasus represent. The observation that different predicates apply to different representations is unilluminating.

This objection is a general objection to predicate nominalism, the doctrine according to which a particular instantiates a property in virtue of satisfying a predicate (I will return to the discussion of predicate nominalism in section 10.2). But even if predicate nominalism is accepted, there is a more specific problem with Goodman's proposal, which is that it relies on an *ad hoc* and controversial claim about the semantics of the word 'depicts' (see Forbes, 2006, 130-147) for detailed discussion of the syntax and semantics of 'depicts'). A better solution to the problem would concern itself not with the word 'depicts', but with the nature of depiction itself.

## 8.3 Denying relations are between existents

Just as it's possible to depict unicorns, although no unicorns exist, it's intuitively possible to resemble a unicorn, although no unicorns exist. And just as it's possible to depict a horse without depicting any horse in particular, it's intuitively possible to resemble a horse without resembling a particular horse. This suggests that exactly the same reasons for denying that depiction is unequivocally relational may be brought forward in favour of denying that resemblance is unequivocally relational. The same motivation that Goodman gives for denying the thesis that all depictions resemble what they represent may be more naturally given in order to deny that resemblance is a relation between existents instead (Hyman, 2006, 65).

The cost of this solution is that it is committed to denying not only the thesis that resemblance is a relation between existents but also the analysis of resemblance as sharing properties. Even though it is intuitively possible to resemble a horse without resembling any particular horse, it is impossible to share properties without sharing properties with at least one particular horse. Similarly, even though it is intuitively possible to resemble Santa, it is not possible to share properties with Santa, since Santa does not have properties. Sharing properties is a relation, so if resemblance is sharing properties, then resemblance is also a relation. One cannot deny that resemblance is a relation without denying that resemblance is sharing properties.

But there is another way to deny the thesis that resemblance is a relation between existents, which does not incur the cost of denying that resemblance is sharing properties. Instead of denying that resemblance is a relation, it is possible to deny that resemblance is between existents. In order to do this it is necessary to posit that there are objects which don't exist, called Meinongian objects, and that depictions can be related to these objects. According to this proposal, Santa, although he does not exist, is a non-existent object who is capable of being resembled by Santa's portrait. In general, depictions that don't depict existents are still supposed by this proposal to bear the relations of resemblance and depiction to non-existent objects.

Postulating Meinongian objects – unlike analysing depiction in terms of other intentional notions – has the advantage that it provides a general solution to the problem of intentionality. In the case of experience, for example, hallucinatory experiences can be construed as relations towards non-existent objects. If, for example, I hallucinate an apple, then the relation that usually obtains between me and the existent apples I normally perceive instead obtains between me and the non-existent apple which I hallucinate. In general, intentional states that are not about objects which exist can be construed as states that are about objects which don't exist.

It might be objected that postulating non-existent objects does not genuinely resolve the trilemma, on the grounds that, since non-existent objects do not have properties, it is not possible to share properties with them and thus not possible to resemble them. For example, it might be argued that since Santa cannot be red without existing, a picture of Santa cannot resemble Santa in respect of being red without Santa existing. According to this objection, postulating non-existent objects is of no help in resolving the problem of the depiction of non-existents, since it is still impossible to resemble those non-existent objects.

But it is standardly argued that Meinongian objects do have properties. Meinong's view holds that sentences such as 'the round square is round', for example, are true, even though no round square exists. In order to do this it's claimed that the round square is a non-existent object which nevertheless has the properties of being round and being square. Similarly, a proponent of this position can argue that although Santa doesn't exist, he still has properties such as wearing a red coat, having a beard, being jolly and so forth. The postulation of non-existent objects to solve problems in other areas is already committed to postulating that non-existent objects have properties.

The proposal is also able to resolve the problem of the depiction of non-particulars by postulating that there are indeterminate non-existent objects. Depicting a horse but no particular horse, for example, can be analysed as a relation towards a non-existent object which has the property of being a horse, but lacks the properties of being Phar Lap, being Bucephalus, being Incitatus or being any other particular horse. In general, a depiction of something but not of anything particular can be analysed as a depiction of a non-existent object which has only the properties which the picture represents it as having. This treatment of the depiction of non-particulars exactly parallels the Meinongian treatment of thoughts and sentences about non-particulars.

The problem of depictive misrepresentation is more difficult to resolve by postulating non-existent objects. Suppose, for example, that my portrait depicts me with three heads, when I in fact have only one head. This cannot be analysed as a relation between my portrait and a non-existent object with three heads, because my portrait is a depiction of me, and I am not a non-existent object. Though this problem is a difficult one for resolving the problem of depictive misrepresentation by postulating non-existents, it is also a problem for Meinongianism in general: if I am thinking of myself with three heads, for example, this cannot simultaneously be a thought about myself and a relation towards a non-existent three headed object (Parsons, 1995).

Furthermore, though the postulation of non-existent objects is an attractive solution to the trilemma, it is less attractive as a general metaphysical position. The thesis that there are non-existent objects seems to be equivalent to the thesis that non-existent objects exist, but this is a contradiction. To avoid this contradiction a distinction has to be drawn between what there is and what exists, so that the claim that there are non-existent objects does not imply the claim that non-existent objects exist. But the Meinongian distinction between what exists and what there is is a distinction without a difference, because the most compelling way to characterise what exists is as everything there is.

(A Meinongian may respond to this objection by agreeing that what exists is the same as what there is, but continuing to argue not that there are things that do not exist, but merely that some things do not exist (Priest, 2005). So although dragons do not exist, and moreover although there are no dragons, some dragons are nevertheless green, so, according to this version of Meinongianism, a depiction may resemble some dragon in respect of being green. In any case, the solution I offer below can be reconstrued as either kind of Meinongianism, by reconstruing possibilia and possible worlds as non-existent Meinongian objects instead of existent non-actual objects.)

## 8.4 Depiction of states of affairs

The first thesis of the trilemma, that all depictions resemble what they represent, together with the second thesis, that resemblance is a relation between existents, together imply that depiction is a relation between existents. It is this implication that produces the inconsistency with the third thesis, that not all depiction is between existents. But that implication is plausible independently of whether or not all depictions resemble what they represent or whether resemblance is a relation between existents. For this reason, it seems that the most plausible resolution of the trilemma is to deny the third thesis, that some depictions represent non-existents. This section argues for doing so by construing depiction as a relation towards states of affairs.

Depictions represent particulars, properties and states of affairs. The Mona Lisa, for example, represents Lisa herself, the property of smiling and the state of affairs of Lisa's smiling. I will argue for denying the thesis that some depictions represent non-existents by arguing that apparent depiction of non-existent particulars is really the depiction of existent states of affairs. I will also argue for denying the first thesis as applied to particulars: not all depictions resemble the particulars they represent. But the first thesis is true as applied to states of affairs: all depictive states of affairs resemble the states of affairs they represent. Thus, the apparent depiction of non-existents is compatible with the platitude that depiction is mediated by resemblance.

A natural way to deny the thesis that some depictions represent non-existents is to deny that apparent depictions of non-existents depict particulars at all. It may be argued that Santa's portrait, for example, does not really depict any particular, on the grounds that Santa, the particular which Santa's portrait is purported to depict, does not exist. The same can be said of pictures of Pegasus and diagrams of Phlogiston: since the particulars these pictures are purported to represent do not in fact exist, it is reasonable to argue that portraits of Pegasus and diagrams of Phlogiston do not in fact depict particulars. Since, in general, non-existent particulars do not exist, it seems that the apparent depiction of non-existents cannot be the depiction of particulars.

But denying that apparent depictions of non-existents depict particulars has the disadvantage that it does not capture the obvious differences between depictions which are apparently of different non-existents. Depictions of Pegasus appear to be different from depictions of Santa because they depict different particulars: depictions of Pegasus depict Pegasus, whereas depictions of Santa depict Santa. If depictions of Santa and depictions of Pegasus do not depict particulars at all, then the difference between what they represent must not reside in the different particulars they represent. Instead, different depictions of non-existents differ primarily by representing different states of affairs.

Holmes does not exist, but in other states of affairs he might have existed (Kripke, 1963). So although depicting Holmes cannot be analysed as a relation towards Holmes himself it can, for example, be analysed as a relation towards the state of affairs of Holmes' smoking a pipe. And although the difference between depictions of Santa and depictions of Pegasus cannot be construed as a difference between which particulars they represent, it can be construed as a difference between the states of affairs which they represent: depictions of Santa depict states of affairs in which Santa exists, whereas depictions of Pegasus depict states of affairs in which Pegasus exists. So analysing depiction as a relation between states of affairs is able to resolve the problem of the depiction of non-existents.

No difficulty for the depiction of states of affairs is posed by inexistence because, unlike particulars which may simply exist or not, states of affairs may fail to obtain without ceasing to exist. Just as there is a fact of the Eiffel Tower's being in Paris, for example, there is a state of affairs of the Eiffel Tower's being in New York, although that state of affairs does not obtain. So since all states of affairs are existents, construing depiction as primarily a relation towards states of affairs – including states of affairs which do not obtain – provides a way to deny the thesis that some depictions represent non-existents, while still accommodating the intentionality of depictive representation and thus resolving the trilemma.

It might be objected that analysing depiction as a relation between states of affairs is still incompatible with the thesis that depictions resemble what they represent, because states of affairs do not resemble each other in the relevant respects. Depictions are supposed to resemble what they represent in ordinary respects such as colour and shape, but states of affairs do not have ordinary properties such as colour and shape. There are, for example, red particulars, but red states of affairs are no more possible than green numbers. If this objection is right, then arguing that depictions represent states of affairs does not solve the trilemma, because it is incompatible with the thesis that all depictions resemble what they represent.

This objection can be answered by invoking resemblances between states of affairs which mirror the more ordinary resemblances which obtain between particulars. Two states of affairs resemble each other – in the relevant sense – if they share the property of being states of affairs of something's having a property. The state of affairs of Santa's portrait's being partly red, for example, resembles the state of affairs of Santa's wearing a red coat, because both states of affairs have the property of being states of affairs of something's having the property of being partly red. The relevant respects of resemblance are not the ordinary properties of having certain colours and shapes, but the closely related properties of being states of affairs of thing's having those colours and shapes.

One clarification. Depictive and depicted states of affairs often differ in some of the properties – sometimes including shape and colour properties – which they are states of affairs of something's having. The state of affairs of a photograph's being black and white, for example, does not resemble the state of affairs of the photograph's subject's being coloured. Nevertheless, there are other properties – such as properties of shape and relative shading – such that the state of affairs of the photograph's having those properties still resembles the state of affairs of the photograph's subject's having those same properties. So as long as it's possible to specify the respects in which depictions usually resemble objects, it's also possible to specify the respects in which depictive resemble depicted states of affairs.

As well as the depiction of non-existents, analysing depiction as a relation towards states of affairs resolves the problem of depicting non-particulars. The state of affairs which obtains if there is a tall man, for example, is distinct from the state of affairs of some particular man being tall. So if depiction is a relation toward states of affairs, then depicting a man without depicting any man in particular can be construed as a relation towards the state of affairs, for example, of a man's being tall, but not to a state of affairs of any particular man being tall. In general, a depiction that doesn't depict something in particular can be analysed as a depiction of a state of affairs of something's, but not any particular thing's, having a property.

Similarly, depictive misrepresentation can be analysed as the depiction of a state of affairs which does not obtain. Although the police's picture, for example, does not resemble the criminal as he is, the state of affairs of the police's picture's having a certain colour resembles the state of affairs of the criminal's having the colour which the police believe him to have, since they are both states of affairs of something's having that colour. In general, depictions are accurate when the states of affairs they are of obtain, and inaccurate when the states of affairs they are of fail to obtain. So although the example of misrepresentation shows that not all depictions resemble the particulars they represent, it does not show that depictive states of affairs do not resemble depicted states of affairs.

One clarification. This solution involves a partial denial of the thesis that all depictions resemble what they represent, since depictions which completely misrepresent particulars, like the police's wanted poster, do not resemble those particulars in any relevant respect. Nevertheless, the first thesis is preserved as the thesis that depictive states of affairs resemble the state of affairs they represent. The state of affairs of the wanted poster's being a certain colour and shape, for example, resembles the state of affairs of the criminal's being similarly coloured and shaped. So as well as denying the third thesis, that some depictions represent non-existents, this solution involves a modification of the first thesis, that all depictions resemble what they represent (in relevant respects).

As well as being compatible with the platitude that depiction is mediated by resemblance, analysing depiction as a relation towards states of affairs has the advantage of being part of a general solution to the problem of intentionality. My hallucination of an apple, for example, can be analysed as a relation between me and the existent but non-obtaining state of affairs of an apple's being in front of me, instead of a relation between me and a non-existent apple. In general, experiences can be analysed as relations towards states of affairs: veridical experiences involve relations towards states of affairs which obtain, whereas hallucinations and illusions involve relations towards existent states of affairs which fail to obtain.

Three objections. First, it might be argued that analysing depiction in terms of states of affairs merely shifts the bump in the rug. The puzzle of the depiction of non-existents, according to this objection, has merely been replaced with the puzzle of how there can be states of affairs with non-existent constituents. The puzzle of how Santa's portrait can depict Santa even though Santa does not exist, for example, has merely been replaced by the puzzle of how there can be a state of affairs of Santa's wearing a red coat if Santa does not exist to be a constituent of that state of affairs. If this is the case, then analysing depiction in terms of states of affairs fails to improve on analysing it in terms of experienced resemblance.

I accept that non-existents pose a problem for the analysis of states of affairs, but it is a problem that most analyses of states of affairs are able to answer. The next chapter argues, for example, for analysing states of affairs in terms of possible worlds. But the solution is available in principle to other analyses of states of affairs and even to the view that states of affairs are primitive and unanalysable (as long as they do resemble each other in relevant respects). All that is essential to the solution is that depictions apparently of non-existents are really depictions of states of affairs which do in fact exist, but may not obtain. Since the solution is available in principle to any theory of states of affairs which allows that there are states of affairs concerning non-existents, it seems best to remain neutral until the next chapter about what the correct theory of states of affairs is.

Second, it might be objected that it is not possible to distinguish between general and particular states of affairs concerning non-existents without holding that some states of affairs have non-existent constituents. The particular state of affairs of Bucephalus' grazing, for example, differs from the general state of affairs of a horse's grazing because the former contains Bucephalus as a constituent whereas the latter does not. But since Pegasus does not exist, the particular state of affairs of Pegasus' flying cannot differ from the general state of affairs of a horse's flying by having Pegasus as a constituent, because Pegasus cannot be the constituent of a state of affairs without existing.

Some theories of states of affairs may accept this consequence. But if states of affairs are analysed in terms of possibility, as in the theory the next chapter argues for, then the problem may be avoided by holding that some states of affairs have non-actual possibilia as constituents and by holding that non-actual possibilia exist. So the state of affairs of Pegasus' flying, for example, could differ from the state of affairs of a unique winged horse's flying because the former contains Pegasus, an existent non-actual possibilia, whereas the latter does not. In general, singular states of affairs apparently concerning non-existents can be reconstrued as singular states of affairs concerning existent but non-actual possibilia.

Sympathisers with this objection might reply that if existent non-actual possibilia must be introduced, it would be better to have analysed depiction as a relation towards those possibilia in the first place, rather than as a relation towards states of affairs. The problem with this proposal is that depictions do not straightforwardly resemble existent non-actual possibilia, since non-actual possibilia have no properties in the actual world and different properties in the different possible worlds in which they occur: Santa, for example, wears a red coat in some possible worlds, but a green coat in others (Walton, 1974, 246). For this reason, depiction still has to be analysed in terms of resemblance between states of affairs, even if it is granted that non-actual possibilia exist. The depiction of non-actual possibilia is another counterexample to the thesis that all depictions resemble the particulars they represent.

Third, it might be objected that analysing the depiction of non-existents, the depiction of non-particulars and depictive misrepresentation in terms of a relation towards non-obtaining states of affairs does not improve upon Meinongianism, because the distinction between obtaining and non-obtaining states of affairs is as controversial as the Meinongian distinction between existent and non-existent particulars. Stipulating that non-obtaining states of affairs merely differ from facts by not obtaining is as uninformative as stipulating that non-existent differ from existent particulars merely by not existing. This suggests that the distinction between facts and non-obtaining states of affairs, like the distinction between what exists and what there is, is a distinction without a difference.

But the distinction between facts and non-obtaining but existent states of affairs is easier to draw than the distinction between what exists and what there is. The reason is that in the case of Meinongian objects there is a prima facie equivalence between objects that there are and objects that exist. In the case of states of affairs, however, there is no prima facie equivalence between states of affairs that exist and states of affairs that obtain. So there is some reason to expect that the distinction between existent and non-existent objects cannot be drawn, whereas a distinction between obtaining and non-obtaining states of affairs can be – as it is in the next chapter.

The analysandum of previous chapters was the conditions under which something depicts another. But if the conclusion of this chapter is correct, the analysandum should have been the conditions under which an object depicts a state of affairs. This leads to the following analysis of depiction:

(23) An object depicts a state of affairs if and only if it is intended that if the object reaches an audience of a certain type then:

　　a. the object's having a property resembles that state of affairs in respect of both being states of affairs of something's having a certain property

b. the audience recognises that the object's having a property resembles that state of affairs in that respect
c. the audience infers at least in part from the fact that the object's having a property resembles that state of affairs in that respect that it is intended that:
d. the object induce an attitude or an action directed towards that state of affairs in the audience
e. this effect be induced by means of providing a reason
f. and the audience recognise intentions (a)-(f).

So the Mona Lisa depicts Lisa's smiling, for example, because Leo intended that the Mona Lisa's appearing a certain way to resemble Lisa's being a certain way in respect of both being states of affairs of something's appearing a certain way and intended his audience to infer his communicative intentions from that resemblance.

Once the depiction of states of affairs is defined, the depiction of objects and of properties can be defined as follows:

(24) An object depicts another if and only if the former depicts a state of affairs of the latter's having a property.

(25) An object depicts a property if and only if the object depicts a state of affairs of something's having that property.

So, for example, the Mona Lisa depicts Lisa and the property of smiling because the Mona Lisa depicts the state of affairs of Lisa's smiling.

## 8.5 Conclusion

I have considered four proposals for resolving the problem of depictive intentionality: analysing depiction in intentional terms, denying that depiction is unequivocally relational, postulating non-existent objects and analysing depiction as a relation toward states of affairs. The final proposal – analysing depiction as a relation toward states of affairs – provides a solution to the problem which is consonant with the platitude that depiction is mediated by resemblance and which also forms part of the most plausible solution to the problem of intentionality. But even for those who believe that a different solution to the problem of intentionality is more plausible, it seems likely that that solution will also be compatible with the platitude that depiction is mediated by resemblance.

The most striking moral of this discussion is not the merits of any particular proposal, but the similarity in the shape of the issues with other areas in which the problem of intentionality arises: the various options for resolving the problem of the depiction of non-existents, for example, are the same as the various options which are available for resolving the problem of intentional inexistence in general. The distinctive role of resemblance in depictive representation adds some extra subtleties to the dialectic, but on closer examination the same problems can usually be raised for other kinds of representation. So the intentionality of depictive representation poses no specific difficulties for the platitude that depiction is mediated by resemblance.

I want to conclude by emphasising that however the general problem of intentionality should be resolved – whether it be by postulating Meinongian objects, denying that representation is relational, analysing representation in terms of experience or, as I have suggested, by analysing representation as a relation towards states of affairs – the problem in the specific case of depiction should not be resolved by denying the platitude that depiction is mediated by resemblance. The reason is that because the platitude that depiction is mediated by resemblance is the only element of the problem which is specific to depictive representation, denying that platitude is the option which is least able to provide a solution to the problem of intentionality in general.

# 9. Perspective and Possibility

Depictions, like thoughts and sentences, distinguish different ways things might be; the Mona Lisa, for example, represents Lisa by distinguishing between the various possible ways which Lisa might have looked. This suggests analysing the states of affairs depictions represent in terms of possible worlds: the state of affairs represented by the Mona Lisa, for example, may be analysed as the set of possible worlds in which Lisa's appearance is as it portrays. This chapter argues that analysing states of affairs in terms of possible worlds addresses the lacuna in the last chapter in a way which is consonant with the platitude that depiction is mediated by resemblance.

The first section introduces the analysis of states of affairs as sets of possible worlds. The next three sections address three problems for this analysis. The second addresses the problem posed by pictures in perspective. The third addresses the problem posed by pictures of metaphysical or a posteriori impossibilities. The fourth addresses the problem posed by pictures of logical or a priori impossibilities. All three problems require revision to the analysis of states of affairs as sets of possible worlds, but the revisions are consonant with both a strong analogy between depiction and description and the platitude that depiction is mediated by resemblance.

## 9.1 The possible worlds analysis of content

A possible world is a consistent and complete way things might be. The actual world, for example, is one consistent and complete way things might be: it includes not just the earth, but also other planets, solar systems, galaxies, intergalactic space, and anything that actually exists. Other possible worlds include different planets and galaxies, but all of them are complete: there is no possible world which leaves any question undecided, since it is impossible for things not to be one way or another. And all of them are consistent: no possible world answers any question inconsistently, since inconsistencies are impossibilities.

The main application of possible worlds is in the analysis of necessity and possibility: necessity may be analysed as truth in every possible world and possibility may be analysed as truth in some possible world. It is necessary that twice two is four, for example, because twice two is four in every possible world. And it's possible that there are alien species, for example, because there are alien species in some possible worlds. Similarly, it's impossible that twice two is five because there's no possible world in which twice two is five and it's not necessary that there are alien species because there are not alien species in every possible world.

Since possible worlds are consistent and complete the rules of classical logic hold within them, so this analysis has the advantage of reducing an ill understood phenomenon – modal logic – to a well understood one – classical logic. It explains, for example, how it is necessary that there either will or will not be a sea battle tomorrow, without being necessary that there will be or necessary that there won't be a sea battle tomorrow, because – since possible worlds are complete – every possible world is one in which there either is or isn't a sea battle tomorrow, even though some possible worlds do have sea battles tomorrow and other possible worlds don't.

A state of affairs can be analysed as a set of possible worlds (Lewis, 1986, 185). The state of affairs of grass' being green, for example, is the set of possible worlds in which grass is green and the state of affairs of Lisa's smiling is the set of possible worlds in which Lisa smiles. The state of affairs of a horse's grazing is the set of possible worlds in which a horse is grazing: since different horses graze in different possible worlds, the state of affairs of a horse's grazing need not be the state of affairs of any particular horse's grazing. Similarly, the state of affairs of Santa's laughing can be analysed as the set of possible worlds in which Santa laughs: the puzzle of Santa's inexistence is overcome by postulating his existence in other possible worlds.

One clarification. The analysis of states of affairs in terms of possible worlds requires no particular assumptions about their nature or existence. Possible worlds may, for example, be concrete entities like the actual world, abstract entities akin to numbers and sets, non-existent objects, or merely useful fictions. If it's correct that there's no distinction between what exists and what there is, then if there are possible worlds they must exist. But if there is a distinction between what exists and what there is, then it's possible to agree with the conclusions of this chapter, but not the last, by construing possible worlds and their constituents as Meinongian non-existent objects.

## 9.2 Centred properties and possible worlds

Many pictures represent what they do from a particular viewpoint or perspective: profile portraits, for example, represent their subjects from their sides, rather than their fronts. The analysis of depictive content simply in terms of sets of possible worlds, as Jeff Ross (1997, 73-97) shows, is unable to accommodate perspective pictures. To illustrate the point, Ross (1997, 73) uses two pictures: whereas the first picture (Fig. 1) depicts a white sphere in front of a black sphere, the second picture (Fig. 2) depicts the same spheres from the opposite direction, with the black sphere in front of the white sphere.

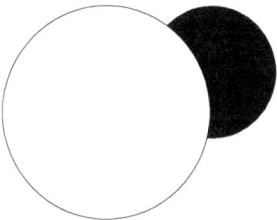

Fig. 1 A white sphere in front of a black sphere. From Jeff Ross (1997), *Semantics of Media* (Dordrecht: Kluwer), p. 73.

Fig. 2 A black sphere in front of a white sphere. From Jeff Ross (1997), *Semantics of Media* (Dordrecht: Kluwer), p. 73.

There is an obvious difference in content between the two pictures, but there is no difference in the set of possible worlds they represent. Every possible world in which the white sphere is in front of the black sphere is also a possible world in which, from another perspective, the black sphere is in front of the white sphere. And every possible world in which the black sphere is in front of the white sphere is also a possible world in which, from another perspective, the white sphere is in front of the black sphere. So every possible world in which the first picture is accurate is a possible world in which, from another perspective, the second picture is accurate: the two pictures represent the same set of possible worlds, but differ in content.

This is an important difficulty for analysing the contents of depictions as sets of possible worlds. However, as Ross (1997, 75-76) points out, the problem is not unique to depictive representation. The analysis of the content of thought and language in terms of possible worlds, for example, also has to be revised to accommodate beliefs and sentences with egocentric content. The rest of this section explains the solution to the problem of accounting for egocentric content in general, the application of that solution to depiction and then the consonance of that solution with the platitude that depiction is mediated by resemblance.

Consider the example, due to Lewis (1979, 139), of two gods. One lives on the tallest mountain and throws down mana; the other lives on the coldest mountain and throws down thunderbolts. Both gods know everything about which possible world they inhabit: for example, both know they inhabit a possible world with two gods, one on the tallest and one on the coldest mountain. However, neither god is omniscient, because both gods are ignorant about which god they are: neither god knows whether he is the god on the tallest mountain who throws down mana or the god on the coldest mountain who throws down thunderbolts.

Because the gods already know which possible world they inhabit, their lack of knowledge cannot be analysed as ignorance about which world is actual; rather, their ignorance is about their location within the world. The solution to the problem is to analyse contents as sets of *centred* possible worlds or, in other words, ordered triples of locations, times and possible worlds. When the gods know the time and everything about their world, the content of their knowledge can be characterised as a set of two triples. The world and time coordinate of each triple is the same, but the location coordinate is different: one triple's location coordinate is the tallest mountain whereas the other's is the coldest mountain.

The difference in content between the picture of the white sphere in front of the black sphere and the black sphere in front of the white sphere can be analysed as a difference in the location coordinates of the centred possible worlds in the sets they represent. The possible worlds coordinates of the centred possible worlds in the sets represented by both pictures are the same, but the location coordinates differ: the location coordinates of ordered triples in the set represented by the first pictures are locations to which the white sphere is closer, whereas the location coordinates of the ordered triples in the set represented by the second are locations to which the black sphere is closer.

Two clarifications. First, Lewis and Ross (1997, 75-83) characterise egocentric belief in terms of the self-ascription of properties rather than triplets of locations, time and worlds. The later proposal was originally suggested by Quine (1969); Lewis (1979, 147) argues the two views turn out to be equivalent. Ordered triples of individuals, times and worlds are often used rather than triples of worlds, times and locations: I prefer locations to individuals because I prefer to leave open the question of whether or not the point of view in some pictures is inhabited by an individual (Walton (1990, 337-348) and Currie (1995, 170-179) discuss this issue).

Second, Figure 3 and Figure 4 show that accommodating every example of difference in perspective requires centred possible worlds to be defined as ordered quadruples of locations, orientations, times and possible worlds. Whereas Figure 3 depicts a sphere to the left, Figure 4 depicts the same sphere to the right. They both depict the sphere from the same location: the difference in content is produced by a difference in the orientation of the viewer, as illustrated by Figure 5, which shows from above the orientation of the viewer in Figure 3, and Figure 6, which shows from above the orientation of the viewer in Figure 4.

Fig. 3 A black sphere to the left.

Fig. 4 A black sphere to the right.

164  *Resemblance and Representation*

Fig. 5 A black sphere to the left from above.

Fig. 6 A black sphere to the right from above.

Similar examples show that the contents of thoughts and sentences must also be defined as ordered quadruples of locations, orientations, time and possible worlds: a change in orientation can change the truth of the sentence 'the sphere is to the left', for example, even while location, time and possible world are kept constant. Alternatively, if centred possible worlds are defined as ordered triples of individuals, times and possible worlds, then orientations may be dispensed with (in the analysis of linguistic, mental and depictive content) on the grounds that orientation and location may both be determined by the direction in which the individual is faced at the relevant time and possible world.

Analysing what depictions represent in terms of sets of ordered quadruples of orientations, locations, times and possible worlds, instead of as sets of possible worlds simpliciter, is not as completely straightforward as it is for the case of egocentric beliefs. Egocentric beliefs represent that the believer is located at the centre of one of the centred possible worlds corresponding to their beliefs; in the case of pictures, this would suggest that what is depicted is the onlooker instead of, as it should be, what they look on. Perspective pictures do not represent that people are located at certain points of view, but the way things look to people when they are seen from those points of view (Ross, 1997, 85).

Depictive representation is not representation of the properties of viewers, but the representation of the properties of depicted objects. To solve the problem of how things can be represented by pictures from particular points of view, properties have to be found which the things have from some points of view but not others. In the case of the pictures of the black and white spheres, a distinction must be drawn between the white sphere having the property of being in the foreground and the black sphere having the property of being in the foreground. I will argue in the rest of this section that the problem can be resolved by accepting a slight and intuitive revision of the standard analysis of properties in terms of possible worlds.

The analysis of properties in terms of possible worlds is motivated by a problem for an extremely naïve theory of properties: the analysis of properties as the sets of objects that possess them. The property of red, for example, is analysed as the set of red things. The problem with this analysis is that it cannot distinguish between properties which happen to be possessed by all the same things. The property of being a creature with a heart differs from the property of being a creature with a kidney, for example, but the analysis of properties in terms of sets cannot distinguish them, because it so happens that the set of creatures with a heart and the set of creatures with a kidney are the same.

This problem can be resolved by analysing properties as functions from possible worlds to extensions, which take each possible world to the set of things possessing the property at that world. So the property of being green, for example, is analysed as the function which takes the actual world to the set of things which are actually green and other possible worlds to the sets of things which are green in those worlds. This analysis can distinguish between the properties of being a creature with a heart and being a creature with a kidney, for example, because the functions associated with each property take possible worlds in which not all creatures with hearts have kidneys to distinct sets.

Since the set of possible worlds in which the black sphere is in the foreground is the same as the set of possible worlds in which, from a different perspective, the white sphere is in the foreground, a function from possible worlds to the set of things that are in the foreground in that world cannot provide a property the representation of which can distinguish between the two pictures. More generally, if properties are functions from possible worlds to extensions, it is not possible to distinguish between different properties that things may have from different perspectives within the same possible worlds.

This problem can be resolved by analysing properties as functions from centred possible worlds, rather than possible worlds simpliciter, to extensions, which take each ordered quadruple of orientation, time, location and possible world to the set of things possessing the property in question relative to that orientation, time location and world (Egan, 2006a, 509-513). The property of being in the foreground, for example, can be analysed as a function which takes centred possible worlds in which the white sphere is closer to the location coordinate to extensions including the white sphere and centred possible worlds in which the black sphere is closer to the location coordinate to extensions including the black sphere.

So perspective pictures can be accommodated by taking the content of a depiction to be the set of centred possible worlds in which the depicted objects have the depicted properties, where those properties are functions from centred possible worlds to extensions, rather than functions from possible worlds simpliciter to extensions. The content of the picture of the white sphere in front of the black sphere, for example, is the set of centred possible worlds relative to which the white sphere has the centred property of being in front of the black sphere; the content of the picture of the black sphere in front of the white sphere is the set of centred possible worlds relative to which the black sphere has the centred property of being in front of the white sphere.

Originally, introducing centred possible worlds may have seemed to be problematic for the claim that depictions resemble what they represent. But the introduction of the corresponding centred properties reveals some attractive features of the combination of a resemblance theory of depiction with the claim that the contents of depictions are sets of centred possible worlds. The natural suggestion is that pictures from particular points of view resemble what they represent because they share centred properties with what they represent. Depictions resemble what they represent because they possess centred properties relative to the intended positions of the viewer which the represented object possesses relative to the points of view represented by the picture.

Take, for example, anamorphic pictures, which appear to resemble what they represent only if viewed from certain angles. This can be explained because the property in which the anamorphic picture resembles what it represents will be one that it has only relative to the unusual position from which the picture has to be perceived. In Holbein's famous detail of the skull, for example, the shape of the details appears to be the same as a shape of a skull only relative to a viewpoint far off-centre. So the recognition of centred properties is important for understanding both the contents and the representational features of depictions, as well as the kinds of respects in which depictions resemble what they represent.

One clarification. To accommodate the point that some pictures, such as anamorphic pictures, only resemble what they represent relative to a certain time and place, the analysis has to be revised as follows:

(26) An object depicts a state of affairs if and only if it is intended that if the object reaches an audience of a certain type at a certain time, place and orientation then:

a. the object's having a property relative to that time, place and orientation resembles that state of affairs in respect of being states of affairs of something's having that property relative to a time, place and orientation
b. the audience recognises the object's having a property relative to that time, place and orientation resembles that state of affairs in that respect
c. the audience infers at least in part from the fact that the object's having a property relative to that time, place and orientation resembles that state of affairs in that respect that it is intended:
d. that the object induce an attitude or an action directed towards that state of affairs in the audience
e. this effect be induced by means of providing a reason
f. and the audience recognise intentions (a)-(f).

So, for example, Holbein's detail depicts a skull because if the detail is seen by an audience at the extreme right of the picture, then the detail's having the property of appearing to be a certain shape at the extreme right of the picture resembles the state of affairs of a skull's having that shape in respect of both being states of affairs of something's appearing to have that shape (see Greenberg (2013, 261-263) for further discussion of centred worlds and properties in the analysis of depiction).

## 9.3 The two-dimensional analysis of content

The introduction of centred possible worlds shows how perspective pictures, even though they require an important revision, can be easily accommodated within the spirit of the possible worlds framework. Impossible pictures, on the other hand, seem more threatening: the possibility of pictures of impossibilities is an obvious difficulty for the analysis of what pictures are of in terms of possibilities. Similar difficulties arise for pictures of necessities and pictures with distinct but necessarily connected subjects. The problems divide into two kinds: depictions of metaphysical or a posteriori and of logical or a priori impossibilities and necessities.

Inexistence and identity are the two main sources of a posteriori necessities and impossibilities. The inexistence of unicorns, for example, is known only empirically. But it's empirical knowledge of a necessary truth, since it follows from the fact that unicorns do not exist that unicorns could not have existed, because although there are numerous possible but inexistent horned horse-like species, no one of these species is uniquely entitled to be identified with the unicorn (Kripke, 1980, 156-158). It follows that depictions of unicorns – and other inexistents whose essential properties are unspecified – are depictions of impossibilities. Their content can't be analysed in terms of the sets of possible worlds in which they are accurate, since they aren't accurate in any.

Similarly, it was an empirical and a posteriori discovery that Hesperus – the brightest star in the evening – is Phosphorus – the brightest star in the morning. Nevertheless, it was an a posteriori discovery of a necessary truth, since it follows from the identity of Hesperus and Phosphorus that Hesperus and Phosphorus are necessarily identical (Kripke, 1980, 97-105). Imagine a star chart produced before the discovery that Hesperus is Phosphorus, which depicts them as simultaneously possessing different locations. The analysis of depictive content in terms of sets of possible worlds predicts that the content of this depiction – and all other depictions of a posteriori impossibilities – is the empty set, since there are no possible worlds in which the depiction is accurate.

One way to escape this problem would be to argue that the chart does not really represent the impossibility of Hesperus and Phosphorus possessing different locations, but merely represents the possibility of the brightest star in the evening possessing a different location from the brightest star in the morning. Similarly, one may argue that pictures of unicorns do not represent any particular impossible species, but merely the general possibility of the existence of horse-like animals with horns. In general, apparent depictions of impossible states of affairs concerning particulars can be reconstrued as depictions of possible states of affairs concerning generalities.

But this strategy obscures an important distinction. There is an important difference in content, for example, between a depiction of Pegasus flying and a depiction of a flying horse – but no horse in particular – which closely resembles Pegasus. Similarly, there is an important difference in content between depictions of stars with certain properties, and of particular stars with which we are familiar: depicting Hesperus is different from merely depicting a star – but no particular star – which rises in the evening. The strategy of arguing that apparent depictions of a posteriori impossible states of affairs concerning particulars are really depictions of possible states of affairs concerning generalities obscures these distinctions.

A better solution is to argue that all depictions of a posteriori impossibilities do depict the empty set, but under different modes of presentation. Although depictions of unicorns and depictions of werewolves, for example, both depict the same impossible state of affairs, they do so under a different mode of presentation: the former represents the impossible state of affairs under a mode of presentation involving horns and horse-like features, whereas the latter represents the impossible state of affairs under a mode of presentation involving teeth and wolf-like features. The rest of this section clarifies this proposal and reconciles it with the platitude that depiction is mediated by resemblance.

Prima facie, the introduction of modes of presentation into the analysis of depictive content is problematic for the platitude that depiction is mediated by resemblance. Depictions of a posteriori impossibilities, for example, seem to resemble neither the impossible states of affairs they depict nor the abstract modes of presentation under which those states of affairs are represented in any relevant respect. Moreover, what a mode of presentation is needs further explanation. Both these problems can be resolved by the two-dimensional theory of modes of presentation, which is naturally reconcilable with the platitude that depiction is mediated by resemblance.

Depictions of a posteriori impossibilities might, if things had turned out differently, have been depictions of possibilities. If, for example, it had turned out that the brightest star in the morning and the brightest star in the evening were distinct, then the chart which represents Hesperus and Phosphorus as having different locations would have represented the genuine possibility of two other possible stars having different locations. Similarly, in other possible worlds in which a horned horse-like species does exist, depictions of unicorns might have depicted the possibility of members of that species appearing in a certain way.

Just as the states of affairs depictions represent may be analysed as sets of possible worlds, the various states of affairs depictions might have represented may be characterised by two-dimensional intensions: functions from possible worlds to the set of possible worlds which a depiction would represent if that world were actual. The various states of affairs which the chart which represents Hesperus and Phosphorus as having different locations might have represented, for example, is characterised by a function which takes the actual world to the empty set, but possible worlds in which the stars appearing in the morning and evening are distinct to sets of possible worlds in which those stars have the locations shown by the map.

A two-dimensional intension determines which states of affairs a depiction represents in each possible world, but they also determine one further state of affairs: the diagonal state of affairs is the set of possible worlds which the function takes to sets in which they're included. To illustrate, suppose there are just two possible worlds: $i$ and $j$. In $i$ the brightest star in the evening is the brightest in the morning, but in $j$ it is not. The rows represent the states of affairs the chart would depict in $i$ and $j$:

|   | $i$ | $j$ |
|---|---|---|
| $i$ | 0 | 0 |
| $j$ | 0 | 1 |

The diagonal from upper left to lower right represents the diagonal state of affairs: in this case, the set of possible worlds in which the brightest stars in the morning and evening are distinct.

One clarification. In some possible worlds, what a picture would have depicted if that world were actual is completely irrelevant to its actual meaning (Schroeter, 2003). The chart representing that Hesperus and Phosphorus differ in location, for example, might have depicted sandwiches instead of stars, but sandwiches are irrelevant to its content. Resolving this problem requires either restricting the possible worlds involved to those compatible with the presuppositions of a representation's perpetrator and audience (Stalnaker, 1978) or arguing a two-dimensional intension is part of a representation's actual content, which reflects the perpetrator and audience's understanding of how its truth depends on the facts (Chalmers, 2000; Jackson, 1998).

Characterising the content of a depiction using a two-dimensional intension distinguishes between depictions of a posteriori impossibilities with different content, because different depictions of a posteriori impossibilities are associated with different diagonal states of affairs by their two-dimensional intensions. The diagonal state of affairs associated with the chart depicting Hesperus and Phosphorus, for example, is the set of possible worlds in which the brightest stars in the morning and evening are differently located, whereas the diagonal state of affairs of a picture depicting unicorns is the distinct state of affairs of there being a horned horse-like species, even though the horizontal state of affairs of both is the empty set.

But characterising the content of a depiction using a two-dimensional intension also distinguishes between depictions of a posteriori impossibilities concerning particular and general states of affairs, because although depictions concerning particular and general states of affairs are associated with the same diagonal states of affairs by their two-dimensional intensions, they are associated with different horizontal states of affairs. A depiction of Pegasus grazing, for example, differs from a depiction of a winged horse, but no horse in particular, grazing, because the non-empty horizontal states of affairs associated with the former all concern particular horses, whereas the horizontal states of affairs associated with the latter do not.

Originally, characterising the content of depiction in terms of modes of presentation might have seemed problematic for the platitude that depiction is mediated by resemblance. But characterising modes of presentation as diagonal states of affairs resolves this prima facie inconsonance, by showing that the state of affairs of the picture's having a certain property may resemble the picture's diagonal state of affairs in respect of both being states of affairs of something's having a certain property. The state of affairs of Pegasus' portrait's being partly white, for example, resembles the diagonal state of affairs of a winged horse's being partly white, because they are both states of affairs of something's being partly white.

## 9.4 Structured intensions and impossible worlds

The possibility of depicting logical or a priori impossibilities is more directly problematic for the analysis of depictive content in terms of possible worlds. The Penroses' (1958, 31) or Reutersvard's triangle (see Fig. 7), for example, is a picture of an a priori, rather than a merely a posteriori, impossibility (see Mortensen (2010, 117-119) for a defence of the logical inconsistency of the impossible triangle). The depicted triangle does not exist in any possible world, nor would the picture have depicted an existent triangle if the world had turned out differently, so the content of the picture cannot be analysed as a set of possible worlds or two-dimensionally.

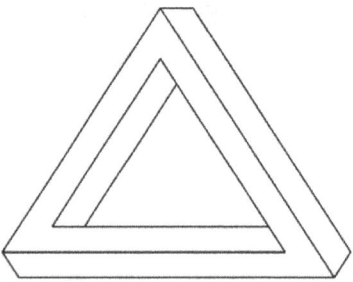

Fig. 7 An impossible triangle.

Impossible pictures like the impossible triangle are a manifestation of a more general problem for the analysis of content in terms of possible worlds: just as it is possible to draw a priori impossibilities, it's possible to believe a priori impossibilities: a person who believes the premises but disbelieves the conclusion of a deductive argument, for example, believes an a priori impossibility. This is problematic for the analysis of the content of belief in terms of possible worlds, because there are no possible worlds in which all their beliefs are true, nor any possible worlds in which, had things turned out differently, their beliefs would have represented something true.

A natural solution to this problem is to argue that inconsistent beliefs divide into consistent partitions: although the beliefs of a person who believes the premises but disbelieves the conclusion of a deductive argument, for example, are logically inconsistent, that person's beliefs divide into consistent partitions corresponding to each premise and the conclusion's negation, and these partitions can be analysed in terms of sets of possible worlds (Stalnaker, 1984; Lewis, 1986, 34-35). Similarly, although the Penroses' triangle is inconsistent, each part is consistent: covering any two of the picture's sides with a piece of paper reveals that the remaining side depicts a consistent part of a triangle.

But not every depiction of, or belief in, a logical impossibility can be treated in this way. Take, for example, a picture of a straight line captioned 'square circle, side view' (Sorensen, 2002, 343). The picture depicts a logical impossibility – a square circle – but not by consisting of individually consistent parts whose combination is inconsistent: every part of the straight line depicts a part of the square circle which is both straight and curved and therefore impossible. Since not even the parts of the straight line depicting a square circle depict possibilities, the inconsistent content of the whole cannot be analysed in terms of the consistent content of the parts.

Side view depictions of square circles do not succeed in representing impossibilities explicitly; the depiction is successful only by representing an impossibility at an angle from which it is invisible. This phenomenon is widespread: depictions which are not composed of consistent, but jointly inconsistent, parts all seem incapable of representing impossibilities explicitly. This suggests an odd disanalogy between depictive and descriptive representation, since sentences seem straightforwardly capable of explicitly representing impossible states of affairs. It seems to follow that depictions differ from descriptions not merely in whether they are mediated by convention or resemblance, but in the kind of contents that they have.

But this apparent disanalogy between depictive and descriptive content can be more neatly explained by the platitude that depiction is mediated by resemblance, which suggests that a picture depicts a property explicitly only if the depictive resembles the depicted states of affairs in respect of both being states of affairs of something's having that property. So the Mona Lisa, for example, represents Lisa's colour explicitly, because the

Mona Lisa resembles Lisa in respect of colour, but represents that Lisa is smiling only implicitly, because the Mona Lisa does not resemble Lisa in respect of smiling.

It follows from this characterisation of explicit depiction of properties that depictions cannot represent things' having inconsistent properties explicitly, because depictions cannot resemble things in respect of having inconsistent properties. A straight line, for example, can resemble a square circle in respect of appearing like a straight line from the side, but a straight line cannot resemble a square circle in respect of being both square and circular, because it cannot be both square and circular. The straight line depicts that the square circle appears straight from the side explicitly, but depicts that it is both square and circular only implicitly.

Even the implicit depiction of impossibilities is problematic for the analysis of depictive content in terms of possible worlds. According to the analysis, the content of a depiction is the set of – or a function from possible worlds to sets of – possible worlds in which it is accurate, but since impossibilities do not occur in any possible world, the analysis predicts that every depiction of an impossibility has the same content: the empty set or the constant function from every possible world to the empty set. Since neither a straight line depicting a square circle nor a straight line depicting a triangular hexagon, for example, are accurate in any possible world, both seem to represent the empty set, when in fact what they represent is obviously different.

There are two options for dealing with this problem. The first option is to replace the analysis of depictive content in terms of sets of possible worlds with an analysis in terms of sets of worlds simpliciter, by allowing the inclusion of impossible – incomplete and inconsistent – as well as possible worlds (Malinas, 1991, 288). This would accommodate depictions of inconsistencies straightforwardly, since depictions of different inconsistencies would depict different sets of impossible worlds. The set of worlds represented by the straight-line depicting a square-circle, for example, would include impossible worlds in which there is a square-circle, whereas the set of worlds represented by the straight-line depicting a triangular hexagon would not.

The introduction of impossible worlds can naturally accommodate the resemblance of depictions to what they represent, by enabling properties to be reanalysed as functions from ordered quadruples of locations, orientations, times and worlds – possible or impossible – simpliciter to extensions. A depiction which represents a triangle as equilateral but not equiangular, for example, represents the triangle as having a property characterised by a function which takes all possible worlds (and other coordinates) to sets of triangles which are both equilateral and equiangular, but which takes some impossible worlds (and other coordinates) to sets of triangles all of which are equilateral but some of which are not equiangular.

However, the introduction of impossible worlds does have some costs. Because possible worlds are consistent and complete, the rules of classical logic hold within them, so that analyses in terms of possible worlds provide an analysis of an ill understood phenomenon in terms of an extremely well understood phenomenon. The possibility of depicting a horse, but no particular horse, for example, is explained by the possible worlds analysis without appealing to non-particular horses in other possible worlds, whereas the possibility of depicting an impossible horse is explained by the impossible worlds analysis only by appealing to impossible horses in the impossible worlds.

The second option is to analyse the content of depictions by introducing more fine-grained contents than sets of possible worlds, such as ordered n-tuples of objects and properties (Soames, 1987; Malinas, 1991, 288). A line depicting a square circle on its side, for example, may depict the ordered quintuple of an object, the property of being square, the property of being circular and the centred property of being viewed from the side. Although ordered n-tuples of objects and properties are more fine-grained than sets of possible worlds, the proposal remains close to the analysis in terms of possible worlds, because each ordered n-tuple of objects and properties determines a set of possible worlds in which the relevant objects possess the relevant properties.

Ordered tuples of objects and properties are fine-grained enough to distinguish between the content of all necessarily equivalent depictions only if it is possible to distinguish between the necessarily equivalent properties represented. The content of a depiction of an equiangular triangle can only differ from the content of a depiction of an equilateral triangle, for example, if it is possible to distinguish between the properties of equiangularity and equilaterality, since if equiangularity and equilaterality are the same property, there is no difference between ordered tuples of objects and properties containing equiangularity and those containing equilaterality.

The solution is to introduce finer-grained properties in addition to states of affairs. Structured properties and relations are ordered tuples of unstructured properties and relations. So equiangularity, for example, can be analysed in terms of an ordered tuple containing the property of being an angle, whereas equilaterality can be analysed in terms of an ordered tuple containing the property of being a length: since the unstructured properties of being an angle and being a length are distinct, so are the structured properties of being equiangular and equilateral and structured states of affairs constituted by ordered tuples of objects and those properties (Lewis, 1986, 56-57).

Since non-particulars do not exist, non-particular states of affairs cannot be analysed as ordered n-tuples of non-particulars and properties. Instead, non-particular states of affairs must be analysed as ordered n-tuples of properties and higher-order properties of properties (Soames, 1987, 224). The state of affairs of something's grazing, for example, can be analysed as the ordered pair of the property of grazing, and the higher-order property of being instantiated. The state of affairs of a horse's grazing can be analysed as the ordered triple of the property of being a horse, the property of grazing, the higher-order relation of being co-instantiated, and so on.

Depictions of non-existents are also problematic for analysing depictive content in terms of fine-grained states of affairs. If Holmes does not exist for example, then the content of a depiction of Holmes smoking cannot be analysed as the ordered pair of Holmes and smoking, because there is no such ordered pair. In general, depictions of non-existents cannot be analysed in terms of ordered tuples of non-existent objects and properties, because there are no ordered tuples of non-existent objects and properties. The analysis of depictive contents as fine-grained states of affairs cannot distinguish between depictions of different non-existents with the same properties.

The solution is to combine fine-grained states of affairs with the two-dimensional solution to the problem of depicting a posteriori impossibilities. Just as a function from centred possible worlds to sets of possible worlds characterises the different states of affairs a depiction might have represented, functions from centred possible worlds to particulars and properties characterise the different particulars and properties it might have represented. A structured two-dimensional intension is an ordered tuple of functions from centred possible worlds to properties and particulars (Chalmers, 2011b). The content of depictions can then be fully characterised by structured two-dimensional intensions.

The structured two-dimensional intension of a depiction of Holmes smoking, for example, is the ordered pair of a function which takes centred possible worlds to detectives called 'Holmes', if anything, and a constant function which takes centred possible worlds to the property of smoking. The structured two-dimensional intension determines an ordinary two-dimensional intension, a function from centred possible worlds to the empty set or sets of possible worlds in which a detective is smoking, as well as the various structured horizontal states of affairs Holmes' portrait might have represented and the structured diagonal state of affairs consisting of the ordered pair of the property of being a detective called 'Holmes' and the property of smoking.

## 9.5 Conclusion

The application of possible world semantics to the contents of depiction requires revision to cope with depictions in perspective and depictions of metaphysical and logical impossibilities, but the revisions that are required are close to the spirit of the possible worlds framework and consonant with the platitude that depiction is mediated by resemblance. The success of these revisions in defending the application of possible world semantics to depiction suggests that similar strategies should be pursued for resolving the similar problems which arise for the analysis of the contents of thought, language and fiction in terms of possible worlds, rather than revisions which depart more radically from the spirit of the possible worlds framework.

Whatever revisions need to be made – even if they depart markedly from the analyses discussed in this chapter – the examples discussed here suggest that most plausible analyses of depictive content will be consonant with the platitude that depictive representation is mediated by resemblance. The reason is that whatever complications are introduced into the analysis of depicted states of affairs, similar complications will need to be made to the analysis of properties, so that depictive will always resemble depicted states of affairs in respect of both being states of affairs of thing's having certain properties. So whatever theory of depictive content is right, that theory seems likely to support the platitude that depiction is mediated by resemblance.

Similarly, whatever revisions need to be made – even if they depart markedly from the analyses discussed in this chapter – the examples discussed here suggest a strong analogy between the content of depictive and other kinds of representation. The reason is that whatever complications are introduced into the analysis of depictive content, analogous complications will need to be made to the analysis of linguistic, mental and other kinds of representation. The few disanalogies – such as the inability of depictions to represent impossibilities explicitly – discovered in this chapter were either incidental or arose from the platitude that depiction is mediated by resemblance.

# 10. Pictures and Properties

The following three theses are individually plausible, but jointly inconsonant:

(1) The degree of realism of a picture is the degree to which it resembles what it represents (in relevant respects)

(2) Properties correspond to (possible) predicates, so the number of properties is the number of (possible) predicates

(3) The degree of resemblance between particulars is their number of properties in common divided by their number of properties in total

This chapter argues for resolving this problem by revising the third thesis.

The first thesis, that a picture's degree of realism is the degree to which it resembles what it represents (in relevant respects), is plausible because it's a natural extension of the analysis of depiction in terms of resemblance to the analysis of depictive realism, as well as a piece of common sense in its own right. It's natural to think the degree of realism of my portrait, for example, is the degree to which it resembles me in relevant respects. And it's natural to think that the Mona Lisa, for example, is more realistic than *Les Demoiselles d'Avignon*, because the Mona Lisa resembles Lisa to a greater degree than *Les Demoiselles d'Avignon* resembles the young women of Avignon.

Not every respect of resemblance between a picture and what it represents is relevant to its degree of realism. A painting of a sailing ship, for example, does not depict the sails more realistically because it resembles them in respect of being canvas. So the degree of realism of a picture is not its degree of resemblance to what it represents simpliciter, but its degree of resemblance to what it represents in relevant respects (Sartwell, 1994, 7). A painting of a sailing ship, for example, does not depict the sails more realistically if it resembles them in respect of being canvas, but it does represent them more realistically if it resembles them in respect of colour.

The second thesis, that because properties correspond to (possible) predicates, the number of properties is the number of (possible) predicates, is plausible on the hypothesis that the meaning of a (possible) predicate is a property: the meaning of the predicate 'is white', for example, is the property of being white. The second thesis is also entailed by predicate nominalism, according to which a particular has a property if and only if it satisfies a (possible) predicate. And it is entailed by class nominalism, according to which an individual has a property if and only if it belongs to the class of individuals which have that property (Lewis, 1983a, 18).

The third thesis, that the degree of resemblance between particulars is their number of properties in common divided by their number of properties, is plausible because it's a natural extension of the analysis of resemblance as having properties in common to the analysis of degree of resemblance. It's natural to suggest, for example, that peas in a pod resemble each other to a high degree because their properties in common – like greenness, roundness and yuckiness – are a high proportion of their properties in total. And it's natural to suggest that the more properties a picture has in common with what it represents, the more closely it resembles what it represents.

These three theses are in tension with each other because the second two theses entail that the degree of resemblance between different particulars is constant if defined (as I will explain below). So in combination with the unqualified version of the first thesis, according to which degree of realism is simply degree of resemblance, the second two theses entail that the degree of realism of any picture different from what it represents is constant if defined. But if this is the case, no two pictures different from what they represent differ in degree of realism. The Mona Lisa and *Les Demoiselles D'Avignon* are both, for example, realistic to the same degree. But this is absurd.

The qualified version of the first thesis, according to which the degree of realism of a picture is its degree of resemblance to what it represents in relevant respects, does not combine with the second two theses to entail that the degree of realism of a picture is constant if defined (Sartwell, 1994, 7). Even if colour photographs do not resemble what they represent more than black and white photographs do, for example, colour photographs resemble what they represent in all relevant respects in which black and white photographs do, but also resemble what they represent in the relevant respect of colour. So colour photographs are more realistic than black and white photographs.

But this solution to the problem merely shifts the bump in the rug. Although not every respect of resemblance between a picture and what it represents is relevant to its degree of realism, a respect of resemblance between a picture and what it represents is relevant to its degree of realism only if it contributes to a greater degree of resemblance between a picture and what it represents. Colour is relevant to the degree of realism of photographs, for example, because it contributes to a greater degree of resemblance between colour photographs and what they represent than between black and white photographs and what they represent.

But if it's accepted that, because the number of properties is the number of (possible) predicates and degrees of resemblance are proportions of properties in common, the degree of resemblance between different particulars is constant if defined, it follows that no respect contributes to a greater degree of resemblance between a picture and what it represents than any other. Colour, for example, would not contribute towards a greater degree of resemblance of colour photographs to what they represent, because although colour photographs resemble what they represent in respect of colour, their degree of resemblance to what they represent would still be constant if defined.

I will argue that the problem should be resolved not by exploiting the qualification in the thesis that degree of realism is degree of resemblance (in relevant respects), nor by denying that the number of properties is the number of (possible) predicates. Instead, the problem should be resolved by analysing degree of resemblance as a weighted proportion of properties in common. The degree of resemblance between particulars, according to this revision, is the sum of the weights of their properties in common, divided by the sum of the weights of their properties in total. I'm unsure if the weights are subjective degrees of importance or objective degrees of naturalness.

The second section explains how predicate nominalism, together with the thesis that degree of resemblance is proportion of properties in common, entails that degree of resemblance between different particulars is constant if defined. The third section explains how the same conclusion follows from class nominalism. The fourth section considers resolving the problem by rejecting both class and predicate nominalism in favour of a sparse conception of properties. The fifth section argues for resolving the problem by revising the analysis of degree of resemblance. Finally, the sixth section concludes by discussing the objectivity of depictive realism.

One clarification. The word 'realism' refers to different doctrines in politics and philosophy. Within philosophy it refers to different doctrines in metaphysics and aesthetics. And within aesthetics it refers to both stylistic and thematic realism, and to literary and depictive realism. Even within the philosophy of pictures, 'realism' may refer to photographic realism, illusionism and a variety of other aesthetic virtues (see Lopes, 2006). I shall defend the thesis that degree of realism is degree of resemblance (in relevant respects) in at least one sense of the word 'realism', but of course I won't deny that there are many other senses which deserve the name equally well.

## 10.1 Predicate nominalism

According to predicate nominalism, particulars have properties in virtue of satisfying predicates (Armstrong, 1978a, 13). The screen before me has the property of being white, for example, because it satisfies the predicate 'is white'. Goodman's position in *Languages of Art* is a version of predicate nominalism; he writes, for example, that "… application of a label [predicate] (pictorial, verbal, etc.) as often effects as it records a classification. The "natural" kinds are simply those we are in the habit of picking out for and by labelling" (Goodman, 1968, 32). Predicate nominalism, since it maintains the properties there are depends on the way we speak, is a kind of subjectivism.

Recall that a predicate is a sentence with a name removed. The predicate 'is white', for example, results from removing 'snow' from 'snow is white'. A (named) particular satisfies a predicate if and only if replacing the gap in the predicate by the name of the particular produces a true sentence. Snow satisfies 'is white', for example, because the sentence 'snow is white' is true. In the sense relevant to predicate nominalism, two predicates which are necessarily satisfied by all the same particulars are the same. The predicates 'is white', 'ist weiß' and 'is not unwhite', for example, although they sound different, are all counted as one (Armstrong, 1978a, 7).

It follows from predicate nominalism that a particular has a property if and only if it satisfies a corresponding predicate. The screen before me has the property of being white, for example, if and only if it satisfies the predicate 'is white'. And so it follows from predicate nominalism that the number of properties is the number of predicates: since the property of being white corresponds to the predicate 'is white', the property of being red corresponds to the predicate 'is red', ... and so on, there is a property corresponding to every predicate and vice versa. It's just this biconditional, and not the purported priority of its left hand side, which leads to the problem raised below.

Some depictions resemble what they represent in ways that are not easily articulated. There is not a word, for example, for every shade of colour in respect of which the Mona Lisa resembles Lisa, so there may not be a predicate corresponding to every property in respect of which the Mona Lisa resembles Lisa. This is a general problem for predicate nominalism. As David Armstrong writes "It is clearly possible, and we believe it to be the case, that particulars have certain properties and relations which never fall under human notice" (Armstrong, 1978a, 21). If so, then it's very likely that there are some properties that do not correspond to any predicate.

The standard solution to this problem is to argue that particulars have properties in virtue of satisfying possible predicates (Armstrong, 1978a, 22). Although there may be no predicate corresponding to the exact shades of colour in respect of which parts of the Mona Lisa resemble Lisa, for example, there are possible predicates which do correspond to those shades which we could introduce, for example, by ostension. If this solution is adopted, then the subjectivism of predicate nominalism is mitigated, because whereas which predicates we in fact employ depends on us, which possible predicates we might employ is a matter of necessity and independent of us.

As well as simple predicates like 'is red' and 'is square' there are complex predicates like 'is red or square' and 'is red and square'. Particulars satisfy complex predicates in virtue of satisfying combinations of simple predicates. *Black Square*, for example, satisfies 'is red or square' but not 'is red and square' in virtue of satisfying 'is black' and 'is square', whereas *Red Square* satisfies both 'is red or square' and 'is red and square' in virtue of satisfying 'is red' and 'is square'. *Black Square* and *Red Square* both satisfy 'is red or not red' but not 'is red and not red' no matter what combination of simple predicates they satisfy.

The combinations of simple predicates are two to the power of the number of simple predicates, or less if some of the simple predicates entail each other, are contraries, or are subcontraries (Watanabe, 1969, 367). If the simple predicates are, for example, 'is red' and 'is square', there are four simple predicate combinations: both 'is red' and 'is square', 'is red' only, 'is square' only and neither 'is red' nor 'is square'. If the simple predicates are 'is red' and 'is coloured', then there are just three combinations, since nothing satisfies 'is red' but not 'is coloured'. And likewise if the simple predicates are 'is red' and 'is black', since nothing satisfies both 'is red' and 'is black'.

If n is the number of simple predicate combinations, the total number of predicates is $2^n$, since there is a predicate which applies in virtue of each combination of simple predicate combinations (Watanabe, 1969, 367). If 'is red', for example, is the only simple predicate, there are two simple predicate combinations and so four predicates in total: 'is red', 'is not red', 'is red or not red' and 'is red and not red'. If 'is red' and 'is square' are the only simple predicates, then there are four simple predicate combinations and sixteen predicates in total, whereas if 'is red' and 'is black' are the only simple predicates, there are three combinations and eight predicates in total.

Each particular satisfies $2^{n-1}$ of the $2^n$ predicates, since all the predicates which apply to it must apply in virtue of the simple predicate combination it satisfies, but may apply in virtue of any combination of the remaining $n - 1$ simple predicate combinations. If 'is red' and 'is square', for example, are the only simple predicates, then *Red Square* satisfies all the predicates which apply to it in virtue of it satisfying 'is red' and 'is square', or eight of the sixteen predicates: 'is red or not red', 'is red or square', 'is not red or square', 'is square', 'is red or not square', 'is red', 'is red if and only if square' and 'is red and square'.

Likewise, any pair of different particulars both satisfy $2^{n-2}$ predicates, since all the predicates which apply to both of them must apply in virtue of the two simple predicate combinations they satisfy, but may apply in virtue of any combination of the remaining $n - 2$ simple predicate combinations (Watanabe, 1969, 377). If 'is red' and 'is square', for example, are the only simple predicates, then *Red Square* and *Black Square* satisfy all of the predicates which apply in virtue of them satisfying either 'is red' and 'is square' or 'is black' and 'is square', or four of the sixteen predicates: 'is red or not red', 'is red or square', 'is not red or square' and 'is square'.

In total, any two different particulars satisfy $2^{n-1} + 2^{n-1} - 2^{n-2}$ predicates, or the sum of the number of predicates satisfied by each minus the number of predicates satisfied by both. If 'is red', for example, is the only simple predicate, then *Red Square* and *Black Square* satisfy two predicates each, one predicate in common and three predicates in total: 'is red', 'is not red' and 'is red or not red'. If 'is red' and 'is square' are the only simple predicates, *Red*

*Square* and *Black Square* both satisfy eight predicates each, four predicates in common, and so eight plus eight minus four or twelve predicates in total.

So if the degree of resemblance between two particulars is their number of properties in common divided by their number of properties in total, and if, since properties correspond to predicates, the number of properties is the number of predicates, then the degree of resemblance between two different particulars is $2^{n-2}$ divided by $2^{n-1} + 2^{n-1} - 2^{n-2}$ or, in other words, one third. If, for example, the only simple predicate is 'is red', then a third of the predicates satisfied by *Red Square* and *Black Square* in total are satisfied by both. If 'is red' and 'is square' are the only simple predicates, then the number is four twelfths or, in other words, still a third.

If properties correspond to possible predicates, instead of predicates simpliciter, and if the number of possible predicates is infinite, then each particular possesses an infinite number of properties, and each pair of different particulars possess an infinite number of properties in common. In this case, if degree of resemblance between particulars is their number of properties in common divided by their number of properties in total, degree of resemblance between particulars is undefined, since it involves the division of an infinite number by the same infinite number. Not all different particulars would have the same degree of resemblance: they would all have none.

So if degree of resemblance is simply proportion of properties in common, predicate nominalism entails that degree of resemblance between different particulars is a third if defined. Though the resemblance between *Red Square* and *Black Square* seems to be greater than the resemblance between a raven and a writing desk, for example, this is an illusion: *Red Square* and *Black Square* and the raven and the writing desk all resemble each other to degree half. And if there's any difference between ducklings in a brood, then the ducklings resemble a cygnet to the same degree they resemble each other, no matter how little the cygnet seems like the ducklings.

## 10.2 Class nominalism

The same conclusions issuing from predicate nominalism can equally be drawn from class nominalism. According to the simplest version of class nominalism, properties are classes of individuals: an individual has a property if and only if it is a member of the class of individuals which have that property (Armstrong, 1978a, 15). The screen before me has the property of being white, for example, because it is a member of the class of white things. Which properties there are, according to class nominalism, does not depend on which predicates we employ, but only on which classes exist, so class nominalism is an objectivist analysis (Armstrong, 1978a, 29).

Nevertheless, although the existence of classes is objective, class nominalism does not escape the counterintuitive consequences of predicate nominalism. Any combination of individuals, no matter how arbitrary or heterogeneous, is a class. Just as there is a class of white things and a class of red things, for example, there's a class of things mentioned in the dictionary and a class containing just a raven and a writing desk. In general, the number of classes of some things is two to the power of the number of the things. If there are just two things, for example, there are four classes of those things: the class of the first, the class of the second, the class of both and the class of neither.

If n is the number of individuals, then each individual is in $2^{n-1}$ classes of individuals, since each individual is in a class corresponding to each combination of the remaining n − 1 individuals. Likewise, any two individuals both belong to $2^{n-2}$ classes of individuals, since any two individuals both belong to a class corresponding to each combination of the remaining n − 2 individuals (Goodman, 1970, 443) and any two individuals belong to $2^{n-1} + 2^{n-1} - 2^{n-2}$ classes of individuals in total. So any pair of individuals are both in $2^{n-2}$ of the $2^{n-1} + 2^{n-1} - 2^{n-2}$ or in other words one third of the classes of individuals either individual is in.

So if degree of resemblance is proportion of properties in common, class nominalism entails that any two individuals resemble each other to degree one third. If *Red Square* and *Black Square*, for example, were the only individuals, there would be four classes: the class of squares, the class of red things, the class of black things, and the empty class. *Red Square* would be a member of the class of squares and the class of red things whereas *Black Square* would be a member of the class of squares and the class of black things. So of the three properties they would have in total – being red, being black and being square – each would have one – being square.

The same conclusion also issues from more complex versions of class nominalism. Suppose, for example, properties are classes of possible individuals (Lewis, 1986, 50) and let n be the number of possible individuals. Then each individual is in $2^{n-1}$ classes of possible individuals, since each is in a class corresponding to each combination of the remaining n − 1 possible individuals. Likewise, any two individuals both belong to $2^{n-2}$ classes of possible individuals, since they both belong to a class corresponding to each combination of the remaining n − 2. So any two individuals are in $2^{n-2}$ of the $2^{n-1} + 2^{n-1} - 2^{n-2}$, or one third, of the classes of possible individuals either is in.

If properties are functions from possible worlds to classes, which take each possible world to the set of individuals possessing the property at that world (Lewis, 1986, 53), and n is the sum of the number of individuals in each possible world, then the number of properties is $2^n$, since there are two possibilities for each individual in each possible world: the function may take the possible world to a class containing the individual, or it may not. All individuals still have $2^{n-1}$ properties and all pairs of individuals still have $2^{n-2}$ properties in common, so the proportion of properties two individuals have in common is still $2^{n-2}$ divided by $2^{n-1} + 2^{n-1} - 2^{n-2}$ or, in other words, still one third.

If properties are functions from centred possible worlds to sets, then the objectivity of class nominalism is mitigated, since particulars will instantiate properties only relative to the indices of the centred possible world, one of which might be a person (Egan, 2006b). But if centred worlds are ordered quadruples of locations, orientations, times and worlds, rather than ordered triples of persons, times and worlds, then the relativity involved in defining properties as functions from centred possible worlds to sets is not relativity to people, and the objectivism of the analysis is unmitigated. This is an issue on which I prefer to remain neutral.

However, the issue bears on the question raised in the first chapter about whether the respects of resemblance between depictions and what they represent are objective or subjective. If depictions resemble what they represent in respect of centred properties which are defined in terms of ordered quadruples of locations, orientations, times and worlds, this "… does not make these properties viewer-dependent. The spectator's point of view coincides with an actual point, and it is only this geometrical point … that is needed…" (Newall, 2011, 73). So the resolution of the issue depends on which definition of centred worlds best captures our conception of properties.

If the number of (possible) individuals or the sum of the number of individuals in each possible world is infinite, then the number of properties is also infinite. For any individual, the number of properties it has is infinite, and for any two individuals, the number of properties they have in common is also the same infinity, so the proportion of properties they have in common is undefined. In this case, if degree of resemblance is proportion of properties in common, then the degree of resemblance between any two individuals is undefined, and it's still the case that no pair of individuals resemble each other to a greater degree than any other (Goodman, 1970, 444).

Because this conclusion is so counterintuitive, the natural solution to the problem is to deny predicate and class nominalism. As John Hyman writes "Goodman's claim that "the criteria of resemblance vary with changes in representational practice" ... is a sign of his allegiance to a form of nominalism. ... If we examine judgements about resemblance in the light of this doctrine the results are striking. ... That is how the doctrine ... challenges the traditional view of realism as an objective quality we can perceive in art ... But the doctrine is demonstrably false" (Hyman, 2006, 185-187). I will argue in the next section that denying nominalism only exacerbates the problem.

## 10.3 Scientific realism

Sparse theories of properties deny there is a property corresponding to every possible predicate, and so deny the number of properties is the number of possible predicates. Which predicates correspond to properties, according to sparse theories, is revealed a posteriori by total science (Armstrong, 1978b, 7-9). Whether the predicate 'is white' corresponds to a property of being white, for example, is an a posteriori question; the existence of the property of being white cannot be deduced from the existence of the predicate 'is white'. Because whether a property exists or not, according to sparse theories, is independent of us, sparse theories are typically objectivist.

As well as simple properties like being red, being black and being square, there are complex properties like the property of being red and square and the property of being black and square. A conjunction of properties, for example, is a property, according to some sparse theories of properties, if and only if a particular instantiates its conjuncts (Armstrong, 1978b, 30). So if being red and being square are properties, for example, then their conjunction being red and square is a property as well. But even if being red and being black are properties, their conjunction being red and black is not a property, since no particulars are both red and black.

Particulars instantiate complex properties in virtue of instantiating combinations of simple properties. *Black Square*, for example, instantiates the property of being black and square in virtue of instantiating the property of being black and instantiating the property of being square. But whereas there is a complex predicate corresponding to every combination of simple predicate combinations, it's important that there's not, according to sparse theories, a property corresponding to every combination of simple property combinations, because if there were and degree of resemblance is proportion of properties in common, degree of resemblance would still be one third if defined.

In particular, it's important that there are not, according to sparse theories, disjunctive properties: if being red and being black are properties, for example, being red or black is not a property, since the redness of *Red Square* and the blackness of *Black Square* is not a respect of similarity between them. As David Armstrong writes, "Suppose *a* has a property P but lacks Q, while *b* has Q but lacks P. It seems laughable to conclude from these premises that *a* and *b* are identical in some respect. Yet both have the "property", P or Q" (Armstrong, 1978b, 20). Ravens don't resemble writing desks in virtue of being ravens or writing desks.

Proponents of sparse theories of properties equally stress the inexistence of negative properties: if being red, for example, is a property, being not red is not a property. As Armstrong writes, "If particulars are identical in a respect, then they resemble each other. But it is surely implausible to suggest that *not being P* is a point in which *a, b, c* ... etc. resemble each other" (Armstrong, 1978b, 23). Peas in a pod resemble each other in respect of greenness because they have the common property of being green, but ravens and writing desks do not resemble each other in respect of being not green, according to the sparse theory, because there is no property of being not green.

So even if the degree of resemblance between particulars is their number of properties in common divided by their total number of properties, sparse theories of properties do not entail that degrees of resemblance are constant if defined, since they deny there is a property corresponding to every possible predicate, and so deny that the number of properties is the number of possible predicates. If the only simple property is being red, for example, the degree of resemblance between *Red Square* and *Black Square* is, according to the sparse theory, zero, because since the property of being red or not red doesn't exist, *Red Square* and *Black Square* have no property in common.

If the simple properties are being red and being square, then there are three properties in total according to the sparse theory: being red, being square, and being both red and square. *Red Square* and *Black Square* have a third of their properties – being square – in common. But if being black is also a property, then *Red Square* and *Black Square* have one property – being square – out of five – being red, being black, being square, being red and square, and being black and square – in common. So proponents of the sparse theory can accept that degrees of resemblance are proportions of properties in common, without concluding that degree of resemblance is one third if defined.

Even if the number of properties is infinite, sparse theories of properties do not entail that degrees of resemblance between particulars are undefined. If every exact shade of colour is a property, for example, then there are infinitely many properties, since there are infinitely many exact shades of colour. But since each particular instantiates only a single shade, each particular may still instantiate only finitely many properties, and so the number of properties two particulars have in common divided by their number of properties in total need not be undefined. So long as two particulars instantiate only finitely many of the infinite properties, their degree of resemblance will be defined.

So since it denies that there are negative and disjunctive properties, the sparse theory of properties does not entail that the number of properties is the number of (possible) predicates and might be expected to be consonant with the thesis that the degree of resemblance between particulars is their number of properties in common divided by their number of properties and the thesis that a picture is realistic to the degree that it resembles what it represents (in relevant respects). But the sparse theory of properties still faces two problems. The first can be avoided, but the second requires revising the analysis of degree of resemblance as proportion of properties in common.

Firstly, the sparse theory of properties is inconsonant with the theses because it is too sparse. According to many proponents of the sparse theory, the sparse properties are only those of fundamental physics. As David Lewis, for example, writes "Physics has its short list of 'fundamental physical properties': the charges and masses of particles, also their so-called 'spins' and 'colours' and 'flavours', ... an inventory of the *sparse* properties of this-worldly things" (Lewis, 1986, 60). But if only fundamental physical properties exist, most pictures have no properties in common with what they represent – the Mona Lisa, for example, does not resemble Lisa in respect of mass.

The problem isn't with the thesis that the degree of realism of a picture is its degree of resemblance to what it represents (in relevant respects), but an inconsonance between the analysis of degree of resemblance as proportion of properties in common and the conception of sparse properties as the properties of fundamental physics. Fundamental physical properties are not the respects in which ordinary objects resemble each other, so the conception of sparse properties as fundamental physical properties is ill suited to feature in the analysis of resemblance (Schaffer, 2004, 94). Resemblances between friends, for example, aren't resemblances in respect of mass either.

However, there are other conceptions of sparse properties which are suited to feature in the analysis of resemblance. If the sparse properties aren't only those which feature in fundamental physics, but those which feature in total science, including chemistry, biology, psychology, and sociology, ordinary objects might be expected to resemble each other in respect of those properties (Schaffer, 2004, 94). Resemblances between friends, for example, are in respects which might feature in psychology or sociology, whereas resemblances between the Mona Lisa and Lisa are in respects which might feature in geometry or colour science.

But secondly, the sparse theory is inconsonant with the thesis that degree of realism is degree of resemblance (in relevant respects) and the thesis that degree of resemblance is proportion of properties in common because it denies the existence of negative and disjunctive properties, even when the respects of resemblance between some pictures and what they represent and other ordinary objects are often negative or disjunctive. Because it's its denial that negative and disjunctive properties exist which allows it to avoid the conclusion that degrees of resemblance are constant if defined, the sparse theory of properties cannot avoid this problem so easily.

Although *Black Square*, for example, is not a realistic depiction of anything, it might have realistically depicted a black night. But Armstrong writes that "... black surfaces turn out to be, as a matter of scientific fact, surfaces which do not emit any light. So the predicate 'black', apparently a positive predicate, applies in virtue of a certain lack or absence in the particulars to which it applies" (Armstrong, 1978b, 52). If blackness is not a property, then *Black Square* does not have any property in common with a black night, and so *Black Square* resembles a black night to degree zero. But even if blackness is not a property, *Black Square* could still realistically depict a black night.

(There are other conceptions of colour according to which blackness is a property, but the problem still arises for any conception of properties according to which negative properties do not exist, because it is possible to depict something as lacking a property by drawing a picture which lacks that property. A more intuitive conception of colour, for example, may allow that particulars may lack colour through being transparent, or in some other way. If so, then it should be possible to depict something as uncoloured by using a picture which is uncoloured. But if being uncoloured is not a property, this involves no resemblance between the picture and what it represents.)

The same problem arises with the rejection of disjunctive properties. *Red Square*, for example, may have been a realistic painting of a peasant women in a red dress, which resembles her in respect of redness. But redness is the disjunction of all the different shades; being red is being scarlet, or being crimson or ... etc. So if the shades of red are properties and disjunctions of properties are not properties, then being red is not a property, and so unless *Red Square* is the same shade of red as the peasant woman's dress, *Red Square* resembles the woman to degree zero (in relevant respects). But the degree of realism of *Red Square* in this case, while low, need not be zero.

(It might be objected that a determinable isn't merely a disjunction of determinates. Being yellow or angry, for example, is not a determinable of which being yellow and being angry are the determinates. But although not all disjunctions are determinables, all determinables are disjunctions of their determinates, since the determinable entails the disjunction, and the disjunction entails the determinable, so the determinable and the disjunction are equivalent. Since being red entails being one of the shades of red, for example, and being one of the shades of red entails being red, being red and being one of the shades of red are equivalent, and being red is their disjunction.)

The problem isn't with the thesis that the degree of realism of a picture is its degree of resemblance to what it represents (in relevant respects), but with the combination of the sparse theory of properties and the thesis that the degree of resemblance between particulars is their proportion of properties in common. Just as *Black Square* might realistically depict a dark night, even if being black is not a property, *Black Square* resembles a dark night, even if being black is not a property. Likewise, just as *Red Square* may realistically depict a peasant women wearing another shade of red, *Red Square* resembles a peasant women wearing another shade of red.

So the sparse theory of properties is inconsonant not just with the thesis that degree of realism is degree of resemblance (in relevant respects), but also with the analysis of resemblance as having properties in common. Instead, a particular resembles another, according to the sparse theory of properties, if and only if a property of the former resembles a property of the latter (Armstrong, 1978b, 96). Oranges resemble lemons, for example, because oranges are a shade of orange which resembles the yellow shade of a lemon. And though the shade of red of *Red Square*, for example, is not the shade of red the peasant woman wears, they resemble each other because their shades do.

Degree of resemblance, according to the sparse theory of properties, is not proportion of properties in common. Rather, the degree of resemblance of something to another is the proportion of the first thing's properties which resemble the second thing's properties, weighted according to those properties' degrees of resemblance. Peas in a pod, for example, resemble each other to a high degree because a high proportion of the peas' properties resemble each other to a high degree. But *Red Square* resembles a peasant woman to a low degree because only a few of their properties, such as their shades, resemble each other to a high degree.

This revision avoids the problem posed by the rejection of disjunctive properties, but not the problem posed by the rejection of negative properties. Since being black, for example, is not a property, *Black Square* not only fails to have a property in common with a black night, but also fails to have any property which resembles any property of a black night. In general, whereas particulars with different properties can resemble each other, according to the sparse theory of properties, in virtue of their different properties resembling each other, particulars which lack properties cannot resemble each other in virtue of the properties they lack resembling each other.

## 10.4 Inegalitarian nominalism

Even if it is not combined with the thesis that the degree of realism of a picture is its degree of resemblance to what it represents (in relevant respects), the thesis that the degree of resemblance between different particulars is constant if defined is absurd: it's simply not the case that all different particulars resemble each other to the same degree. So the problem should be resolved by denying that since there is a property corresponding to every (possible) predicate, the number of properties is the number of (possible) predicates, or by denying that degrees of resemblance are proportions of properties in common.

But since denying that because there is a property corresponding to every (possible) predicate the number of properties is the number of (possible) predicates leads to a revision of the analysis of degree of resemblance as proportion of common properties in any case, the most conservative solution is to just revise the analysis of degree of resemblance. Different properties, according to this revision, have different weights in determining degrees of resemblance: the degree of resemblance between particulars is the sum of the weights of the properties they have in common divided by the sum of the weights of the properties they have in total (Watanabe, 1969, 382).

If being red, for example, is the only simple property, then the degree of resemblance between *Red Square* and *Black Square* is the weight of being red or not red divided by the sum of the weights of being red, of being not red, and of being red or not red. If the weight of being red or not red is less than half the sum of the weights of being red and of being not red, then the degree of resemblance between *Red Square* and *Black Square* is less than one third, whereas if the weight of being red or not red is greater than half the sum of the weights of being red and of being not red, then the degree of resemblance between *Red Square* and *Black Square* is more than one third.

Whether it is combined with a subjectivist theory of properties, such as an unqualified version of predicate nominalism, or an objectivist theory of properties, such as an unqualified version of class nominalism, analysing degrees of resemblance in terms of weighted proportions of properties in common potentially introduces a new source of subjectivity into the analysis of resemblance. As Goodman writes "... $a$ and $b$ are more alike than $c$ and $d$ if the cumulative importance of the properties shared by $a$ and $b$ is greater than that of the properties shared by $c$ and $d$. But importance is a highly volatile matter, varying with every shift of context and interest ..." (Goodman, 1970, 444).

But even if degree of resemblance is a weighted proportion of properties in common, the weights need not be subjective degrees of importance, but may also be objective degrees of naturalness. As Lewis writes, "... an *adequate* theory of properties is one that recognises an objective difference between natural and unnatural properties; preferably, a difference that admits of degree ... Natural properties would be the ones whose sharing makes for resemblance" (Lewis, 1983a, 14). So while introducing weights into the analysis of degree of resemblance can introduce a new source of subjectivity, it needn't do so; whether it does or not depends on underlying metaphysical issues.

Because it doesn't deny that there are negative properties, this revision accommodates the fact that there is a degree of resemblance between *Black Square* and a black night, because even if being black is being not coloured, it does not follow that being black has no weight. But since properties differ in their weights, the revision accommodates the fact that there is a low or no degree of resemblance between ravens and writing desks in respect of being not green, because although it doesn't deny that the property of being not green exists, the property of being not green may have low or no weight. So there is no problem corresponding to that of the rejection of negative properties.

Likewise, because it doesn't deny that there are disjunctive properties, this revision accommodates the fact that there is a degree of resemblance between *Red Square* and a peasant woman wearing a different shade of red. But because disjunctive properties may differ in their weights, the revision accommodates the fact that the more closely the shade of *Red Square* resembles the shade of the peasant woman's clothes, the more closely *Red Square* resembles the peasant woman, because disjunctions of like shades of colour are weightier than disjunctions of unlike shades of colour. So there is no problem corresponding to that of the rejection of disjunctive properties.

If there is a property corresponding to every (possible) predicate, then each particular possesses either the property corresponding to that (possible) predicate or its negation. So if the number of (possible) predicates is infinite, then each particular possesses an infinite number of properties and, since if there is a property corresponding to every (possible) predicate different particulars have one third of their properties in common, all particulars have an infinite number of properties in common. If the weights have a positive minimum, then the sums of the weights of properties in common and in total are infinite as well, and degrees of resemblance are undefined.

So if the number of properties is the number of (possible) predicates, the number of (possible) predicates is infinite and degree of resemblance is a weighted proportion of common properties, then weight of properties has no positive minimum unless degree of resemblance is undefined. If there is an infinite number of properties which weigh more than a positive minimum, then degrees of resemblance are defined only between particulars possessing only a finite number of those properties. If there is an infinite number of determinate shades of colour with positive equal weight, for example, then each particular can possess only a single shade of colour.

So by accepting that the number of properties is the number of (possible) predicates and analysing degrees of resemblance as weighted proportions of common properties, the conclusion that degree of resemblance between particulars is constant if defined is avoided in a way which is consonant with the platitude that the degree of realism of a picture is its degree of resemblance to what it represents (in relevant respects). The Mona Lisa has a high degree of realism, for example, because the sum of the weights of the (relevant) properties in common of the Mona Lisa and Lisa is high compared to the sum of the weights of the (relevant) properties in total of the Mona Lisa and Lisa.

## 10.5 Conclusion

The theses that degree of realism is degree of resemblance (in relevant respects), that the number of properties corresponds to the number of (possible) predicates, and that degree of resemblance is proportion of common properties are individually plausible, but jointly inconsonant, since the second two theses entail that degree of resemblance between different particulars is constant if defined, which entails, in combination with an unqualified version of the first thesis, that the degree of realism of pictures which differ from what they represent is constant if defined. These conclusions are absurd, so one of the theses must be revised or rejected.

I have argued for resolving the inconsonance by revising the analysis of degrees of resemblance in terms of proportions of properties in common, and not by denying that there is a property corresponding to every predicate nor by denying or exploiting the qualification in the thesis that degree of realism is degree of resemblance (in relevant respects). Instead, degree of resemblance should be analysed as a weighted proportion of properties in common: the degree of resemblance between two particulars is the sum of the weights of their properties in common divided by the sum of the weights of their properties in total.

However the problem is resolved, it should not be resolved by denying the thesis that degree of realism is degree of resemblance (in relevant respects), because the thesis that degree of resemblance is constant if defined is implausible even in isolation. Any adequate theory of properties and resemblance, whether it is sparse or abundant, must accommodate the Moorean facts about which things resemble each other – facts more certain than any philosophical theory. And amongst these facts is the fact that pictures resemble what they represent, and that realistic pictures resemble what they represent to a high degree. So any adequate theory will have to accommodate these facts too.

But whereas all theories must accommodate the platitude that the degree of realism of a picture is its degree of resemblance to what it represents (in relevant respects), they may differ on the question of whether the degree of realism of a picture is subjective or objective. Goodman, for example, argues the platitude undermines the objectivity of depictive realism because "... insofar as resemblance is a constant and objective relation, resemblance between a picture and what it represents does not coincide with realism: and ... insofar as resemblance does coincide with realism, the criteria of resemblance vary with changes in representational practice" (Goodman, 1968, 39).

But the thesis that degree of realism is degree of resemblance (in relevant respects) is consistent with the thesis that degree of realism is objective as well as the thesis that degree of realism is subjective. If combined with an objective analysis of properties, such as an unqualified version of class nominalism, and an analysis of degree of resemblance as proportions of properties in common weighted by degrees of objective naturalness, then it entails degree of realism is objective. The objectivity of degree of realism depends on the objectivity of resemblance, which depends on the objectivity of properties and their weights: as long as the latter are objective, so are the former.

But if combined with a subjective analysis of properties, such as unqualified versions of predicate nominalism, or an analysis of degrees of resemblance as proportions of properties in common, weighted by degrees of subjective importance, then the thesis that degree of realism is degree of resemblance (in relevant respects) entails degree of realism is subjective. The subjectivity of degree of realism depends on the subjectivity of resemblance, which depends on the subjectivity of properties and their weights: as long as the latter are subjective, so are the former. So the analysis of degree of realism in terms of resemblance is consonant with its subjectivity or its objectivity.

But although the thesis that degree of realism is degree of resemblance (in relevant respects) is equally consistent with the thesis that degree of realism is subjective and with the thesis that degree of realism is objective, it should be emphasised that which thesis is correct is determined by its metaphysical underpinnings. The presupposition of predicate nominalism in Goodman's argument against the objectivity of depictive realism is not illegitimate, because the objectivity of depictive realism is dependent on the objectivity of resemblance. To avoid Goodman's conclusions one must not merely renounce predicate nominalism; one must embrace metaphysical realism.

# References

Abell, Catharine (2005a), "Pictorial Implicature", *The Journal of Aesthetics and Art Criticism* 63(1): 55-66. http://dx.doi.org/10.1111/j.0021-8529.2005.00181.x

Abell, Catharine (2005b), "Against Depictive Conventionalism", *The American Philosophical Quarterly* 42(3): 185-197.

Abell, Catharine (2009), "Canny Resemblance: An Account of Depiction", *Philosophical Review* 118(2): 183-223. http://dx.doi.org/10.1215/00318108-2008-041

Armstrong, David (1978a), *Nominalism and Realism* (Cambridge: Cambridge University Press).

Armstrong, David (1978b), *A Theory of Universals* (Cambridge: Cambridge University Press).

Avramides, Anita (1989), *Meaning and Mind* (Cambridge, MA: MIT Press).

Bennett, John (1974), "Depiction and Convention", *The Monist* 58(2): 255-268. http://dx.doi.org/10.5840/monist197458212

Bennett, Jonathan (1976), *Linguistic Behaviour* (Cambridge: Cambridge University Press).

Blumson, Ben (2008), "Depiction and Convention", *dialectica* 62(3): 335-348. http://dx.doi.org/10.1111/j.1746-8361.2008.01156.x

Blumson, Ben (2009a), "Defining Depiction", *British Journal of Aesthetics* 49(2): 143-157. http://dx.doi.org/10.1093/aesthj/ayp003

Blumson, Ben (2009b), "Images, Intentionality and Inexistence", *Philosophy and Phenomenological Research* 79(3): 522-538. http://dx.doi.org/10.1111/j.1933-1592.2009.00292.x

Blumson, Ben (2010a), "Maps and Meaning", *Journal of Philosophical Research* 35: 123-127. http://dx.doi.org/10.5840/jpr_2010_6

Blumson, Ben (2010b), "Pictures, Perspective and Possibility", *Philosophical Studies* 149(2): 135-151. http://dx.doi.org/10.1007/s11098-009-9337-2

Blumson, Ben (2011), "Depictive Structure", *Philosophical Papers* 40(1): 1-25. http://dx.doi.org/10.1080/05568641.2011.560026

Blumson, Ben (2012), "Mental Maps", *Philosophy and Phenomenological Research* 85(2): 413-434. http://dx.doi.org/10.1111/j.1933-1592.2011.00499.x

Braddon-Mitchell, David and Frank Jackson (1996), *Philosophy of Mind and Cognitive Science* (Cambridge, MA: Blackwell Publishers).

Bronner, Ben (forthcoming), "Maps and Absent Symbols", *Australasian Journal of Philosophy*.

Calvino, Italo (1982), *If On a Winter's Night a Traveller* (London: Picador).

Carroll, Lewis (1871), *Through The Looking Glass* (London: Macmillan). Reprinted in Gardner (2000): 133-288.

Casati, Roberto and Achille Varzi (1999), *Parts and Places: The Structures of Spatial Representation* (Cambridge, MA: MIT Press).

Chalmers, David (1996), *The Conscious Mind* (Oxford: Oxford University Press).

Chalmers, David (2000), "On Sense and Intension", *Philosophical Perspectives* 16: 135-182. http://dx.doi.org/10.1111/1468-0068.36.s16.6

Chalmers, David (2011a), "Verbal Disputes", *Philosophical Review* 120(4): 515-566. http://dx.doi.org/10.1215/00318108-1334478

Chalmers, David (2011b), "Propositions and Attitude Ascriptions: A Fregean Account", *Nous* 45(4): 595-639. http://dx.doi.org/10.1111/j.1468-0068.2010.00788.x

Currie, Gregory (1990), *The Nature of Fiction* (Cambridge: Cambridge University Press). http://dx.doi.org/10.1017/cbo9780511897498

Currie, Gregory (1995), *Image and Mind: Film, Philosophy and Cognitive Science* (Cambridge: Cambridge University Press). http://dx.doi.org/10.1017/CBO9780511551277

Davidson, Donald (1967), "Truth and Meaning", *Synthese* 17(1): 304-323. Reprinted in Davidson (1984): 17-36. http://dx.doi.org/10.1007/bf00485035

Davidson, Donald (1970), "Semantics for Natural Languages", in *Linguaggi nella Società e nella Tecnica* (Milan: Edizioni di Comunità). Reprinted in Davidson (1984): 55-64. http://dx.doi.org/10.1093/0199246297.003.0004

Davidson, Donald (1984), *Inquiries into Truth and Interpretation* (Oxford: Oxford University Press). http://dx.doi.org/10.1093/0199246297.001.0001

Davidson, Donald (1986), "A Nice Derangement of Epitaphs", in R. Grandy and R. Warner (eds.) *Philosophical Grounds of Rationality* (Oxford: Oxford University Press). Reprinted in Davidson (2005): 90-97. http://dx.doi.org/10.1093/019823757x.003.0007

Davidson, Donald (2005), *Truth, Language and History* (Oxford: Oxford University Press). http://dx.doi.org/10.1093/019823757x.001.0001

Davies, Martin (1981a), *Meaning, Quantification and Necessity* (London: Routledge and Keegan Paul).

Davies, Martin (1981b), "Meaning, Structure and Understanding", *Synthese* 48(1): 135-161. http://dx.doi.org/10.1007/bf01064632

Davies, Martin (1983), "Meaning and Structure", *Philosophia* 13(1-2): 13-33. http://dx.doi.org/10.1007/bf02380987

Davies, Martin (1987), "Tacit Knowledge and Semantic Theory: Can a Five Per Cent Difference Matter?", *Mind* 96(384): 441-462. http://dx.doi.org/10.1093/mind/xcvi.384.441

Eaton, Marcia (1969), "Art, Artifacts and Intentions", *American Philosophical Quarterly* 6(2): 165-169.

Egan, Andy (2006a), "Appearance Properties?", *Nous* 40(3): 495-521. http://dx.doi.org/10.1111/j.1468-0068.2006.00621.x

Egan, Andy (2006b), "Secondary Qualities and Self-Location", *Philosophy and Phenomenological Research* 72(1): 97-119. http://dx.doi.org/10.1111/j.1933-1592.2006.tb00492.x

Evans, Gareth (1981), "Semantic Theory and Tacit Knowledge", in Steven Holtzman and Christopher Leich (eds.) *Wittgenstein: To Follow a Rule* (London: Routledge and Keegan Paul). Reprinted in Evans (1985): 322-422.

Evans, Gareth (1985), *Collected Papers* (Oxford: Oxford University Press).

Fodor, Jerry (2008), *LOT 2: The Language of Thought Revisited* (Oxford: Oxford University Press).

Forbes, Graeme (2006), *Attitude Problems: An Essay on Linguistic Intentionality* (Oxford: Oxford University Press). http://dx.doi.org/10.1093/acprof:oso/9780199274949.001.0001

Gardener, Martin (2000), *The Annotated Alice: The Definitive Edition* (New York: Norton).

Goodman, Nelson (1968), *Languages of Art: An Approach to a Theory of Symbols* (Indianapolis and New York: The Bobbs-Merrill Company, Inc.). Second edition 1976.

Goodman, Nelson (1970), "Seven Strictures on Similarity", in L. Foster and J. W. Swanson (eds.) *Experience and Theory* (Boston: University of Massachusetts Press). Reprinted in Goodman (1972): 437-447.

Goodman, Nelson (1972), *Problems and Projects* (Indianapolis: Hackett).

Greenberg, Gabriel (2013), "Beyond Resemblance", *The Philosophical Review* 122(2): 215-287. http://dx.doi.org/10.1215/00318108-1963716

Grice, H. P. (1957), "Meaning", *The Philosophical Review* 66(3): 377-388. Reprinted in Grice (1989): 213-223. http://dx.doi.org/10.2307/2182440

Grice, H. P. (1968), "Utterer's Meaning, Sentence Meaning and Word Meaning", *Foundations of Language* 4(3): 225-242. Reprinted in Grice (1989): 117-137.

Grice, H. P. (1969), "Utterer's Meaning and Intentions", *The Philosophical Review* 78(2): 147-177. Reprinted in Grice (1989): 86-116. http://dx.doi.org/10.2307/2184179

Grice, H. P. (1989), *Studies in the Way of Words* (Cambridge, MA: Harvard University Press).

Harman, Gilbert (1974), "Meaning", *The Journal of Philosophy* 71(7): 224-229. http://dx.doi.org/10.2307/2025349

Harman, Gilbert (1977), "Eco Location", in M. Cohen and G. Mast (eds.) *Film Theory and Criticism* (New York: Oxford University Press). Second edition: 234-236.

Hollander, John (1981), *Rhyme's Reason* (London: Yale University Press). Third edition 2001.

Hopkins, Robert (1994), "Resemblance and Misrepresentation", *Mind* 103(412): 421-438. http://dx.doi.org/10.1093/mind/103.412.421

Hopkins, Robert (1998), *Picture, Image, and Experience* (Cambridge: Cambridge University Press).

Hospers, John (1946), *Meaning and Truth in the Arts* (Chapel Hill, NC: University of North Carolina Press).

Houser, Nathan and Christian Kloesel (eds.) (1992), *The Essential Peirce: Selected Philosophical Writings Volume 1 (1867-1893)* (Bloomington and Indianapolis: Indiana University Press).

Hyman, John (2006), *The Objective Eye: Colour, Form and Reality in the Theory of Art* (Chicago and London: The University of Chicago Press). http://dx.doi.org/10.7208/chicago/9780226365541.001.0001

Jackson, Frank (1998), "Reference and Description Revisited", *Philosophical Perspectives* 12: 201-218. http://dx.doi.org/10.1111/0029-4624.32.s12.9

Kaplan, David (1968), "Quantifying In", *Synthese* 19(1-2): 178-214. http://dx.doi.org/10.1007/bf00568057

Kaplan, David (1989), "Demonstratives: An Essay on the Semantics, Pragmatics, Logic, Metaphysics and Epistemology of Demonstratives and Other Indexicals", in Joseph Almog, John Perry and Howard Wettstein (eds.) *Themes from Kaplan* (New York: Oxford University Press): 481-564.

Kulvicki, John (2006), *On Images: Their Structure and Content* (Oxford: Oxford University Press). http://dx.doi.org/10.1093/019929075x.001.0001

Kripke, Saul (1963), "Semantical Considerations on Modal Logic", *Acta Philosophica Fennica* 16: 83-94.

Kripke, Saul (1980), *Naming and Necessity* (Oxford: Basil Blackwell).

Larson, Richard and Gabriel Segal (1995), *Knowledge of Meaning* (Cambridge, MA: MIT Press).

Lewis, David (1969), *Convention* (Cambridge, MA: Harvard University Press). http://dx.doi.org/10.1002/9780470693711

Lewis, David (1975), "Languages and Language", *Minnesota Studies in the Philosophy of Science* VII: 3-35. Reprinted in Lewis (1983b): 163-188. http://dx.doi.org/10.1093/0195032047.003.0011

Lewis, David (1979), "Attitudes *De Dicto* and *De Se*", *The Philosophical Review* 88(4): 513-543. Reprinted in Lewis (1983b): 133-159. http://dx.doi.org/10.2307/2184843

Lewis, David (1983a), "New Work For a Theory of Universals", *Australasian Journal of Philosophy* 61(4): 343-377. Reprinted in Lewis (1999): 8-55. http://dx.doi.org/10.1080/00048408312341131

Lewis, David (1983b), *Philosophical Papers I* (Oxford: Oxford University Press). http://dx.doi.org/10.1093/0195032047.001.0001

Lewis, David (1986), *On The Plurality of Worlds* (Oxford: Basil Blackwell).

Lewis, David (1994), "Reduction of Mind", in Samuel Guttenplan (ed.) *A Companion to Philosophy of Mind* (Oxford: Blackwell Publishers). Reprinted in Lewis (1999): 291-324. http://dx.doi.org/10.1017/cbo9780511625343.019

Lewis, David (1999), *Papers in Metaphysics and Epistemology* (Cambridge: Cambridge University Press). http://dx.doi.org/10.1017/cbo9780511625343

Livingston, Paisley (2005), *Art and Intention: A Philosophical Study* (Oxford: Oxford University Press). http://dx.doi.org/10.1093/0199278067.001.0001

Lopes, Dominic (1996), *Understanding Pictures* (Oxford: Clarendon Press). http://dx.doi.org/10.1093/acprof:oso/9780199272037.001.0001

Lopes, Dominic (2005), "The Domain of Depiction", in Mathew Kieran (ed.) *Contemporary Debates in the Philosophy of Art* (Oxford: Blackwell): 160-174.

Lopes, Dominic (2006), "The Special and General Theory of Realism: Reply to Abell, Armstrong and McMahon", *Contemporary Aesthetics* 4. http://www.contempaesthetics.org/newvolume/pages/article.php?articleID=373

Lycan, William (2000), *Philosophy of Language* (New York: Routledge).

Malinas, Gary (1991), "A Semantics for Pictures", *Canadian Journal of Philosophy* 21(3): 275–298.

McKinsey, Michael (1983), "Psychologism in Semantics", Canadian Journal of Philosophy 13(1): 1-25.

Mortensen, Chris (2010), *Inconsistent Geometry* (London: College Publications).

Newall, Michael (2011), *What is a Picture?* (London: Palgrave Macmillan). http://dx.doi.org/10.1057/9780230297531

Novitz, David (1977), *Pictures and Their Use in Communication* (The Hague: Martinus Nijhoff). http://dx.doi.org/10.1007/978-94-010-1063-4

Orwell, George (1945), *Animal Farm* (London: Secker & Warburg).

Parsons, Terence (1995), "Meinongian Semantics Generalized", *Grazer Philosophische Studien* 50: 145-161. http://dx.doi.org/10.5840/gps1995508

Peacocke, Christopher (1976), "Truth Definitions and Actual Languages", in Gareth Evans and John McDowell (eds.), *Truth and Meaning* (Oxford: Oxford University Press): 162-188.

Peacocke, Christopher (1987), "Depiction", *The Philosophical Review* 96(3): 383-410. http://dx.doi.org/10.2307/2185226

Peirce, Charles (1868), "On a New List of Categories", *Proceedings of the American Academy of Arts and Sciences* 7: 278-298. Reprinted in Houser (1992): 1-10.

Penrose, Lionel and Roger Penrose (1958), "Impossible Objects: A Special Type of Visual Illusion", *The British Journal of Psychology* 49(1): 31–33. http://dx.doi.org/10.1111/j.2044-8295.1958.tb00634.x

Priest, Graham (2005), *Towards Non-Being: The Logic and Metaphysics of Intentionality* (Oxford: Oxford University Press). http://dx.doi.org/10.1093/0199262543.001.0001

Putnam, Hilary (1981), *Reason, Truth and History* (Cambridge: Cambridge University Press). http://dx.doi.org/10.1017/cbo9780511625398

Quine, Willard (1940), *Mathematical Logic* (Cambridge, MA: Harvard University Press).

Quine, Willard (1969), "Propositional Objects", in Willard Quine, *Ontological Relativity and Other Essays* (New York: Columbia University Press): 139-160.

Quine, Willard (1970), "Methodological Reflections on Current Linguistic Theory", *Synthese* 21(3-4): 386-398. http://dx.doi.org/10.1007/bf00484806

Recanati, Francois (2004), *Literal Meaning* (Cambridge: Cambridge University Press). http://dx.doi.org/10.1017/cbo9780511615382

Rescorla, Michael (2009), "Predication and Cartographic Representation", *Synthese* 169(1): 175-200. http://dx.doi.org/10.1007/s11229-008-9343-5

Ross, Jeff (1997), *Semantics of Media* (Dordrecht: Kluwer). http://dx.doi.org/10.1007/978-94-011-5650-9

Sachs-Hombach, Klaus (2003), "Resemblance Reconceived", in Heiko Hecht, Robert Schwartz and Margaret Atherton (eds.), *Looking Into Pictures: An Interdisciplinary Approach to Pictorial Space* (Cambridge, MA: The MIT Press): 167-178.

Saint-Exupéry, Antoine de (1943), *The Little Prince* (New York: Reynal & Hitchcock).

Sartwell, Crispin (1994), "What Pictorial Realism is", *British Journal of Aesthetics* 34(1): 2-12. http://dx.doi.org/10.1093/bjaesthetics/34.1.2

Saussure, Ferdinand de (1972), *Course in General Linguistics* (London: Duckworth).

Schaffer, Jonathan (2004), "Two Conceptions of Sparse Properties", *Pacific Philosophical Quarterly* 85(1): 92-102. http://dx.doi.org/10.1111/j.1468-0114.2004.00189.x

Schier, Flint (1986), *Deeper Into Pictures* (Cambridge: Cambridge University Press). http://dx.doi.org/10.1017/cbo9780511735585

Schiffer, Stephen (1972), *Meaning* (Oxford: Oxford University Press). Paperback edition 1988.

Schiffer, Stephen (1987), *Remnants of Meaning* (Cambridge, MA: MIT Press).

Schiffer, Stephen (1993), "Actual-Language Relations", *Philosophical Perspectives* 7: 231-258. http://dx.doi.org/10.2307/2214124

Schroeter, Laura (2003). "Gruesome Diagonals", *Philosophers' Imprint* 3(3): 1–23. http://hdl.handle.net/2027/spo.3521354.0003.003

Scruton, Roger (1983), *The Aesthetic Understanding* (Manchester: Carcanet Press).

Searle, John (1979), "Metaphor", in Andrew Ortony (ed.) *Metaphor and Thought* (Cambridge: Cambridge University Press): 83-111. http://dx.doi.org/10.1017/cbo9781139173865.008

Sellars, Wilfrid (1962), "Philosophy and the Scientific Image of Man", in Robert Colodny (ed.) *Frontiers of Science and Philosophy* (Pittsburgh, PA: University of Pittsburgh Press). Reprinted in Sellars (2007): 369-409.

Sellars, Wilfrid (2007), *In the Space of Reasons: Selected Essays of Wilfrid Sellars* (Cambridge, MA: Harvard University Press).

Soames, Scott (1987), "Direct Reference, Propositional Attitudes and Semantic Content", in Scott Soames and Nathan Salmon (eds.) *Propositions and Attitudes* (New York: Oxford University Press): 197-239.

Sorensen, Roy (2002), "The Art of the Impossible", in Tamar Szabo Gendler and John Hawthorne (eds.) *Conceivability and Possibility* (Oxford: Clarendon Press): 337-368.

Stalnaker, Robert (1978) "Assertion", in *Syntax and Semantics* 9 (New York: Academic Press). Reprinted in Stalnaker (1999): 78-95. http://dx.doi.org/10.1093/0198237073.003.0005

Stalnaker, Robert (1984), *Inquiry* (Cambridge, MA: MIT Press).

Stalnaker, Robert (1997), "Reference and Necessity", in Crispin Wright and Bob Hale (eds.) *Blackwell Companion to the Philosophy of Language* (Oxford: Basil Blackwell). Reprinted in Stalnaker (2003): 165-187. http://dx.doi.org/10.1093/0199251487.003.0010

Stalnaker, Robert (1999), *Context and Content* (Oxford: Oxford University Press). http://dx.doi.org/10.1093/0198237073.001.0001

Stalnaker, Robert (2003), *Ways a World Might Be: Metaphysical and Anti-Metaphysical Essays* (Oxford: Oxford University Press). http://dx.doi.org/10.1093/0199251487.001.0001

Walton, Kendall (1974), "Are Representations Symbols?", *The Monist* 58(2): 236-254. http://dx.doi.org/10.5840/monist197458216

Walton, Kendall (1984), "Transparent Pictures: On the Nature of Photographic Realism", *Nous* 18(1): 67-72. Reprinted in Walton (2008): 70-109. http://dx.doi.org/10.2307/2215023

Walton, Kendall (1990), *Mimesis as Make-believe* (Cambridge, MA: Harvard University Press).

Walton, Kendall (2008), *Marvelous Images: On Values and the Arts* (New York: Oxford University Press).

Watanabe, Satosi (1969), *Knowing and Guessing* (New York: Wiley).

Weitz, Morris (1956), "The Role of Theory in Aesthetics", *The Journal of Aesthetics and Art Criticism* 15(1): 27-35. http://dx.doi.org/10.2307/427491

Wollheim, Richard (1980), *Art and Its Objects* (Cambridge: Cambridge University Press). Second edition.

Wollheim, Richard (1987), *Painting as an Art* (London: Thames and Hudson).

Woods, Michael (1972), "Reasons for Actions and Desires", *Proceedings of the Aristotelian Society, Supplementary Volumes* 46: 189-201.

Wright, Crispin (1986), "Theories of Meaning and Speakers' Knowledge", in *Realism, Meaning and Truth* (Oxford: Blackwell): 31-44.

Ziff, Paul (1967), "On H. P. Grice's Account of Meaning", *Analysis* 28(1): 1-8. http://dx.doi.org/10.2307/3327605

# Index

Abell, Catharine  12, 28, 32, 35, 44–48, 55, 128
allegory  11, 59
ambiguity  133, 134–135, 136–137, 146–147
analysis  23–27
  reciprocal  25
  reductive  21, 25–26, 31, 42, 144–145
anamorphism  167
a posteriori necessity  168
arbitrariness  22, 67–70, 72–73, 75–76, 77–79, 90, 99–100, 114, 186
Armstrong, David  183, 189, 191
assertion  35, 144–145

Braddon-Mitchell, David  100, 101, 114

Casati, Roberto  100, 103–104, 106, 113
causation  21, 22, 54, 56–57, 63, 66, 121, 144
chess diagrams  69, 80, 101, 102, 108, 109, 110, 112, 115, 122–124, 126
cinema  54, 114, 124
colour  15, 27, 191
commands  35
compositionality  99–101, 102–103, 106, 107, 110–116, 117–138
conditionals  23–24, 48–49, 59, 88
context  128–130, 136, 137
convention  40, 73–76, 88, 94
Currie, Gregory  35, 114, 136, 163

Davidson, Donald  118
dispositions  118–121

experience  12, 27, 44, 142–144, 147, 149, 154

fiction  11, 35, 38–39, 140
finite axiomatization constraint  106–108, 113
Fodor, Jerry  100

Goodman, Nelson  18, 67, 68–70, 82, 145–148, 148, 182, 188, 194
grammar  100, 101, 115–116, 146
Greenberg, Gabriel  168
Grice, Paul  28, 31, 47, 118

hallucination  143–144, 147, 149, 154
Harman, Gilbert  40, 85
Hopkins, Robert  15, 17, 26, 36, 55, 142
Hyman, John  11, 15, 16, 188

imperatives  32, 80–81
impossible pictures  168–170, 172–173
impossible worlds  174, 175
indexicals  128–129
indication  10, 21–23, 56, 144
indicatives  32, 80–81
infinitary conjunction  107–108, 109, 111
infinity  104–106, 114, 185, 187, 190, 195–196
intensions
  diagonal  170–171, 177
  horizontal  171, 177
  structured  176, 177
  two-dimensional  170–171, 176, 177
intention  41, 42, 52
  necessity of  45, 47, 52–57, 79
  sufficiency of  60–63
intentionalism  52
intentionality  47, 49, 139–145, 147, 149, 152, 154, 157, 158

Jackson, Frank  100, 101, 114

Kulvicki, John  83, 137

language  70–71
  innate  89, 111
  in the abstract  72, 97
  in use  72, 86–87, 90, 94–98
  non-literal  23, 45, 94–96
Lewis, David  14, 76, 86, 162, 163, 190, 194
Lopes, Dominic  69

malapropisms  61, 132–133
maps  10, 70, 88–89, 100, 103–104, 106–107, 113–114, 123
meaning
  sentence  31, 32, 47, 60–61, 63, 67, 79, 87, 97, 98, 134, 137–138, 144
  speaker  31–41, 47, 54–55, 57–58, 60–61, 63–64, 67, 87–89, 96, 97, 98, 133–134, 137–138, 144
  theories of  101, 102, 105–107, 128, 129, 134, 135
Meinongianism  149–151, 156–157, 160
metaphor  61, 95, 132, 133
mirror constraint  108–111
misrepresentation  47–49, 139–143, 146, 147, 150, 153, 156
modes of presentation  169, 171
mood  80–81

Newall, Michael  15, 16, 44, 187
nominalism
  class  165, 180, 185–188, 194, 197
  predicate  148, 180, 182–185, 194, 197–198
non-existents  47–49, 139–145, 146, 148–158, 160, 168, 176
non-particulars  47, 48, 139–143, 146–147, 148–150, 153, 156, 171, 176

objectivity  15–16, 186–188, 194–195, 197–198
onomatopoeia  19, 20, 46–47, 79–80

performatives  39
perspective  161, 163–165
photography  10, 22, 54–57, 63–66, 180–181

physicalism  24–25, 27, 31, 144–145
possibilia  48, 150, 155, 186
possible worlds  150, 155, 156, 159–165, 175, 187
  centred  162–165, 168, 187
predicates  14, 103, 121, 145–147, 180, 182–185
properties  14–21, 165–167, 174, 180, 182–183, 185–188
  abundant  14–15, 16, 19, 43
  centred  166–168, 187
  conjunctive  188
  disjunctive  189–193, 195
  negative  189, 191–193, 195
  sparse  14–15, 16, 43, 188–193
  structured  175

quantification  144
  substitutional  5, 107–108
Quine, Willard  5, 100, 163

rationality  63, 64, 66, 91
realism  182
  degrees of  179–182, 190–193, 196–198
reasons  64–66, 91–92
recognition  12, 43, 110–111, 112–113, 124
representation
  conventional  21, 22, 23
  intentional  21, 22–23, 32, 49, 51
  mental  25, 144–145
  natural  21–23, 54, 56–57, 63
  non-natural  21–23, 25, 54, 57, 63
  theories of  102–108
resemblance  13
  as a relation  139, 147, 148
  as sharing properties  13–19, 43, 140, 148–149, 180, 193, 194
  degrees of  179–182, 185, 186, 188, 189–198
  experienced  36–39, 44, 142–145
  necessity of  13, 16, 17, 59, 142
  reflexivity of  17, 19, 35, 37, 70
  sufficiency of  13, 16–20, 21, 35, 36–39, 41, 52, 70, 78, 141
  symmetry of  17–18
Ross, Jeff  161, 162

Schier, Flint  101
Scruton, Roger  100, 101, 114
Sellars, Wilfrid  31, 118
states of affairs  80–82, 151–158, 160, 170, 175–176
structural constraint  111–116
subjectivity  15–16, 182–183, 187, 194–195, 197–198
symbol systems  12, 67–70, 71
  depictive  22, 69–70, 73, 77–83, 88–89, 97–98
  in the abstract  72–73, 82, 92
  in use  72–73, 79, 82, 86, 88–98

tacit knowledge  117–126, 130, 135–137
truthfulness  76, 79–81, 86–87

Varzi, Achille  100, 103–104, 106, 113

# This book need not end here...

At Open Book Publishers, we are changing the nature of the traditional academic book. The title you have just read will not be left on a library shelf, but will be accessed online by hundreds of readers each month across the globe. We make all our books free to read online so that students, researchers and members of the public who can't afford a printed edition can still have access to the same ideas as you.

Our digital publishing model also allows us to produce online supplementary material, including extra chapters, reviews, links and other digital resources. Find Ben Blumson's *Resemblance and Representation* on our website to access its online extras. Please check this page regularly for ongoing updates, and join the conversation by leaving your own comments:

http://www.openbookpublishers.com/isbn/9781783740727

If you enjoyed this book, and feel that research like this should be available to all readers, regardless of their income, please think about donating to us. Our company is run entirely by academics, and our publishing decisions are based on intellectual merit and public value rather than on commercial viability. We do not operate for profit and all donations, as with all other revenue we generate, will be used to finance new Open Access publications.

For further information about what we do, to donate to OBP, to access additional digital material related to our titles or to order our books, please visit our website: www.openbookpublishers.com.

www.ingramcontent.com/pod-product-compliance
Lightning Source LLC
Chambersburg PA
CBHW071841230426
43671CB00012B/2033